I0889278

LYDIA SIGOURNEY

LYDIA SIGOURNEY

CRITICAL ESSAYS AND CULTURAL VIEWS

EDITED BY

Mary Louise Kete

and

Elizabeth Petrino

University of Massachusetts Press

Amherst and Boston

Printed in the United States of America

ISBN 978-1-62534-345-1 (paper); 344-4 (hardcover)

Designed by Jen Jackowitz
Set in Adobe Garamond Pro
Printed and bound by Maple Press, Inc.

Cover design by Milenda Nan Ok Lee
Cover art: Stipple engraving of Lydia H. Sigourney, by George Parker. Henry W. and Albert A. Berg Collection of English and American Literature, The New York Public Library, Astor, Lenox and Tilden Foundations.

Library of Congress Cataloging-in-Publication Data
Names: Kete, Mary Louise, editor. | Petrino, Elizabeth A., 1962– editor.
Title: Lydia Sigourney : critical essays and cultural views / edited by Mary Louise Kete and Elizabeth Petrino.
Description: Amherst : University of Massachusetts Press, 2018. | Includes bibliographical references and index. |
Identifiers: LCCN 2017050253 (print) | LCCN 2017055747 (ebook) | ISBN 9781613765845 (e-book) | ISBN 9781613765852 (e-book) | ISBN 9781625343444 (hardcover) | ISBN 9781625343451 (pbk.)
Subjects: LCSH: Sigourney, L. H. (Lydia Howard), 1791–1865—Criticism and interpretation. | Sigourney, L. H. (Lydia Howard), 1791–1865—Political and social views. | Women and literature—United States—History—19th century. | Politics and literature—United States—History—19th century. | Literature and society—United States—History—19th century.
Classification: LCC PS2833 (ebook) | LCC PS2833 .L93 2018 (print) | DDC 811/.3—dc23
LC record available at https://lccn.loc.gov/2017050253

British Library Cataloguing-in-Publication Data
A catalog record for this book is available from the British Library.

Elegy for Lydia

Mrs. Sigourney, 1791–1865

How can you die in us? You are still love
who roots us and flowers. Sweet singer, forgive
the hard, warning questions we've turned the wheel of.
How can you die in us? You are still love,
long-generous giver. You need us to live,
to bless, touch, believe in—know—what we're made of.
How can you die in us? You are still love
who roots us, to flower. Sweet singer, forgive.

—Ani (Annie Finch)

CONTENTS

ACKNOWLEDGMENTS

Over the course of bringing this collection of essays to light—from realizing "You know, there still isn't a collection of essays on Sigourney," to seeing our manuscript into print—we have had the great pleasure of working with a wonderful and diverse set of authors and have received significant support from many individuals and institutions. We would like to thank the Lattie Coor Fund and the Department of English of the University of Vermont and the Humanities Institute at Fairfield University for funding our research and a public forum on Sigourney and other women poets. We also want to thank both universities for their generosity and their commitment to scholarship, which made it possible for us to enjoy overlapping sabbaticals so that we could work on this project at the same time.

We thank Brian Halley of the University of Massachusetts Press, who provided sage advice at crucial moments, as well as the anonymous reviewers whose careful and informed critique of the collection and its individual essays was a great help. Our contributors were extraordinarily dedicated to the project, and their essays demonstrate that Sigourney has become a central figure for innovative scholarship in the American tradition. We also thank our colleagues Nancy Welch, Laura Korobkin, Kathleen Kete, Robert Epstein, Johanna Garvey, and Shannon Kelley, who offered insight, humor and enthusiasm. Finally, we would like to thank our husbands, John Howe and Thomas Hefferon, as well as our children, Madeline and David, for feeding us and picking up the domestic slack while we talked on the phone, worried, edited, and wrote. When we first proposed this collaboration, we did not anticipate how challenging and fruitful it would be nor how our own friendship would produce such substantial work. We hope our collection of critical essays on Lydia Sigourney is a beacon for future collaborative projects that work to recover nineteenth-century female authors.

Mary Louise Kete and Elizabeth Petrino

LYDIA SIGOURNEY

INTRODUCTION

Mary Louise Kete and Elizabeth Petrino

As Nina Baym wrote in a 1990 essay, if "Lydia Howard Huntley Sigourney had not lived, it would have been necessary to invent her."[1] One of the most prolific authors writing between the American Revolution and the Civil War, Sigourney (1791–1865) retold her life history multiple times in various genres and reinvented herself in ways that became a blueprint for a successful literary career in America. If, as Baym speculates, this canny reinvention began during Sigourney's own lifetime, then it has surely continued in the views of critics who have seen her, variously, as historian, essayist, infant elegist, social reformer, educator, literary entrepreneur, cosmopolite, and more.[2] Like most of the American women who helped to shape America's values during the nineteenth century, Sigourney and her contributions were "disremembered" (to borrow Toni Morrison's term) in the official literary histories that twentieth-century Americans wrote for themselves.[3] In fact, by the mid-twentieth century, Emily Dickinson, Sigourney's much younger contemporary, had become the lone nineteenth-century American woman writer with a secure, prominent place in the canon of literature taught in college and high school.

But as a new generation of scholars worked to reveal the importance of nineteenth-century women as writers, readers, buyers, sellers, and givers of literature, they found Sigourney's name everywhere—on the dusty shelves of libraries, in the yellowed pages of old magazines, and among the records of publishing houses and bookstores. She had begun publishing during the second decade of the nineteenth century and went on to dominate the literary marketplace as it took shape during the decades before the Civil War. Sigourney's work appeared in every available print venue. Her poems were featured in newspapers, magazines, anthologies, and holiday gift books. She also published schoolbooks, essays, memoirs, short fiction, and novels. She expressed powerful opinions about the role of women in society and was not afraid to advocate against government policies that undermined what she saw as the promise of America. At the same time, she became a paragon of American womanhood and middle-class rectitude in ways similar to today's public personae of Martha Stewart and Oprah Winfrey. Despite the extraordinarily public nature of their actual lives, Stewart and Winfrey have created an intimate sense of sympathy and collaboration with their audiences and thus have fashioned themselves into celebrity embodiments of the American everywoman.[4] In her nineteenth-century version of that self-invention, Sigourney became such a ubiquitous presence that her oppositional politics and her sometimes radical innovations in education, publishing, and aesthetics were perceived not as threatening but as necessary to the formation of a more perfect Union.

Thus, in her epigram, Baym was being only slightly hyperbolic in substituting Sigourney for God in Voltaire's famous phrase "if God did not exist, it would be necessary to invent him." It gave her a way to express her astonishment over the fact that so many of the new questions that students were asking about the past—especially about the role of women in American culture—were leading to a woman whose life and works had left so little trace in the official accounts of American literary and cultural history. Yet since Baym wrote those words in 1990, Sigourney's work has proliferated in literary anthologies, poetry collections, and syllabi and been analyzed in articles, books, theses, and graduate dissertations. As recently as 2010, Natalie Merchant (formerly of the band 10,000 Maniacs) set one of Sigourney's most famous poems, "Indian Names," to music and included it in her album *Leave Your Sleep*.[5]

Given this shift, we felt we were reprising Baym's astonishment when we discovered that, until now, there had been no collection of essays devoted to reconsidering nineteenth-century America's most popular and consequential woman poet.[6] In conceptualizing this project, we have been conscious that digital research platforms now make primary documents and secondary criticism easily accessible. One of our aims, then, has been to curate a collection that represents a wide variety of the new work being done on Sigourney, not only to make these critical studies easily available in one place but also to promote scholarly conversations that cross methodological and disciplinary lines. As the first editors of a collection of essays devoted to Sigourney's writings, we have also have focused on foregrounding the scholarly practice of reconsideration, which becomes possible only after the initial work of recovery. Thus, we have included new essays by four scholars who played key roles in Sigourney's contemporary reinvention:

Sandra A. Zagarell, Paul Lauter, Annie Finch, and Paula Bernat Bennett. In our invitation to contribute, we asked them to reconsider Sigourney in light of their inaugural thoughts about her and their subsequent scholarship and teaching. As a result, their essays reflect the significance of larger disciplinary changes that have accompanied a resurgence of interest in women's contributions to nineteenth-century culture. One need look only at the notes that follow many of the other contributed essays to see how this quartet's early work, and that of others such as Baym, Ann Douglas, and Mary DeJong, continues to influence critical conversations.

A conventional goal of an edited collection is to allow readers to conceive of the essays as conversations with one another. We have attempted to amplify this effect by inviting our authors to reconsider their own essays in light of at least one of the other essays we have collected here. In addition, we have sorted the essays into two broad categories to reflect the main trajectories in Sigourney scholarship and allow for a reconsideration of the apparent differences between critical approaches and methodologies that privilege the literary text versus the cultural text. Following a main trend in Sigourney studies, the essays in part 1 place her writing at the center of their attention, focusing primarily on poetics, rhetoric, and generic innovation. Those in part 2 unpack her participation in the cultural movements of her day or concentrate on the functions that she serves in our contemporary cultural arena, where we still struggle with issues of American identity, mourning, gender conventions, and poetics.

How do we interpret Sigourney's poetics? How do we understand her role in the cultural movements of her day? To these standard academic questions, we add a third: How does reading Sigourney affect current readers and writers? In answer to this last question, the scholar and poet Annie Finch provides an epigraph addressed directly to Sigourney, who has served as muse and warning in Finch's own efforts to negotiate what it means to be a woman poet at the end of the twentieth century and the beginning of the twenty-first. We are equally fortunate to close the collection with the renowned scholar Paula Bernat Bennett's afterword, which offers a very different way to answer this last question. In reconsidering Sigourney and the essays of this collection, Bennett posits that, "as for Whitman," Sigourney's "multiplicity was the essence of her literary mission because it was and is the essence of America in all its contradictions, excrescences, and moments of genius . . . [and] she wrote, first and foremost, as the American she was."

What had been the major obstacle to Sigourney's place in the canon of American literature, becomes, for Bennett, its foundation.

In chapter 1, we open the collection with our own feminist reassessment of Sigourney's biography, weaving together the dramatic story of her life and the history of her popular and critical reception. Chapters 2 through 7 reconsider Sigourney's poetry, nonfiction, and fiction. In chapter 2, Jennifer Putzi argues that scholars misrepresent her as uninterested in issues of originality and inspiration. Through a series of rigorous, contextualized readings, she unpacks Sigourney's early poetics of collaboration with her readers to establish a new kind of authorial ethos that initially allowed for professional success. In chapter 3, Joan R. Wry also takes up the question of Sigourney's poetics, this time by examining her career-long fascination with the material elements of women's culture and with the powerful trope of the apostrophe. Wry reads her oft-studied fabric poems as extensive, metaphysical conceits that offer traces of a Christian meditative and spiritual exercise: the expansion of one's spiritual self by extending empathy to the most recalcitrant, most material of objects. Wry argues that, like John Donne and Edward Taylor before her, Sigourney used her spiritual practices to inform and enrich her poetics.

In chapter 4, Sandra A. Zagarell focuses on Sigourney's innovative choices in her prose piece *Sketch of Connecticut, Forty Years Since.* As she critiques the monumentalizing narrative of America's founding years, which compresses the experiences of the Revolutionary years into a triumphalist, unitary plotline, Sigourney experiments with ways to narrate the overlapping but incommensurable experiences of that time and place as they diverged along class and ethnic lines. Zagarell notes that the sketch is one of several examples of Sigourney's personal ambivalence about the treatment of the First Nations; throughout her life, she continued to imagine an America that did not depend upon the actual and figurative disappearance of its native people. In chapter 5, Sean Epstein-Corbin considers Sigourney's adaptation of the travelogue genre to map a sentimental geography for a distinctly American yet cosmopolitan identity. In this way, he argues, she attempted to counter the nationalist and patriarchal model of American identity that was already ascendant. More importantly, he suggests what contemporary theorists of cosmopolitanism might gain from seriously engaging with Sigourney's extensive efforts to negotiate this still contentious territory.

In chapter 6, Gary Kelly, who compiled the first important reprinting of Sigourney's selected works, wrestles with relationships among her poetics, her politics, and her lived experience by situating her in the context of transatlantic debates about feminism. In his discussion of Sigourney's relationship to ambition, Kelly offers a dense and sophisticated description of newly found archival material that throws light on a key moment in her invention of herself as a literary woman. His chapter captures the drama of her dangerous negotiation of competing demands as played out in the circulation of published and private texts. In chapter 7, Angela Sorby considers one of Sigourney's favorite, and least studied, topics: the cuteness of children and animals. Grounding her observations in careful readings of some of Sigourney's liveliest works, Sorby focuses on the babies, girls, and cats that populate Sigourney's poems. Like authors who make use of the sentimental, she argues, Sigourney used her mode of cuteness to place the reader into a powerful collaborative relationship. Yet unlike sentimentality, that cuteness engages the reader in a relationship of playful reciprocity that is structured on capitalist exchange rather than gift exchange.

In chapters 8 through 13, the contributors consider Sigourney's role in the emergence of a new, modern culture of authorship and feminine authority during the nineteenth century and the way in which she functions within our own contemporary culture. In chapter 8, Ann Beebe reminds us that Sigourney was one of a constellation of women trying to make a space, or establish an ethos, for women as authors. Her essay works through the previously unnoted connections between one of Sigourney's protagonists and one of the novelist E.D.E.N. Southworth's. Both authors, Beebe argues, were working on the same project: they were theorizing, through narrative fiction, what it would mean for a woman author to advocate for social and political change and forge a new aesthetic in nineteenth-century poetry. In chapter 9, Janet Dean also suggests the importance of reading Sigourney within the context of her women peers. She traces the intertextual resonances between Sigourney's long poem *Pocahontas* (1841) and Felicia Hemans's epic *The Forest Sanctuary* (1825). Both use the same uncommon stanza form, and both focus on transatlantic exile during the age of colonization. Sigourney, Dean argues, did not take up Hemans's forms and themes to mimic her British counterpart or simply to burnish her own reputation. Rather, she was working to reframe American history by telling a less Eurocentric narrative of national ascendancy.

In chapter 10, Amy J. Lueck marshals archival evidence of nineteenth-century reconsiderations of Sigourney, carefully tracing the way in which her authorial identity circulated and morphed as her works circulated through reprinting. Lueck provides important insight into Sigourney's iconicity by showing the productive tensions among the various identities that the author herself constructed at particular times and in particular contexts. She also considers the tension between these authorized Sigourneys and those that various editors constructed for their own purposes. In chapter 11, Paul Lauter seeks to account for the inscrutability of Sigourney's poetry of mourning in the twentieth century. For Lauter, this reflects not only a shift in American norms but reflects a larger shift in the American imaginary, in which the notion of metropolitanism has replaced the notion of rural virtue.

In chapter 12, Ricardo Miguel-Alfonso thinks about the way in which conventional scholarship struggles to conceptualize Sigourney's relationship to transcendentalist culture. He stresses the parallels between Ralph Waldo Emerson's more familiar educational ideals and Sigourney's own theory of education, which she began to posit and practice in the 1820s. As Miguel-Alfonso argues, she played a crucial role in the spread of what we now recognize as transcendentalist values. In chapter 13, Annie Finch reconsiders Sigourney's influence on her own development of a poetic ethos. Looking back on her changing relationship with Sigourney, she recounts how these changes reflect the struggles of finding her voice as a poet and reminds us of Sigourney's ongoing importance to contemporary women who would be poets: she made it possible for a person to imagine herself as a woman and poet.

Together, these essays challenge us to reconsider what Sigourney herself might have meant by declaring, as she did in her posthumously published *Letters of Life,* that the "literary course of her life" had been "happy." Such a modest adjective hardly seems adequate to describe her achievements as a professional author, an educational theorist, a political activist, an entrepreneur, and a cultural icon. Nor does it seem to accurately characterize the uneasy and shifting critical reception of her works in the years since her death. Within the American context, as the essays in this collection suggest, the pursuit (much less the achievement) of happiness is no modest endeavor.

NOTES

1. Nina Baym, "Reinventing Lydia Sigourney," *American Literature* 62 (1990): 385–404.
2. Following are a few of the critical essays that have revived Sigourney: Ann Douglas Wood, "Mrs. Sigourney and the Sensibility of Inner Space," *New England Quarterly* 45 (1972): 163–81; Mary DeJong, "Legacy Profile: Lydia Howard Huntley Sigourney," *Legacy* 5 (1988), 35ff; Wendy Dasler Johnson, "Reviving Lydia Huntley Sigourney," *Romanticism on the Net* 29 (2003); Sandra A. Zagarell, "Expanding 'America': Lydia Sigourney's *Sketch of Connecticut,* Catharine Sedgwick's *Hope Leslie,*" *Tulsa Studies in Women's Literature* 6 (1987): 225–45; Elizabeth A. Petrino, "'Feet so precious charged': Dickinson, Sigourney, and the Child Elegy," *Tulsa Studies in Women's Literature* 13 (1994): 317–38; and Annie Finch, "The Sentimental Poetess in the World: Metaphor and Poetic Subjectivity in Lydia Sigourney's Nature Poetry," *Legacy* 5 (1988): 3–18. More recent critical reappraisals include Joan R. Wry, "Lydia Sigourney's 'To a Shred of Linen': Lineaments of the Domestic and the Sublime," *American Transcendental Quarterly* 22 (2008): 403–14; Paula Bernat Bennett, "Was Sigourney a Poetess? The Aesthetics of Victorian Plenitude in Lydia Sigourney's Poetry," *Comparative American Studies* 5 (2007): 265–89; and Melissa Ladd Teed, "A Passion for Distinction: Lydia Huntley Sigourney and the Creation of a Literary Reputation," *New England Quarterly* 77 (2004): 51–69.
3. For Toni Morrison, the terms *rememory* and *disremembering* emphasize both the conscious, intentional work of constructing meaning out of the vestiges of the past and the limits of the rational mind's ability to control the violence inherent to both acts. In *Beloved,* her narrator says of the title character, "Disremembered and unaccounted for, she cannot be lost because no one is looking for her, and even if they were, how can they call her if they don't know her name?" (New York: Vintage, 1987, 321).
4. Neither Winfrey's wealth nor Stewart's felony conviction has undercut American women's trust in their advice about everything from what to read, to how to cook, to how to raise children.
5. Natalie Merchant, *Leave Your Sleep* (New York: Nonesuch Records, 2010).
6. Mary Loeffelholz describes at least three distinct and not always overlapping constructs of Sigourney: "the staunch republican historical writer, . . . the ur-sentimentalist poetess," and the "nature poet" (*From School to Salon: Reading Nineteenth-Century American Women's Poetry* [Princeton: Princeton University Press, 2007], 34). Gary Kelly addresses this fragmented sense of Sigourney in *Lydia Sigourney: Poetry and Prose* ([Toronto: Broadview, 2008], 11–56).

1

LYDIA SIGOURNEY

FROM REINVENTION TO RECONSIDERATION

Mary Louise Kete and Elizabeth Petrino

Who was Lydia Sigourney? It's hard to separate this question from the story of American literary history. Born in 1791, just a year after the ratification of the American Constitution, she invented and reinvented herself as an author during the years that her fellow Americans were inventing and reinventing a literary culture for their new nation. Sigourney's contemporaries eagerly read her poetry, novels, memoirs, and pedagogical theories, and she became one of America's first celebrity artists. Yet given the cultural shifts that followed the American Civil War, this level of fame did not survive after her death in 1865. In the first decades of the twentieth century, as scholars established the major plotlines of America's literary history, Sigourney was relegated to a supporting role or forgotten altogether. Her aesthetic was too romantic; her writings too didactic. She was, frankly, too feminine. At best, she was a footnote to the story of nineteenth-century American poetry; at worst, she was the paradigm of everything the twentieth-century modernists rejected. She became known as a genteel sentimentalist who wrote accessible yet overwrought poetry for low- and middle-brow audiences. Critical attention to her work languished, and assumptions about it remained unchallenged until the end of the twentieth century.

Even Sigourney's biographer, Gordon S. Haight, who published a book-length study of her in 1930, declared that the "reputation she enjoyed for half a century as America's leading poetess" was not only unwarranted but incomprehensible. He saw it as an example of an earlier America's utter lack of taste, a predilection that was best forgotten.[1] Haight's cartoonish version of Sigourney portrays her as both unprofessional and overly commercial, a conveyer of saccharine, moralizing, unoriginal, and conventionally metered verse. Worse, as far as Haight was concerned, she was not only unable to transcend what he saw as the natural limitations of her sex, but she also failed as a mother and a wife. The most damning accusation appears in a slightly later literary history, Fred Lewis Pattee's notorious *The Feminine Fifties,* which argues that Sigourney had damaged literary history by facilitating women's dominance in the literary marketplace, a misfortune that forced important male authors to struggle to create an authentically American literary culture.[2]

By the 1970s and 1980s, however, feminist literary historians and students had begun finding new answers to the question "Who is Lydia Sigourney?" They revealed large and consequential bodies of prose and verse; a public career as a professional author, an educator, and a political activist; and a private life as a wife and a mother. The disjunction between the older claims and this new information was so great that Judith Fetterley, in the introduction to her important *Provisions: A Reader from 19th-Century Women* (1985), questioned whether "authorities" such as Pattee and Haight had even "bothered to read the material they discuss."[3] This was the context for what Nina Baym has seen as the reinvention of Lydia Sigourney or, as Mary Loeffelholz has said more recently, the reinventions of several, slightly different, but overlapping Sigourneys.[4] In Sandra A. Zagarell's 1987 essay "Expanding 'America,'" for instance, Sigourney appears as a deliberately political author, a historian, who dares "to critique restrictive, masculinist" government policies through her depiction of "an America grounded in inclusiveness and communitarianism."[5] Mary DeJong's influential 1988 "Profile" maps Sigourney's cultural importance in opening professions such as education and social activism to women. For this Sigourney, poetry is less the "spontaneous overflow of powerful feelings" or "emotion recollected in tranquility" (as William Wordsworth contends in his 1802 preface to the *Lyrical Ballads*) but more an extension of her womanly duty to nurture and improve American society.[6] This is the Sigourney that Baym elaborates: a woman for whom writing is an adjunct to a conscious aspiration to "enter the public sphere and influence the formation of public opinion" as a "public mother" of America's republic.[7]

Yet another 1988 essay, Annie Finch's "The Sentimental Poetess in the World," asked readers to consider Sigourney's poetry on its own terms.

Finch found in Sigourney an alternative paradigm for poetic authority or voice: the poetess, a persona whose ethos is distinctively feminine (anti-masculine, anti-individualistic, and anti-transcendent), whose interests and sensibilities are aligned with nature, and whose aesthetic mode is sentimentality.[8] This Sigourney is first and foremost an artist whose medium is verse and whose choices of topic, genre, and voice consciously and subversively embrace an experience of the world that is inflected by conventions of femininity. As Loeffelholz points out, Finch's notion of Sigourney preceded an explosion of critical interest in sentimentality and sentimentalism among scholars in the late 1990s and early 2000s. By that time, sentimentality had come to connote unwarranted, inauthentic, and manipulative displays of emotion; it had been detached from its roots in eighteenth-century philosophical discourse and from its historical association with the positive and powerful force of sympathy. Thus, for a new generation of critics, Finch's essay was critically important in the reconsideration of the sentimental as a powerful discursive mode while it also opened a door into fresh appreciations of the aesthetic aspects of Sigourney's poetics.[9]

As subsequent scholars and students have been introduced to Sigourney's work in class or through the work of contemporary artists, the outlines of these reinvented Sigourneys have become filled in, expanded, and qualified. Since 2003, when Paul Lauter published a revolutionary revision of the American canon in his *Heath Anthology of American Literature,* selections by Sigourney have been added to most major literature anthologies designed for undergraduate classrooms, including those published by Norton, Broadview, Longman, and McGraw-Hill. In 2008, Gary Kelly released the first modern collection of Sigourney's works, thus enlarging her presence in the "new" canon of nineteenth-century American literature alongside other recovered authors such as Lydia Maria Child, Frederick Douglass, Harriet Beecher Stowe, Frances Harper, William Cullen Bryant, Henry Wadsworth Longfellow, and Julia Ward Howe.[10] Kelly's comprehensive biographical sketch of Sigourney, included in his edited collection, has been especially important, for it reflects much of the recovery research done since the late 1980s. Yet while scholarship has helped to open up new fields of study—for instance, book and periodical history, disability studies, women's history, transatlantic studies, and feminist poetics—there has yet to be a book-length, critical biography to make sense of the multiple, sometimes competing, Sigourneys.[11]

Who was Lydia Sigourney? One challenge to answering that question arises from the fact that, like other romantic authors, she revised the story of her life several times over the years. Her memoirs *Letters to Young Ladies, Letters to Mothers,* and *Letters to My Pupils* and her posthumously published memoir *Letters of Life* are our main sources for tracing her own version of the major plotlines and salient details of her story. By the close of the eighteenth century, the epistolary form was common in both fiction and nonfiction, and for Sigourney it became a signature device that she gradually developed into a kind of autobiography. But the self that she constructed through these epistolary memoirs differs fundamentally from the autonomous, self-possessed individual who features in Wordsworth's autobiographical "Prelude," or Douglass's several memoirs, or Walt Whitman's ever-expanding "Song of Myself." Rather, Sigourney's books of letters portray a less unified, more collaborative self who is produced and sustained dialogically through the intimate exchange of sentiments. As figure 1 demonstrates, she almost always pictures herself in relation to other people, whether as a daughter, a teacher, a mother, or, most importantly, a poet.

In many ways, Sigourney's personal history and public career epitomize the nineteenth-century ideal of the American woman, a conception that numerous novelists embodied in their heroines—for instance, in the beloved characters Gerty, from Susan Maria Cummins's *The Lamplighter* (1854), and Jo, from Louisa May Alcott's *Little Women* (1868).[12] Both of these novels are American versions of female bildungsroman: stories of moral and spiritual development that focus on heroines whose struggles begin in girlhood poverty and are alleviated by hard work and the timely help of benefactors and whose success is marked by a self-sufficiency that leads to marriage, children, a secure home, and a respected place in the community. Sigourney's own life, which can be seen as laying the groundwork for such stories, was shaped by a conflict between similar conceptions of what it means to be a woman and what it means to be an American. As we have mentioned, she was born in 1791, two years after the ratification of the U.S. Constitution. Her father, Ezekiel Huntley, had served in the Revolutionary War before marrying Lydia Howard, who died of tuberculosis before their first wedding anniversary. His second wife, Zerviah Wentworth, gave birth to the couple's only child on September 1. By naming the child Lydia Howard in honor of Huntley's first wife, they reinforced the importance of remembering the names, at least, of the women who had come before.

FIGURE 1. Frontispiece of Lydia Sigourney's *Letters to My Pupils, with Narrative and Biographical Sketches* (New York: Carter and Brothers, 1853).

The Huntley family lived in Norwich, Connecticut, on property owned by Dr. Daniel Lathrop and his wife, Jerusha. Huntley worked for the Lathrops as what is variously described as a gardener, a handyman, and a groundskeeper; and he continued in that position after Dr. Lathrop's death in 1782. As a result, Lydia had the good fortune to be raised in a household dominated by strong women. Like the characters Gerty and Jo, she was lucky in attracting mentors and patrons. Jerusha Lathrop was famously well educated, politically informed, and opinionated, and together she and

Sigourney's mother oversaw the child's early education. Both were devoted to fostering Lydia's precocious intelligence and creativity, and they were determined to make sure that she could take advantage of the promise of a new nation in a new century. As they trained her in the onerous and complicated business of housework and household management, Zerviah and Jerusha offered equally valuable instruction in belles lettres (the period's term for light, entertaining, artistic compositions), serious academic subjects such as religion and history, and emerging empirical sciences such as geology, botany, and astronomy.

As the nexus of the private domain of the home and the public sphere of the market and politics, education became the social arena that most shaped Sigourney's sense of self.[13] She studied both with tutors at home and at a variety of local, or common, schools, where she experienced a wide variety of teaching practices from which she later drew as she developed her own theories of pedagogy.[14] In *Letters of Life,* Sigourney humorously described the limitations of the conventional educational opportunities for young ladies such as herself, in which mastery of fine needlework was succeeded by "what were termed the higher branches, including music, painting, and embroidery."[15] But she stressed the importance of her less conventional training in mathematics, spelling and grammar, literature and elocution, and classical languages—Latin, Greek, and Hebrew—which enriched her sense of herself and broadened her sense of the world. Importantly, it was these studies that prepared her to be independent and financially secure. Though her family was hardly well off, young Lydia had one of the most advanced educations it was possible for girl to have at that time. For her, every aspect of education, even the experience of walking to a new schoolhouse "on the green plain near the meeting-house, half a mile from home," "gave [her] a spirit of self-reliance and a sense of liberty and power never before realized."[16] Education would become her main platform, providing the resources that she would draw on in her attempts to resolve the apparent conflict between notions of gender that restrict "the spirit of self-reliance" and notions of nationality that expand the "sense of liberty and power."

Sigourney's private reading and her formal education did much to shape her taste for romantic and especially sentimental literature. At the same time, her mother and Jerusha Lathrop encouraged self-expression, in nonfictional and fictional forms, for its own sake. With unlimited access to the

Lathrops' library, she was able to read Edward Young's "Night Thoughts" (1742), Salomon Gessner's "Death of Abel" (translated into English in 1758), James Hervey's *Meditations among the Tombs* (1746), and other eighteenth-century works that cultivated in her the deep and ready feeling that became a staple element of both British and American romanticism. Like many young girls of the time (and like Alcott's Jo), she nurtured this taste by surreptitiously reading popular, sensational, gothic novels such as Ann Radcliffe's *The Mysteries of Udolpho* (1794). She shared with other authors of her generation, such as the American poets Hannah F. Gould and William Cullen Bryant and the British poets John Keats and Felicia Hemans, an early appreciation for the formal prosody of neoclassical verse forms (such as the ode and ekphrasis) and a desire to use them to express the new sensibility that would come to be called romanticism. This sensibility valued nature and the natural over artifice and convention, strong feelings and intuition over composure and rationalism, authenticity and originality over conformity and convention, individual experience and idealism over received norms and cynicism. Generally optimistic, this sensibility led to efforts to reform the exploitation of the disadvantaged and to improve the condition of humankind. In painting, sculpture, literature, and music, artists were particularly interested in eliciting and depicting the strong feelings of transcendence that can come through the experience of radical sympathy with others (the aesthetics of sentimentality) or radical confrontation with the infinite (the aesthetics of sublimity).

Sigourney's taste leaned toward the sentimental aspects of romanticism, as reflected in a letter she received from her friend Hannah Flag Gould. Gould was nearly her exact contemporary and also published a number of influential books of poetry in the early part of the nineteenth century: "Walking the streets, and in the most exuberant spirits, talking with a companion, if a trembling, white-haired aged man passes before me, I feel the tears gushing hot, and rolling down to quench the smile upon my lips, before I am aware of the change in my emotions. But it is not mourning nor sorrow that does this. I can only call it melting."[17] This kind of sentimentalism, neither "mourning nor sorrow" but a physical, supraverbal experience of sympathy, formed the basis of much of Sigourney's later writing and informed her ideas about gender, education, and politics. Her taste for the experience of overwhelming emotions, her fascination with the relationship between the self and others, her closeness to nature, and especially her belief in the value of intuition and sympathy would only grow stronger.

Like her fictional avatars, Gerty and Jo, Sigourney began contributing to her family's support by teaching what she had learned to other young women and girls. She "kept" two schools, one that closed after her partner died and another that continued until she married in 1819 at the age of twenty-eight. Her classroom experience laid the groundwork for a life-long interest in how people learn and in the possibility that there are modes of communication besides those that are verbal and rational.[18] Like Emma Willard (1787–1870), who became a close friend, Sigourney was invested in developing ways to educate girls to face the challenges of the new century. Her explicitly didactic publications, such as her memoirs, etiquette guides, and advice manuals, were rooted in these early experiences as a teacher, but so were her poetry and fiction. Sigourney was unapologetic about having designs (as Jane Tompkins put it) on her readers' morality.[19] To do this, she relied on what she called "the language of affections" as conveyed by physical touch, nonverbal signs, and the gaze, which both preceded and exceeded verbal language.[20] This is illustrated in the engraving that Sigourney chose as a frontispiece to her 1851 *Letters to My Pupils* (figure 1) in which she is depicted with her arm around a younger woman's shoulders, their hands and eyes joined in what appears to be an active scene of nonverbal communication.[21]

Sigourney's sense of self-reliance, which arose from being both educated and an educator, was expressed as the ability to take care of herself and others. It also led to increased opportunities for self-invention. During this early period, she came to the attention of Daniel Wadsworth of Hartford, Connecticut, who shared and fostered many of her values regarding the new country's need for education and culture. Wadsworth, who also patronized the romantic painters Thomas Cole and Frederic Church, sponsored the publication of Sigourney's first volume, *Moral Pieces, in Prose and Verse,* in 1815. This small book, Haight explained, attracted "advance subscriptions amounting to nearly a thousand copies at a dollar each."[22] Keeping in mind that one dollar in 1815 would buy what fifteen dollars can buy in 2017, we can see that Sigourney's words met the felt needs of a new generation of young readers, women and men alike. Just as importantly, perhaps, critics heralded her as a new literary light. For instance, a contributor to the *North American Review* called her "a most deserving and interesting young woman" who had "emancipated herself from the humblest penury, and still found leisure at a very early age, to compose this volume."[23] Along with Bryant's "Thanatopsis" (which the *North American Review* would publish in 1817) and paintings by Cole and Church, *Moral Pieces* helped usher in what has come to be known as the American Romantic Era, with its celebration of feelings, nature, individualism, and originality.[24]

Although Sigourney clearly embraced writing as a means to "emancipate herself" financially, she expected to continue supporting herself and her parents by teaching. She wrote at least half of the content of *Moral Pieces* for use in her own classroom and revised much of the rest for other teachers to use in their classrooms and homes. In the second decade of the nineteenth century, most Americans would have struggled to imagine supporting themselves and their families as professional authors. Presses were proliferating, but American publishers could reprint British materials for free, so they had no reason to pay American authors much, if anything. Later in the decade, when Longfellow confessed to his father that he aspired to be a professional author, his father reminded him that a writer had to be either independently wealthy or beholden to a patron: "A literary life, to one who has the means of support, must be very pleasant. But there is not wealth enough in this country to afford encouragement and patronage to merely literary men."[25] Given conventions about gender and class, which held that respectable middle-class women should not put themselves forward in the marketplace, this prospect would have been even more daunting for Sigourney. Even in republican America, women were broadly divided into those worthy of respect—ladies—and those who were not. Young, unmarried, and poor, Sigourney had only a tenuous claim to the status of lady, despite her education, her whiteness, and her association with established families such as the Lathrops and the Wadsworths. The challenge of imagining how to be both self-reliant and a lady, both emancipated and "a true woman," remained ongoing throughout Sigourney's career.

The commercial literary marketplace, which Sigourney would dominate by the 1840s, had not yet supplanted the conventional system of literary patronage. She was lucky, then, to have a patron like Wadsworth, who not only advised her but also encouraged members of his social network to preorder copies of her book. In later years, her own name would open the kinds of doors that Wadsworth had opened for her when she first arrived in Hartford. Largely to gratify the desires of her husband, Charles, she published her next two books anonymously; but by 1827, she chose to use her full name, Lydia H. Sigourney, on her collection *Poems.* Thereafter, although she occasionally employed the initial "H.," she more frequently used her married name and became known as Mrs. Sigourney. Wadsworth's patronage did not merely establish Sigourney as an author and help her earn much needed money, but it also helped ensure the respectability that underwrote her future success as an educator.

Authorship, then, was initially an adjunct to teaching, not a status to which Sigourney aspired for its own sake. Neither, perhaps surprisingly, was the status of wife. The success of her schools and *Moral Pieces* had allowed her to imagine a version of womanly emancipation that was at odds with marriage. She had made up her mind "never to leave my parents" but to continue in the role of dutiful daughter.[26] This rationale became a trope in midcentury American domestic fiction. After demonstrating their ability to be self-sufficient and to support their loved ones in a secure home, protagonists such as Gerty and Jo have to overcome their own ambivalence about marriage before this final sign of their success can occur. Sigourney's notion of a daughter's duty had powerful, liberatory potential.[27] She had begun to think of herself as a literary woman in the mold, as Gary Kelly explains, of an earlier generation of transatlantic bluestockings, such as Mary Wollstonecraft, Hannah More, Mercy Warren, Priscilla Wakefield, and Jerusha Lathrop, who had laid a foundation for modern Anglo-American feminism.[28] As a daughter, she could pursue a career as a means to support her parents, and she could resist what she understood as the possibly limiting state of marriage. In *Letters of Life,* she clearly revealed her anxiety about marriage as she described her concern that it would threaten her ability to take care of her parents by forestalling her personal economic emancipation. Sigourney understood that common law determined that a wife's economic and political interests were subsumed into her husband's. It was a husband's duty to provide the income for his family and a wife's duty to care for him and to bear children. It would be up to her husband to decide whether or not to continue to support his wife's parents with his money. Even if he did choose to support his wife's family, it would no longer be seen as necessary or appropriate for her to work for money.

In 1819, however, Lydia Howard Huntley met and then married Charles Sigourney (1778–1854). Thirteen years older than his bride, Charles was a successful businessman and a widower with three children, who seems to have genuinely attracted her with his "pair of deep set and most expressive black eyes."[29] Initially, Kelly explains, the couple seemed to share opinions on politics, religion, and art. They went on to have five children together, though, as was common at that time, only two survived infancy—Mary and Alexander. (Alexander later died at the age of nineteen from tuberculosis.) Charles Sigourney's wedding gifts are suggestive of his plans for their future union as well as his admiration for her intellect. Did the copy of Samuel Richardson's *Sir Charles Grandison* (1757) provide a model for the kind of husband he hoped to be: a moral guide and loving authority who would shape his much younger wife into the woman he hoped she would become? Did the gift of a microscope, a rare and expensive piece of scientific equipment, and a copy of the bluestocking Priscilla Wakefield's *An Introduction to Botany* suggest his approval of her intellectual talents?[30]

Although Sigourney confessed to have found it hard to marshal as much enthusiasm for Richardson's old-fashioned novel as she did for the new romantic novels of Sir Walter Scott, the botany book, written by one of Britain's leading feminist authors, deeply influenced her and strengthened her connections to what Kelly calls the "feminist literary Atlantic."[31] The couple seemed to be well matched, collaborating on a variety of charitable causes (including the founding of what would become Trinity College) that supported Hartford's goal of becoming a forward-looking, vibrant cultural center.

Sigourney continued writing and publishing during the first decade of her marriage but in a manner that suggests the couple's shared ambivalence about her role as a public figure. They worked together on her ambitious, book-length historical poem of 1822, *Traits of the Aborigines,* with Charles helping to write (or at least to edit) the extensive documentation included in the book. Yet he insisted on its anonymous publication, for he was uneasy about her entry into public life and her artistic talent. Consequently, Sigourney composed her two subsequent books, *Sketch of Connecticut, Forty Years Since* (1824) and *Poems* (1827), during her husband's absences from home. The Sigourneys' marriage suffered the burdens of several different kinds of stresses. Their family was growing, yet it also endured the painful loss of three babies; at the same time, Charles's businesses were doing much less well than he had expected. Most important, as Gary Kelly makes clear in chapter 6, was the rift between the couple's notions of the other's duties as husband or wife. While Charles's ideas of what it meant to be a man and a husband had been forward-looking during the first decades of the nineteenth century, he was threatened by the same challenges that Sigourney was embracing in her reinvention of what it meant to be a woman, a wife, and an author. Nevertheless, they remained married until Charles died in 1854, by which time Lydia Sigourney had become the family's main financial support and was publishing most of her works under her married name.

Sigourney's experiences as a teacher continued to shape her sense of self and inform her work at all levels. As Loeffelholz persuasively argues, she had entered "her new life" as a wife while "still thinking of herself as 'schoolmistress and a literary woman,'" for the schoolroom acted as a "matrix of the social relations of Sigourney's poetic and prose genres."[32] This is most evident in the advice literature she directed at adults, who were eager for her views about, for example, marital bliss and household management in *How to Be Happy* (1833) or courtship, marriage, and motherhood in *Letters to Young Ladies* (1833) and *Letters to Mothers* (1838). In expressing the feelings and concerns of her readers (the aspiring "young ladies" or anxious "mothers"), Sigourney addressed how they might reshape their own experiences to match or exceed their unique potential as individuals. She had a similar goal in the literature she wrote for children, which was both romantic in sensibility and republican in political orientation. In her verse and stories for children, the ideals of sentimental or sympathetic appreciation for nature, the weak or the poor, the careful nurturance of strong emotions, and the pursuit of personal authenticity were bound up in her notions of the kind of citizen the still fledgling democracy required.

Although Sigourney never returned to classroom teaching after 1819, her essays on both pragmatic innovations in pedagogy and theoretical investigations into the nature of language and the process of learning were influential. These popular and often reprinted essays advanced the position (shared by educational reformers such as Elizabeth Peabody and Horace Mann) that widespread education was the key to America's prosperity and that every segment of the population—blacks, Native Americans, the deaf, the blind—could and should be educated. As a schoolmistress, Sigourney had had firsthand experience with the challenge of educating a deaf girl, Alice Cogswell. At that time, deafness was often considered a sign of intellectual deficiency; but with Sigourney as a teacher, Cogswell began to read and to write. She became one of Thomas Hopkins Gallaudet's first students in what became known as the American School of the Deaf in Hartford. Inspired by Cogswell, Sigourney developed a theory and a set of educational methods based on an appreciation of different modes of experiencing and communicating with the world.[33]

The notion of womanly duty that Sigourney was developing through the 1820s and 1830s, and that she would later claim was key to her success as an author, extended her responsibility from her personal household and family to the national family. Education reform, linked as it was for her to Christian evangelicalism and to her politics, was the context in which she came early to the debate about race relations. Her epic poem, *Traits of the Aborigines,* challenged the negative and dehumanizing image of Native peoples that dominated the American imaginary in the era of Indian removals and national expansion and thus undercut the notion that it was the Euro-American's Manifest Destiny to dominate the continent. Sigourney remained a life-long opponent of the American government's policies toward the sovereign First Nations. The title poem of her 1835 collection, *Zinzendorff, and Other Poems,* is yet another of her experiments in providing an explanatory narrative history—an epic—that not only integrates Native peoples into the story of America but also models a mutually beneficial, non-exploitative relationship between Euro-Americans and Native Americans.[34] Yet the book as a whole also illustrates the diversity of social and political issues that concerned Sigourney throughout her life as well as the range of genres that she co-opted to this task. It contains poems on the status of the First Nations people; Greek nationalism; Christian missionary work in New Zealand, Greenland, and Africa; female education; the treatment of prisoners and the mentally ill; and the harmful environmental effects of technological "progress." Her work to widen the reader's frame of reference, as she does in both these poems and her more conventional travelogues, bespeaks a consistent effort to imagine an American identity that could be both exceptional and cosmopolitan.

By the 1850s, Sigourney had been writing and publishing for more than thirty years and had actively participated in establishing a literary marketplace in which authors competed against one another for sales to readers rather than for the support of a few wealthy or elite patrons.[35] Having come to understand the value that her poetry and prose had for publishers, she had been able to drive up the amount they paid her (and other authors). Especially in the 1840s and 1850s, major periodicals such as *Godey's Lady's*

Book and *Graham's Magazine* had to compete to publish her work, but Sigourney understood her role in supplying them with material: "Promptitude was the life-blood of these contributions. Hungering presses must be fed, and not wait."[36]

For at least three decades, what the "hungering presses" and their readers most wanted was Sigourney's poetry. In general, her verse was inflected by sentimentality. Devoted to depicting strong emotional states and eliciting sympathy for her subjects, she distinctively melded everyday expressions with highly embellished, literary language to represent lost homes, dying relatives or friends, and threatened landscapes. Her adult readers looked to their "Sweet Singer of Hartford," as she was popularly known, for consolation and for reflections of, and on, their own lives. During her lifetime she spoke to her readers in a range of genres, but her fame as an elegist remained attached to her reputation long after her innovative work in the long narrative poem, humorous and children's verse, and hybrid genres was forgotten. In a culture in which elegy was both highly valued and widely practiced (they were commonly composed by men and women who made no claim to being artists), poems such as Sigourney's "Death of an Infant"—with its concentrated attention on what it feels like to see one's child change from living to dead—were celebrated.[37] Even poems such as "To a Shred of Linen," which begins as a humorous answer to the criticism and scrutiny that literary women (but not literary men) endure, invoke the power of a deathbed scene in their arguments about the interrelationship between domestic work and artistic work.

Like her British contemporary, Felicia Hemans (1793–1835), Sigourney participated in the transatlantic shift toward a romantic aesthetic by embracing and expanding the persona of the poetess. The role or ethos of the poetess in America and Britain was an exaggerated and studied performance of what were considered to be the defining qualities of femininity, especially the performance of an acute emotional and moral sensibility about the world. The poetess complimented rather than competed for the conventional authority granted to the poet, for her poems were imagined as the irrepressible expression of her natural experience of inspiration about such topics as love, beauty, nature, and the family. Sigourney's career, like Hemans's much shorter one, shows the subversive potential of such deference to gender difference and masculine authority. Paradoxically, the intensively feminine stance of the poetess facilitated Sigourney's emancipation, not only freeing her from penury but also freeing her to imagine and depict changes in racial, gender, and national politics. This poetic ethos allowed her to consistently foreground the experiences of women as inherently interesting and worthy of representation, even as Sigourney herself approached representative status as a nineteenth-century American icon.

One indication of Sigourney's celebrity status in antebellum America is the fact that 1840s-era issues of *Godey's Lady's Book,* a popular mainstream magazine for middle-class and aspiring middle-class women, used her signature as an endorsement to help secure its share in the crowded and competitive magazine market. Sigourney never lacked evidence for what her writing meant personally to her readers and her editors. Not only did her readers continue to buy her books, but they also thanked her directly in notes and letters, named their children after her, and organized clubs (known as literary societies) in her name. And when advances in photography led to a fad for the circulation of cartes-de-visite (studio photographs mounted on cardboard, which could be purchased in stationery stores, collected, and exchanged), Sigourney's was one of the most popular in America. Even when she was in her seventies, after the peak of her fame, Sigourney estimated that her "epistolary intercourse . . . exceeds a yearly exchange of two thousand letters."[38] Despite the burden of this volume of correspondence, she was uplifted by "the hope of disseminating through this quiet vehicle, some cheering thought or hallowed principle."[39] Her readers bought, gave, kept, and cherished pictures such as the one reproduced in figure 2. In her dress and her pose, she modeled the kind of feminine authority she had spent her life inventing. Yet iconicity has its costs. Even in her own lifetime, Sigourney's success began to obscure the radicalism of her claim to the right to represent herself, her opinions, and her imagination in her own way: to be an artist in a political world. By signaling established respectability, financial security, and unimpeachable femininity through the lace and furbelows of her fashionable mourning dress, Sigourney also erased the story of the active role she had played in shaping the terms through which respectability and femininity would be judged. On reconsideration, however, one may read the picture as a sign of how far she had come from her origins on the margins of culture, due to her innovative work as an artist and an educator as well as her opposition to government policies.

FIGURE 2. Lydia Sigourney, carte-de-visite photograph, circa 1855–65. Courtesy, Library of Congress, Prints and Photographs Division, Washington, D.C. LC-DIG-cwpbh-02747.

NOTES

1. Gordon S. Haight, *Mrs. Sigourney: The Sweet Singer of Hartford* (New Haven: Yale University Press, 1930), i.
2. Fred Lewis Pattee, *The Feminine Fifties* (New York: Appleton-Century, 1940).
3. Judith Fetterley, *Provisions: A Reader from 19th-Century Women* (Bloomington: Indiana University Press, 1985), 21. For an early yet comprehensive analysis of the gender anxiety of twentieth-century American literary historians, see Peter Stoneley, *Mark Twain and the Feminine Aesthetic* (Cambridge: Cambridge University Press, 1992), intro.
4. Mary Loeffelholz, *From School to Salon: Reading Nineteenth-Century American Women's Poetry* (Princeton: Princeton University Press, 2007), 34.
5. Sandra A. Zagarell, "Expanding 'America': Lydia Sigourney's *Sketch of Connecticut,* Catharine Sedgwick's *Hope Leslie,*" *Tulsa Studies in Women's Literature* 6 (1987): 225.
6. William Wordsworth, "Preface," in *Lyrical Ballads, with a Few Other Poems,* by Samuel Taylor Coleridge and William Wordsworth, ed. R. L. Brett and A. R. Jones (London: Routledge, 1988), 266.
7. Nina Baym, "Reinventing Lydia Sigourney," *American Literature* 62 (1990): 391.
8. Annie Finch, "The Sentimental Poetess in the World: Metaphor and Poetic Subjectivity in Lydia Sigourney's Nature Poetry," *Legacy* 5 (1988): 5–6. In this landmark essay, Finch argues that Sigourney wrote in an era that privileged the subjective tradition in romantic poetry—that is, a poetry that focused on nature as a way to extend and objectify the writer's inner state. It was practiced by a line of primarily male poets who used the subjective lyric *I* and related their external visions of nature to their inner lives.

9. On sentimentality as a discursive mode and its place in eighteenth- and nineteenth-century romantic culture in general and American culture in particular, see Jane Tompkins, *Sensational Designs: The Cultural Work of American Fiction, 1790–1860* (Oxford: Oxford University Press, 1986); Shirley Samuels, *The Culture of Sentiment: Race, Gender, and Sentimentality in 19th-Century America* (Oxford: Oxford University Press, 1992); Mary Louise Kete, *Sentimental Collaborations: Mourning and Middle-Class Identity in Nineteenth-Century America* (Durham: Duke University Press, 2000); Marianne Noble, *The Masochistic Pleasures of Sentimental Literature* (Princeton: Princeton University Press, 2000); and Lauren Berlant, *The Female Complaint: The Unfinished Business of Sentimentality in American Culture* (Durham: Duke University Press, 2008). The study of sentiment has been part of a general turn to affect in the fields of the humanities, education, and social sciences.
10. For a summary of the current state of the canon and current responses, see "Forum: The End of the End of the Canon?" in *J19* 4 (Spring 2016): 125–80.
11. See Carolyn L. Karcher, *The First Woman of the Republic: A Cultural Biography of Lydia Maria Child* (Durham: Duke University Press, 1995); Joan D. Hedrick, *Harriet Beecher Stowe: A Life* (Oxford: Oxford University Press, 1994); and Melba Joyce Boyd, *Discarded Legacy: Politics and Poetics in the Life of Frances E. W. Harper, 1825–1911* (Detroit: Wayne State University Press, 1995).
12. See Maria Cummins, *The Lamplighter* (Boston: Jewett, 1854); and Louisa May Alcott, *Little Women,* vols. 1 and 2 (Boston: Roberts, 1868–69).
13. Loeffelholz, *From School to Salon,* 35.
14. Lydia Sigourney, *Letters of Life* (New York: Appleton, 1866), 342. In the memoir, Sigourney mentions compiling *The Girl's Reading Book* as part of an effort to "elevat[e] the condition of Common Schools in the State of New York" (342–43).
15. Ibid., 55.
16. Ibid., 59.
17. Quoted in Haight, *Mrs. Sigourney,* 5.
18. Sigourney's poem "Unspoken Language" articulates the power of supralingual communication (in *Illustrated Poems by Mrs. L. H. Sigourney* [Philadelphia: Carey and Hart, 1849], 34–39).
19. Jane Tompkins's *Sensational Design* played a key role in the reconsideration of the didactic aesthetic of nineteenth-century American fiction.
20. Lydia Sigourney, *Letters to My Pupils, with Narrative and Biographical Sketches* (New York: Carter, 1853), 249.
21. It is possible that this dual portrait features Sigourney signing with a deaf woman. Her former student, Alice Cogswell (1805–30), could neither hear nor speak and introduced Sigourney to the possibility of communicating through signs. Cogswell inspired Thomas Gallaudet, who founded the American School for the Deaf in Hartford. Sigourney strongly supported this school and remained active in the reformation of deaf education throughout her life.
22. Haight, *Mrs. Sigourney,* 13–14.
23. Ibid., 14.
24. William Cullen Bryant, "Thanatopsis," *North American Review* 5 (September 1817): 338–40. Founded in 1815, the *North American Review* was published without interruption until 1940 and was the first American magazine to be exclusively devoted to literature.
25. Samuel Longfellow, *The Life of Henry Wadsworth Longfellow: With Extracts from His Journals and Correspondence* (Boston: Ticknor, 1886), 1:56.
26. Sigourney, *Letters of Life,* 241.
27. Critics have argued that, like other prominent women writers, Emily Dickinson also adopted the role of daughter to gain more leverage and subvert social roles. In

Dickinson and the Strategies of Reticence, Joanne Dobson explores the tendency toward submission and revolt evinced by the little girl figure in her poems ([Bloomington: Indiana University Press, 1989], 146, note 8). Examining Dickinson's poems from a Jungian standpoint, Barbara Mossberg argues that the child figure occupies a dual role: "Both daughters, the dutiful and the rebellious, are necessary for the manufacture of poetry" (*Dickinson: When a Writer Is a Daughter* [Bloomington: Indiana University Press, 1982], 198).

28. Gary Kelly, *Lydia Sigourney: Selected Poetry and Prose* (Toronto: Broadview, 2008), 268.
29. Sigourney, *Letters of Life,* 244.
30. Ibid., 254–56.
31. In her memoir, Sigourney admitted, "Richardson's novel did not fare as well as the scientific treatise. It was so diffuse" that she skipped the boring parts. In contrast, Sir Walter Scott's early works "effected a revolution" in the idea of what could be done in the novel (ibid., 255).
32. Loeffelholz, *From School to Salon,* 36.
33. Scholars note that Sigourney's interest in advocating for the deaf began early in her career as an educator. See Edna Edith Sayers and Diana Gates, "Lydia Huntley Sigourney and the Beginnings of Deaf Education in Hartford: It Takes a Village," *Sign Language Studies* 8 (Summer 2008): 369–411; and Elizabeth Petrino, "'Language of the Eye': Communication and Sentimental Benevolence in Lydia Sigourney's Poems and Essays about the Deaf," in *Sentimentalism in Nineteenth-Century America: Literary and Cultural Practices*, ed. Mary DeJong (Teaneck, N.J.: Fairleigh Dickinson University Press, 2013), 69–88.
34. Christopher Phillips, *Epic in American Culture: Settlement to Reconstruction* (Baltimore: Johns Hopkins University Press, 2012).
35. For early feminist discussions of Sigourney's importance to the literary marketplace, see Patricia Okker, *Our Sister Editors: Sarah J. Hale and the Tradition of Nineteenth-Century American Women Editors* (Athens: University of Georgia Press, 1995); and Susan Coultrap-McQuin, *Doing Literary Business* (Chapel Hill: University of North Carolina Press, 1990). By the early 2000s, Sigourney was figuring to some degree in most discussions of the nineteenth-century American literary marketplace. See, for instance, Michael Davit Bell, *Culture, Genre, and Literary Vocation: Selected Essays on American Literature* (Chicago: University of Chicago Press, 2001); and Meredith McGill, *American Literature and the Culture of Reprinting, 1834–1853* (Philadelphia: University of Pennsylvania Press, 2013). For an excellent discussion of Sigourney's role as a mentor to a younger generation of authors, see Susan Williams, *Reclaiming Authorship: Literary Women in America, 1850–1900* (Philadelphia: University of Pennsylvania Press, 2006). Also see most of the essays in Earl Frank Yarington and Mary DeJong, eds., *Popular Nineteenth-Century American Women Writers and the Literary Marketplace* (Newcastle, U.K.: Cambridge Scholars, 2007).
36. Sigourney, *Letters of Life,* 366.
37. See Kete, *Sentimental Collaborations.*
38. Sigourney, *Letters of Life,* 377.
39. Ibid.

PART ONE
SIGOURNEY'S WORKS

2

REMODELING THE KITCHEN IN PARNASSUS

SIGOURNEY'S POETICS OF COLLABORATION

Jennifer Putzi

On December 24, 1831, Lydia Sigourney responded to a letter from Amelia Champlin, the wife of a wealthy sea captain in Essex, Connecticut, just thirty miles from Sigourney's home in Hartford. While Champlin's letter does not survive, she seems to have requested a poem from Sigourney in memory of her daughter, Louisa Champlin, who had died in February at just three years of age. In response to this request, Sigourney wrote, "Your letter containing the affecting account of the death of your little girl was perused with deep commiseration. Sorrows of such a nature will not fail to awaken sympathy in the bosom of every mother. . . . Stricken indeed, the heart must be, that is called upon to resign so sweet and cherished a being, as the one whom you have described."[1]

Regarding the memorial poem, Sigourney says only, "I have at your request put in a poetical form some of these thoughts which the recital of your grief awakened, and enclose them with assurances of regret for your affliction."[2] The attached manuscript poem, titled "The Lost Darling," was written from the point of view of the mother and opens with the assertion "She was my idol." After the speaker recounts the delight she once took in observing her daughter's everyday activities—playing with her dolls and her kitten, reciting her alphabet and her prayers—she imagines that she hears a sound coming from the child's bed:

I start,
Half fancying from her empty crib there comes
Some restless sound. I breathe the accustomed words,
"Hush, hush, Louisa dearest,"—then I weep.[3]

While the mother attempts to console herself with the assurance that her "darling" now experiences "a seraph's bliss," she is unable to erase the memories not only of her child's happy days but also of her suffering while ill.

Just a month after Sigourney wrote the letter to Champlin, "The Lost Darling" appeared in print in the *Ladies' Magazine and Literary Gazette,* a periodical edited by Sarah Josepha Hale that later merged with the *Lady's Book and Magazine* to become *Godey's Lady's Book.* The poem was quickly reprinted, with minor changes, in a number of Christian periodicals and women's magazines (as well as the *Youth's Companion*), but apparently it retained in those reprints some connection to its original purpose. In a note that accompanies the reprinted poem in the *Religious Intelligencer,* an evangelical magazine published in Connecticut, a subscriber explained, "The following tender and beautiful lines are from the pen of Mrs. Sigourney, and were sent to a mother who had been bereaved of a darling child." Not until the poem appeared in Sigourney's collected *Poems* (1834) did that origin become obscured: in the collection, the author replaced the line "Hush, hush, Louisa, dearest" with "Hush! Hush thee, dearest." While subtle, the change makes the poem more widely applicable, the subject position of the speaker inhabitable by any woman who has lost a child.

In noting Sigourney's appeal to both individual readers and a broader audience, Eliza Richards argues that the "elegiac poetic realm" in her work "offered an opportunity for interpersonal identification when sentiment overcame the physical boundaries that separated individuals and texts."[4] Yet an examination of the composition and circulation of "The Lost Darling" reveals that the collaborative process that produced this and many other of Sigourney's elegies had already overcome these boundaries. That is, readers such as Amelia Champlin (whose letter, Sigourney attested, contained an "affecting account" of her daughter's death) provided the subject matter, while Sigourney provided the form of the poems. Such collaborations, I argue, are central to any understanding of Sigourney's early success as a poet and to the long history of critical assessment of her work.

Scholars of nineteenth-century American women's poetry are familiar with Sigourney's practice of writing poems to order, but their understanding of the creative process involved in the production of such poems as well as the resulting quality of the work is based almost entirely on Sigourney's posthumous autobiography, *Letters of Life* (1866). Recounting the success of her early career, Sigourney noted that, "with the establishment of a poetic name" in the "monthly magazines," her readers came to feel a sense of ownership over her work, prompting frequent requests for original poetry.[5] She explained:

> Churches requested hymns, to be sung at consecrations, ordinations, and installations; charitable societies, for anniversaries; academies and schools, for exhibition. Odes were desired for the festivities of New Year and the Fourth of July, for silver and golden weddings, for the voyager wherewith to express his leave-taking, and the lover to propitiate his mistress. Epistles from strangers often solicited elegies and epitaphs. . . . But to gratify all was an impossibility.[6]

Sigourney then catalogued a number of the requests she had received for poems written to order, including a "poem, intended as a school premium for a young lady," another "on the feather of a blue-bird picked up by the road-side," and a third "to copy in the album of a lady . . . , requested by a gentleman 'to be sent as soon as Saturday afternoon, because then he is more at leisure to attend to it.'"[7] Many of these requests solicited elegies written to order. One, for example, presented a "canary-bird, which had accidentally been starved to death" as the subject for "some elegiac verses," while another requested an elegy on "a young child," although the only piece of information offered was that he or she "'drowned in a barrel of swine's food.'" Another grieving parent was vague about the child to be elegized, explaining only that his or her nine-month-old son had been "just thirteen pounds," but very specific about the finished presentation and purpose of the product requested: "some poetry to be framed, glazed, and hung over the chimney-piece, to keep the other children from forgetting him."[8]

Most scholars assessing this early period in Sigourney's career have assumed that such requests hindered her development as a poet in one way or another; in this, they follow Sigourney's lead in the most quoted sentence from *Letters of Life:* her declaration that "If there is any kitchen in Parnassus, my Muse has surely officiated there as a woman of all work, and an aproned waiter."[9] This jest has had an inordinate influence on the critical evaluation of Sigourney's work. For example, Gordon S. Haight, author of *Mrs. Sigourney: The Sweet Singer of Hartford,* published in 1930, concluded that Sigourney "was not altogether deceived about the quality of her work," reserving his harshest criticism for her tally, in the spring of 1861, of lines of poetry written, books read, garments made, and social calls exchanged.[10] "To her," he insisted, "they all represented much the same sort of toil, and she saw no incongruity in classifying them together."[11] While Sigourney has received more favorable critical attention in recent decades, both Cheryl Walker and Joanne Dobson, among others, have reiterated Haight's use of Sigourney's reference to her muse in the "kitchen in Parnassus" as a way of insisting on the poet's awareness of the inferior quality of her work.[12] Judith Fetterley has more generously read this description of Sigourney's muse as an acknowledgment of poetry as an extension of the "service role conventionally assigned to women," but she also seems to imply that this role carried with it an aesthetic price.[13]

Other critics, such as Patricia Crain and Paula Bernat Bennett, have either refuted Haight's legacy of disparaging Sigourney's poetry, insisting usefully that such arguments represent a "confusion of social class with literary merit," or have simply seen the question of aesthetics as irrelevant.[14] While both gestures seem to me to have value, they share with Haight's attitude a tendency to make a synecdoche of Sigourney's "kitchen in Parnassus" statement, ignoring the fact that *Letters of Life* is a retrospective assessment of a career that had begun more than fifty years earlier. This is not to say that Sigourney did not at times regard the writing of poetry as a form of domestic labor or service to others. It is also not to contradict the point that class played an important role in her self-definition as a poet as well as in her approach to the literary marketplace. Yet if we are to understand the importance of Sigourney's lengthy career, we need to avoid condensing it in such a way that her posthumous autobiography is allowed to stand as the defining statement of her poetics.

Critics who treat Sigourney's "kitchen in Parnassus" statement as if it were made out of time, without cultural context, have often paired that reading with a refusal to attend to the chronological and aesthetic development of the poet's career. Sigourney's work (like that of many nineteenth-century American women poets) is often treated as a monolithic whole, with no distinction made between, for example, her volumes of poetry, the stages of her professional life, or her participation in literary and aesthetic movements.[15] In this chapter, I look at print and archival evidence as I reassess the importance of a collaborative poetics in Sigourney's career beyond and before the kitchen in Parnassus. As I did with "The Lost Darling," I trace the genealogy of a handful of poems—from letter of request, to manuscript poem, and frequently to published poem—to argue that, although Sigourney effectively disavowed such a collaborative poetics later in her career, the writing of poems in response to epistolary requests was central to, rather than disruptive of, the establishment of her "poetic name." By examining these letters and the poems that followed—in manuscript and in print—I demonstrate that Sigourney collaborated with her readers to produce a body of work that would speak to their experiences while furthering her reputation as a poet.

In *Sentimental Collaborations,* Mary Louise Kete has productively examined such collaborations in her poems about death and mourning. In such a gift economy, she explains, "individuals can join together in solving the seemingly local problem of grief in the face of death."[16] What is being exchanged in this system is sentiment itself, creating "a continued circulation of affection among an increasing circle of associations."[17] Sigourney's letter to Champlin reveals that she participated actively in this process, exchanging her sympathy for the narration of the mother's grief, the text of her poem for the text of Champlin's letter. Building on Kete's argument, I am interested in how this process leads to the practical composition, publication, and circulation of poems. I define *collaboration* broadly here, following Bette London's claim that "collaborations exist in a range of 'authorial' activities not necessarily named authorship: acts of assistance and inspiration; acts of mentoring or mutual influence; acts of revision or editorial input."[18] In nineteenth-century American literary studies, collaboration has been analyzed most thoroughly as a way to rethink the role of marginalized individuals whose access to authorship was mediated by a more privileged (usually white, usually middle- or upper-class) individual—a patron, an amanuensis, an editor.[19] Rather than attempting to recover the often elided presence of such collaborators, I aim to examine the marginalization of collaborative practices in nineteenth-century American women's poetry, with an understanding of authorship, as Karen Weyler puts it, "not as a singular act, but as a process."[20] In doing so, I differentiate between different stages and styles of authorship in Sigourney's career, positioning this transition within a framework of thinking about women's poetics in the period.

Sigourney's establishment of a "poetic name" in antebellum America was no easy task, given cultural prohibitions against middle-class white women living public lives. As Gary Kelly points out, women writers on either side of the Atlantic often risked their reputations and their domestic happiness if they attempted to publish their work and claim authority in the literary marketplace.[21] Although Charles Sigourney knowingly married Lydia Huntley, the author of *Moral Pieces, in Prose and Verse* (published in 1815), he soon objected to her immersion in her writing and publishing career. Sigourney seems to have struggled with her response to her husband's concerns, publishing her 1827 *Poems* without her name on it but clearly marked as "By the Author of 'Moral Pieces in Prose and Verse'" and then moving into the publication of more conventional books for children and young adults as well as advice literature for women.[22] Her periodical poetry, often signed "L. H. S." and marked as originating in Hartford, Connecticut, seems to have been recognized as her work, particularly within her home state; and in the early 1830s, she began to sign her work as "Mrs. Sigourney" or "Mrs. L. H. Sigourney." It wasn't until 1834 that she put her name on the title page of a collection of poetry. The extant evidence suggests that written requests from readers for poems and Sigourney's epistolary and poetic responses date from the early 1830s and into the mid-1840s, clearly a response to the growing popularity of her work and her increasing willingness to sign her name to her poems, in one form or another. While Champlin's letter was likely not the first of these requests, it is indicative of both Sigourney's reputation as a poet and her accessibility to her readers as early as 1831.

There can be no doubt that Sigourney wrote dozens if not hundreds of poems for individual readers, many of them by request. While a number of these requests survive, others are evident in letters written by Sigourney herself or in printed versions of the resulting poem. All indicate confidence in her willingness to place her poetic gifts at the disposal of her readers, whether she knew them personally or not. One such letter, written on October 13, 1842, from Richmond, Virginia, is from a Methodist minister named George W. Nolley, who asked Sigourney to write a poem for a grieving couple who had lost all four of their children to illness within a few years.[23] On the first page of the letter, Sigourney noted that she responded to this request on October 20, "with Lines."[24] There was no apparent social benefit to be gained by writing a poem for Nolley: while Champlin's social status and position in a community relatively close to Hartford may have rendered her a useful connection for Sigourney, Nolley and his congregation lived more than four hundred miles away, making it unlikely that she would ever actually meet them. While I have been unable to locate a copy, the resulting poem may have been published, as some years earlier Nolley appears to have requested another poem ("in the form of a farewell of the wife of a missionary, at the grave of her husband in Africa"), which was then "published and greatly admired in this State." What is clear in the 1842 case is that Nolley's parishioners had Sigourney's poem in hand within two weeks of her receipt of his letter.

Another letter, this time from John M. Niles, the editor of the *Hartford Weekly Times,* indicates that Sigourney also wrote poems for acquaintances. In late 1842, he wrote to Sigourney to thank her for her "acceptable present as a tribute to the memory of my dear wife" and noted that "The 'Lines' will appear in the Times of this city & I will cause a copy to be sent to you."[25] It is unclear if Niles had requested this poem or if Sigourney had simply offered it as a gift. While she did at times offer unsolicited poems in response to the immediate grief of others, the fact that Niles's wife had died almost twenty years before the composition of the "Lines" might indicate that the poem did, in fact, originate in a request rather than an instigating event.[26] Even though Niles's gratitude was accompanied by his plans for publication, it is clear that he saw this poem as more than just a submission to his newspaper: he apologized for the brevity of his letter by insisting that he could "say no more, for grief deep seated hath neither words nor eloquence," and the original handwritten copy of the poem was in his papers when he died in 1856.[27] While Niles asserted that he could not "say how [the 'Lines'] may strike others as the subject of them was so near and dear to my heart," he was clearly aware that Sigourney would not object to publication and that the "Lines" would be acceptable to a broader readership, many of whom had also lost a spouse or could imagine doing so. Part of Sigourney's growing popularity in the 1830s and 1840s (and therefore part of the reason readers wrote to her requesting poems) can be attributed to the fact that she was able to address the grief of others both particularly and generally, writing made-to-order poems that could then be published and read more widely as applicable to the grief of others and simultaneously, perhaps, writing generalized poems that could be copied by many readers and applied to their own particular circumstances. The letter writer (or those for whom the letter was written, in Nolley's case) received an affirmation of his or her grief in print as well as a way to revisit the life and death of a loved one throughout the grieving process. For readers, experiencing such a poem in print provided them with the knowledge that others shared their experience of grief; the poem contributed to a repository of feeling that connected mourners despite geographical distance and social barriers.

Of course, such requests were advantageous to Sigourney as well, providing social connections, opportunities for publication, and an increased readership for her books. The exchange with Amelia Champlin provides one such example. Another exchange began with an 1840 letter from Eliza T. H. Banks, who asked Sigourney to write "some lines to [the] memory" of her mother, who had died more than three years prior.[28] She opened her letter by apologizing for presuming to write "without having any previous personal acquaintance with you." "In offering an excuse," Banks said, "I can only point to the favor I am about to ask at your hands, and to your character as a Christian."[29] By this date, Banks would also have been aware that Sigourney had composed and published other poems in response to readers' requests. She followed her own request with a lengthy description of her mother's life and, in even more detail, her illness and death. Nonetheless, Sigourney did not receive the letter until 1842, when it reached her with a note:

> The enclosed communication was addressed to you about two years ago, with a view then, and ever since, of finishing it, and forwarding it to you. And now, that another and heartrending calamity has befallen me, I must ask a double favor of you. My Nephew, L. B. Sanders, will make known to you my wishes, and give you any information you may desire. By complying with my request, you will pour Balm and Oil on a deeply wounded Heart, and be entitled to its everlasting gratitude.[30]

The "calamity" was the death, on January 13, 1842, of her husband, Linn Banks, a lawyer and a member of the U.S. House of Representatives.

In response to Eliza Banks's request, Sigourney wrote two poems, both of which she presumably sent to Banks but which also appeared in April 1842 in the *Southern Literary Messenger*. Sandwiched between articles on the dangers of free trade to the U.S. economy and the unfairness of a British critique of George Washington, "On the Death of the Hon. Linn Banks," extols his service to the "public weal" and insists that all "Virginia sighs" over the death of this patriot. But the poem turns quickly to "she, whose heart with his, was early bound, / That kindred spirit, whom he held so dear,— / The fond companion of his cherished home," thus giving central place to the wife's grief and her eventual consolation in the assurance that she will "join the lov'd one, in Eternity." The second poem, "To the Memory of Mrs. Edith Sanders," appears a few pages later, after an article titled "Blackwood's Magazine vs. George Washington." The poem celebrates Banks's mother's devotion to her children as well as her continued faith in God, carefully locating the mother figure in "Vale Evergreen," the name of the Banks estate in Virginia.[31]

The letters from Eliza Banks provided Sigourney with material for poems that were suitable for publication, and they appeared in the *Southern Literary Messenger* under the editorship of U.S. Navy officer Matthew Fontaine Maury. Like the poem written for Champlin, these two also established connections between Sigourney and wealthy, white, women readers, who, by sharing these poems with friends and acquaintances, would no doubt increase her national reputation. Such poems indicate that, as Karen Weyler has said of Phillis Wheatley's poetics, "writing and publishing were . . . profoundly social and collaborative acts. They were acts of connection."[32] Sigourney's response to her readers also demonstrates that, even early in her career, she was bridging what critics such as Mary Louise Kete often identify as two very different economies: "the commercial economy in which [Sigourney] was a path-breaker for women's rights, and the kind of noncommercial gift economy which . . . enabled community through the establishment of reciprocal bonds of affection and responsibility among individuals otherwise only tenuously associated."[33]

Poems written in response to epistolary requests were beneficial to the letter writers, to Sigourney, and to readers who encountered those poems in print. Yet most scholars have glossed over this fact, instead following Sigourney's lead in *Letters of Life* and dismissing such requests as mere annoyances. These exchanges, however, clearly demonstrate not only readers' role in establishing her "poetic name," but also Sigourney's sense of indebtedness to them, a circuitry that resulted in more solicitations for letters, more poems, and more readers while also influencing what I am defining here as a collaborative poetics. The details in letters such as those from Champlin and Banks indicate that such requests allowed mourners a space in which to rehearse their grief as well as an understanding that, should Sigourney respond with a poem, she would use their own words as the basis for her composition. That is, such letters did not simply prompt poems, as we can see when we compare the impetus behind Sigourney's elegy for Linn Banks. The note requesting that poem does not mention Banks's name, let alone the details of his life or death. Sigourney had to rely on common knowledge about this illustrious politician and the words of Eliza Banks's nephew, who presumably delivered the note to the poet. In contrast, most other exchanges show that the composition, circulation, and publication processes involved in the production of a requested poem were collaborative, which implies not just that Sigourney valued her readers but that at this point in her career she saw poetry as a collective endeavor. After she published a poem in a collected volume, Sigourney erased the collaborative processes—she did not include identifying names or narrative explanations—but that does not negate their importance in our understanding of her career or, more generally, of how nineteenth-century Americans experienced and used poetry in their daily lives.

These processes are illustrated in the exchange that led to Sigourney's composition and publication of "The Daughter's Dream." In late 1846, Sigourney had received a detailed letter from Mrs. T. L. A. Gooking of Terre Haute, Indiana, which described the deaths of Gooking's two young sons as well as what she calls the "*principal* object of this communication"—her fourteen-year-old daughter's dream, in which the gown-wearing, harp-playing deceased were reunited in Heaven under the watchful eye of a beautiful angel.[34] This dream, the mother admitted, might not have been unusual "under all the circumstances, but still to a mother's partial eye, presenting a scene of singular beauty, and a strong desire to see your graphic pen employed in presenting this scene to the eye of the mind, by the aid of the *Muses,* has alone induced me to trouble you."[35] Here, Gooking clearly indicated her understanding of the collaborative process involved in producing such a poem. She expected that Sigourney, presented with the scene of such grief, would, with the aid of her "graphic pen" and creative inspiration, re-present this scene back to Gooking in a slightly different but still recognizable way. Sigourney's acceptance of this subject matter seemed to validate both the singularity of the narrative and the mother's grief for her children. Interestingly, it was Gooking who made publication central, rather than accidental, to this process: "Should you comply with my request," she continued in her letter, "I should like very much to see the production in the Mother's Magazine, of which I have been a constant and admiring reader from its commencement."[36] Indeed, in January 1847, less than two months after Sigourney received the original letter, "The

Daughter's Dream" was published in the *Mother's Magazine*.[37] While she frequently did publish her work in this periodical (a few years later, her name appeared on a list of principal contributors), her compliance with Gooking's request indicates that letter writers had some sort of control over the circulation of poems created out of their personal tragedies.

Another collaboration is hinted at in a note preceding "The Unchanged of the Tomb," a poem that Sigourney originally published in the Boston-based *Bunker Hill Aurora* and reprinted in the *Youth's Companion* on February 1, 1834.

> A few weeks after W. B. A. was interred, his parents were called to follow an infant to the grave. Anxious to behold once more the face of their dear son, they went down into the tomb. They saw him; his countenance had remained unchanged; the same apparent smile seemed to rest upon it, and his hair had grown to a considerable length. These interesting facts were communicated to a lady, who gave them the following poetical dress.[38]

While this note establishes the fact that Sigourney was willing to write poems to order and that writing such poems presumably generated more such requests, it also illuminates her poetic process. These "interesting facts"—the deaths of two children; the parents' request to see the corpse of their elder son, dead for several weeks; the appearance of life that they found there—are said to have been "communicated" to Sigourney, who then "gave them . . . poetical dress." The subject matter of the poem and its almost gothic details originated in the parents' experience (presumably narrated by one of the parents), while Sigourney contributed her poetic talent and knowledge.

The phrase "poetic dress" seems to encompass everything from rhyme and meter to a careful use of sentiment and point of view. As in "The Lost Darling," Sigourney focused throughout "The Unchanged of the Tomb" on the grief of the mother figure, even though the note explains that both parents had seen their son's body in the tomb. While "they" are described as bringing "an innocent infant" to the "vaulted tomb," the fourth stanza shifts to the mother's feelings about her infant's death and her witnessing of her elder child's body:

> She is drooping low at her idol's side,
> With her wild eyes on his face.

But the pestilent damps of the dread abode
Have fallen on a changeless cheek,
And it seem'd that the warmth of the living blood
Through his ruby lip might speak.

And his glossy locks to a fearful length
Have grown in that bed of clay,
In a clustering mesh they have wreath'd their strength,
Who will part those curls away?[39]

The "interesting facts" of the dead child's physical appearance are shocking in that they convey both life and death simultaneously. The boy's "changeless cheek" and "ruby lip" give him a lifelike appearance, yet his abundant hair indicates both an excessive life that is perhaps attempting to escape or exceed the grave as a well as a method of tying him to the grave and preventing such release. The mother's response is one of distress and even mental instability, begging her child to "rise" and being "borne . . . away in her deep despair," crying "till her eyes are dim." It is up to the poet to remind the mother, this figure of unrelenting grief, not only that the "world where the angels sing" is more important than the "tomb" but also that the mother must attend to her own salvation in order to "*see that ye meet him there!*"[40] Sigourney's elevation of the gothic tone, her use of alliteration (the boy's "changeless cheek," his "clustering" "curls" grown long in their "bed of clay"), the rhetorical "Who will part those curls away?" were all her own, the "poetic dress" that clothes the narrative provided by the original request for the poem.

The sentimental appeal of the poem was also, no doubt, part of what those who requested it expected to see in Sigourney's response. While the experience at the heart of "The Unchanged of the Tomb" was unusual and unlikely to be shared by many (if any) of Sigourney's readers, the experience of losing more than one child in quick succession was a fairly common one in nineteenth-century America. The urge to give in to uncontrollable grief over the death of a child was familiar to many readers and must have made this poem interesting to more than just the grieving parents. Sigourney obviously thought so, as she republished the poem, with minor changes, in her 1834 collected *Poems.* As one of many selections in the book, however, the poem became disconnected from its collaborative process and was now presented as the creation of an individual author, "Mrs. L. H. Sigourney."

Sigourney highlighted this shift in her preface to the volume, insisting that its poems "were suggested by passing occasions, and partake of the nature of extemporaneous productions." Such a claim not only devalued Sigourney's own labor but also erased the contributions of those who had provided the "occasions," the narrative, and often the language of her poetic response to their grief. This devaluation is reiterated when Sigourney framed her experience as a poet in romantic terms:

> They have sprung up like wild flowers in the dells, or among the clefts of the rock; wherever the path of life has chanced to lead. The hand that gathered and now presents them, borrows for their motto the sweetly eloquent words of Coleridge:
>
> > "I expect from them neither profit nor general fame; and I consider myself amply repaid without either. Poetry has been to me its own exceeding great reward. It possesses power to soothe affliction,—to multiply and refine enjoyment,—to endear solitude, and to give the habit of discovering the *good* and the *beautiful* in all that meets or surrounds us."[41]

Here, Sigourney's narration of her poetic process is contradictory. Poems such as "The Daughter's Dream" and "The Unchanged of the Tomb," she explained, are like "wild flowers," fully formed and simply gathered by the poet. In this she might have seemed to acknowledge the efforts of the letter writers; yet by associating her process with Coleridge and the other romantic poets, she positioned herself as writing for herself alone, unconcerned with her accessibility to or relationship with her readership. Poetry, she implied, was "its own exceeding great reward," a solitary pleasure rather than a collective effort. While Sigourney would answer requests for poems for many years to come, this was perhaps the beginning of the road that would lead to her to disavow her collaborative poetics in *Letters of Life.*

By the time Sigourney was writing *Letters of Life,* poetry as a profession had changed drastically, particularly for women, and her autobiography was at least in part an effort to reframe her place in a literary tradition that seemed to be quickly forgetting about her. While Sigourney's popular influence remained strong at the time of her death, her status with critics waned significantly in the last twenty years of her life, and her poetic name was increasingly seen as representing a particular type of sentimental and religious poetry rather than a distinctively individual style. As early as 1848, Rufus Wilmot Griswold introduced a selection of Sigourney's poetry in *The Female Poets of America* by essentially attributing her success to being in the right place at the right time. "Mrs. Sigourney has acquired a wider and more pervading reputation than many women will receive in this country" he wrote. "The times have been favorable for her, and the tone of her works such as is most likely to be acceptable in a primitive and pious community."[42] The implication, of course, was that American literature had progressed beyond the "primitive and pious" and that the critical establishment represented by Griswold demanded something far more sophisticated from the female poet. When compared to other female poets, then, Sigourney was clearly seen as lacking: "Though possessing but little constructive power, she has a ready expression, and an ear naturally so sensitive to harmony that it has scarcely been necessary for her to study the principles of versification in order to produce some of its finest effects. She sings impulsively from an atmosphere of affectionate, pious, and elevated sentiment, rather than from the consciousness of subjective ability."[43] It is worth noting that the things that Griswold dismissed here were the things that had drawn readers to her in the decades before his assessment. Many of them had requested poems from Sigourney precisely because of her piety, her "elevated sentiment," her "ready expression," and her "ear . . . so sensitive to harmony" as well as to the emotions of others.

While Griswold did not mention the poems that Sigourney wrote by request, it is clear that such exchanges underlay his assessment of her work, especially in comparison with the writings of other women poets of the day. Indeed, the only elegies that Griswold reprinted in his selection of Sigourney's work were her "Monody on Mrs. Hemans" and "Monody on the Late Daniel Wadsworth, Esquire." The first, a memorial for the well-known British poet Felicia Hemans, was acceptable in that it positioned Sigourney within a transatlantic tradition of women poets. The second, commemorating the death of Sigourney's early mentor and patron, focuses on a wealthy and socially established man with whom Sigourney had a long-standing relationship. Neither, however, reflects Sigourney's pattern of reaching out to and collaborating with readers. Griswold went on to emphasize that Sigourney's natural and impulsive power was not equivalent to the sincere expression of emotion that he saw in those whom he named "our female poets." Despite the fact that Sigourney was one of the earliest practitioners of the romantic aesthetic in America, he insisted that she had not suffered enough to claim the sort of passionate transparency that he placed at the center of his notion of the poetess. The best of her work, he wrote, "suggest[s] that it is only because the flower has not been crushed that we have not a richer perfume."[44] Meanwhile, female poets such as Maria Brooks, Frances Sargent Osgood, and Sarah Helen Whitman gained visibility and critical approval for their success within an aesthetic and a professional mode of operation that Sigourney herself had set into motion. According to Griswold, their poetry shows a subjectivity that Sigourney's clearly lacks, rendering her plodding, methodical route to success a thing of the "primitive and pious" past. He commended Brooks, for example, for her "power and passion" as well as her "imagination, fancy, command of poetical language, and intense feeling" and said that Whitman "abandon[ed] herself to her inspirations" with "luxuriant delight."[45] Alongside his effusive admiration of Osgood's work, Griswold emphasized that "throughout all appears the poet, and the affectionate and enthusiastic woman."[46]

This assessment of Sigourney and her work was persistent. In a dismissive review of *Letters of Life* published almost twenty years after Griswold's *The Female Poets of America,* Timothy Dwight V, a fellow native of Norwich, Connecticut, and a professor of sacred literature at Yale University, agreed with Sigourney's claim in the autobiography that her life was "little varied by incident."

> Man's life, in general, has been said by some one to consist of three great things—being born, getting married, and dying. If ever a life drew near to this simplicity, we may almost say that Mrs. Sigourney's was that life; and the really interesting volume, which she has made as it were out of nothing, seems to justify the undoubting trust in her powers, which was manifested by so many strangers in sending to her for poems for every occasion and on every subject. We smile, as she tells us of the letter which she once received, requesting an elegy on a young man, "who was one of the nine children of a judge of probate, and quite the Benjamin of the family, the member of a musical society, and who, had he lived, would likely have been married in about a year," but of whose character and life she knew nothing beyond these interesting facts. Yet as we finish this account of her own life, we hardly wonder that these few things were deemed sufficient to excite her poetic fervor, and we have a prevailing

> belief that the wished-for elegy can now be found somewhere among her published or unpublished works.[47]

Dwight's emphasis on the "simplicity" of Sigourney's life echoed Griswold's lament that "the flower has not been crushed" in order to produce superior poetry. Yet unlike Griswold, who granted Sigourney "little constructive power," Dwight mockingly complimented her on her ability to produce something out of nothing—or at least something out of the bare materials of her own life and the letters of strangers. Although Sigourney herself attempted in *Letters of Life* to disavow this poetic process, Dwight denied her that gesture, insisting that she responded to even the most ridiculous of requests and that these responses could "now be found somewhere among her published or unpublished works." The implication here is that her body of work was so immense and homogenous that, while the "wished-for elegy" could be found, no one other than the correspondent who had requested the poem would care to locate it. To Dwight, finding these poems and the correspondence concerning them was a nonsensical task, yet it is exactly this, I argue, that allows us to rethink Sigourney's approach to composition and circulation and distinguish her self-representation in *Letters of Life* from her earlier identity as a poet.

After their publication in periodicals and books, Sigourney's written-to-order poems were disembedded from the social circumstances in which they were generated; but as Griswold's dismissal of her talent reveals, they were tainted by their collaborative past once a different kind of aesthetic began to dominate the literary marketplace. This poetics of collaboration distinguished her work and her career from her peers, such as Osgood, and her successors, such as Julia Ward Howe. It also distinguished the Sigourney of the 1830s and 1840s from the Sigourney of the 1860s, rendering her in both instances a savvy reader of her audience and her cultural moment. Sigourney's "kitchen in Parnassus" statement demonstrates her own participation in the shift in American women's poetry as marked by Griswold's anthology. By framing her collaborative work as a charity of sorts in *Letters of Life,* a reluctant gesture that she could not shake even after she had established a "poetic name," Sigourney reconstructed her early career as if professional authorship for women had always been the endgame rather than just one way in which women's poetry would come to have meaning in the nineteenth-century American literary marketplace.

NOTES

1. Lydia Sigourney, letter to Mrs. A. [Amelia] P. Champlin, December 24, 1831, Lydia Huntley Sigourney Papers, Connecticut Historical Society, Hartford (hereafter LHS Papers).
2. Ibid.
3. Ibid.
4. Eliza Richards, *Gender and the Poetics of Reception in Poe's Circle* (Cambridge: Cambridge University Press, 2004): 67.
5. Lydia Sigourney, *Letters of Life* (New York: Appleton, 1866), 367, 365. Sigourney's sense that her reading public felt proprietary about her is confirmed by letters in her papers, one of which begins, "Esteemed Lady, Your name & fame have become so much the property of the public, that I hope to escape the imputation of presumption in thus venturing to address you without the usual form of introduction" (John Fanning Watson, letter to Lydia Sigourney, February 1, 1833, LHS Papers).
6. Sigourney, *Letters of Life,* 368.
7. Ibid., 372, 373, 372.
8. Ibid., 373.
9. Ibid., 376.
10. Gordon S. Haight, *Mrs. Sigourney: The Sweet Singer of Hartford* (New Haven: Yale University Press, 1930), 46. Haight refers here to Sigourney's "Memoranda of Employments" (LHS Papers). The document is reprinted in Gary Kelly, *Lydia Sigourney: Selected Poetry and Prose* (Peterborough, Ont.: Broadview, 2005), 320–21.
11. Haight, *Mrs. Sigourney,* 45.
12. See Cheryl Walker, *The Nightingale's Burden: Women Poets and American Culture before 1900* (Bloomington: Indiana University Press, 1982), 56–57; Cheryl Walker, ed., *American Women Poets of the Nineteenth Century: An Anthology* (New Brunswick: Rutgers University Press, 1992), xxvii; and Joanne Dobson, *Dickinson and the Strategies of Reticence: The Woman Writer in Nineteenth-Century America* (Bloomington: Indiana University Press, 1989), 31.
13. Judith Fetterley, *Provisions: A Reader from Nineteenth-Century American Women* (Bloomington: Indiana University Press, 1985), 107. In their discussion of Sigourney's professionalism and economic success as a poet, Joanne Dobson and Sandra A. Zagarell read the "kitchen in Parnassus" quotation as Sigourney "assess[ing] her career in domestic terms" but ignore the way in which she imagines her muse as a "servant" in the "kitchen" rather than its mistress ("Women Writing in the Early Republic," in *An Extensive Republic: Print, Culture, and Society in the New Nation, 1790–1840*, ed. Robert A. Gross and Mary Kelly [Chapel Hill: University of North Carolina Press, 2010], 377). While I argue in this chapter that the quotation has had an inordinate influence on Sigourney scholarship, I do think that it is important to read it as part of Sigourney's larger awareness of the intersections of gender, class, and labor in nineteenth-century America.
14. Patricia Crain, "Lydia Hunter Sigourney," in *Encyclopedia of American Poetry: The Nineteenth Century,* ed. Eric L. Haralson (Chicago: Fitzroy Dearborn, 1998): 381. See also Paula Bernat Bennett, "Was Sigourney a Poetess? The Aesthetics of Victorian Plenitude in Lydia Sigourney's Poetry," *Comparative American Studies* 5, no. 3 (2007): 271–74.
15. Haight instituted this tendency, claiming that "the simple formulas . . . established in" Sigourney's first volume of poetry "remained practically unchanged throughout her life" (*Mrs. Sigourney,* 13). Mary Loeffelholz, on the other hand, recommends a more contextualized analysis of her work, insisting that "over her lifelong writing career

[she] monitored her own reception and shifted her own self-construction as an author, including the field of her own interdependent literary genres, in response to a changing field of literary possibles" (*From School to Salon: Reading Nineteenth-Century American Women's Poetry* [Princeton: Princeton University Press, 2014], 36).

16. Mary Louise Kete, *Sentimental Collaborations: Mourning and Middle-Class Identity in Nineteenth-Century America* (Durham: Duke University Press, 2000), 3.
17. Ibid., 53.
18. Bette London, *Writing Double: Women's Literary Partnerships* (Ithaca: Cornell University Press, 1999), 19.
19. See Doveanna Fulton and Reginald Pitts, eds., *Speaking Lives, Authoring Texts: Three African American Women's Oral Slave Narratives* (New York: State University of New York Press, 2009); Joycelyn Moody, ed., *Memoirs of Elleanor Elldridge* (Morgantown: West Virginia University Press, 2014); and Karen Weyler, *Empowering Words: Outsiders and Authorship in Early America* (Athens: University of Georgia Press, 2013). See also Gary Kelly, chapter 6 of this volume.
20. Weyler, *Empowering Words,* 23.
21. See Kelly, chapter 6.
22. For a detailed account of the influence of Sigourney's marriage on her writing career, see Gary Kelly, ed., *Lydia Sigourney: Selected Prose and Poetry,* (Peterborough, Ont.: Broadview, 2008), 19–24.
23. George W. Nolley, letter to Lydia Sigourney, October 13, 1842, LHS Papers.
24. Ibid.
25. John M. Niles, letter to Lydia Sigourney, December 2, 1842, LHS Papers.
26. See Lydia Sigourney, letter to Mrs. Thomas Smith, March 6, 1842 (LHS Papers), which begins, "Will you accept a few verses written yesterday, after looking with you at the beautiful remains of your beloved little one, whom God has seen fit to transfer from your arms to His own?"
27. John M. Niles Papers, Connecticut Historical Society, Hartford.
28. Eliza Banks, letter to Lydia Sigourney, [1840], LHS Papers.
29. Ibid.
30. Eliza Banks, letter to Lydia Sigourney, March 11, 1842, LHS Papers.
31. Lydia Sigourney, "On the Death of the Hon. Linn Banks," and "To the Memory of Mrs. Edith Sanders," *Southern Literary Messenger* 8 (April 1842): 282–83, 286.
32. Weyler, *Empowering Words,* 38.
33. Kete, *Sentimental Collaborations,* 138.
34. Mrs. T. L. A. Gooking, letter to Lydia Sigourney, November 19, 1846, LHS Papers.
35. Ibid.
36. Ibid.
37. I have not been able to find the original issue of the *Mother's Magazine;* but in its reprint of Lydia Sigourney, "The Daughter's Dream," the *Youth's Companion* (March 11, 1847) credits that periodical as the poem's first publisher (180).
38. Lydia Sigourney, "The Unchanged of the Tomb," *Youth's Companion,* February 1, 1834, 148. The poem is reprinted in the *Youth's Companion* as "From the Bunker Hill Aurora," but I have not been able to locate that publication.
39. Ibid.
40. "The Unchanged of the Tomb" is especially interesting in that it was published in the same year as Sigourney's best-known short story, "The Father" (in *Sketches* [Philadelphia: Key and Biddle], 1834). That story has been frequently anthologized and has received attention from scholars such as Fetterley, who see it as more interesting than her poetry: "Although Sigourney was not primarily a writer of fiction, 'The Father' exhibits an imaginative power rarely found in her poetry" (*Provisions,* 108).

41. Lydia Sigourney, *Poems* (Philadelphia: Key and Biddle, 1834), v-vi.
42. Rufus Wilmot Griswold, *The Female Poets of America* (Philadelphia: Carey and Hart, 1849), 93.
43. Ibid.
44. Ibid.
45. Ibid., 80, 166.
46. Ibid., 273.
47. Timothy Dwight, "Mrs. Sigourney," *New Englander* 25 (April 1866): 331–32.

3

A SENSE OF THE MATERIAL OBJECT

SIGOURNEY'S FABRIC POEMS

Joan R. Wry

"Nineteenth-century Americans understood that objects tell stories," Laurel Thatcher Ulrich states in the opening pages of *The Age of Homespun,* adding that the owners of objects routinely transcribed those stories in "speeches, memoirs, and poems, and on scraps of paper that they pinned, pasted, or sewed to the things they saved."[1] Yet among the more than 2,000 poems that Lydia Sigourney wrote over the span of a half-century are a number of verses in which objects—especially common household ones such as cleaning rags, clothing remnants, fabric scraps, sewing machines, and rocking chairs—go further than mere storytelling. Three of these poems—"To a Fragment of Silk" (1833), "To a Shred of Linen" (1838), and "To a Fragment of Cotton" (1841)—typify Sigourney's innovative use of direct address to request, or even demand, a story from an inanimate object. The speaker of each of these poems not only assumes that the fragments of cloth can listen to her but also that they are able to respond with a story about themselves. The apostrophe in these poems, moreover, serves as a vehicle through which the fictional persona of the speaker is also animated. Both the imagined speaker and the imagined object are joined in a dynamic fiction of agency that is consistent with Barbara Johnson's understanding of apostrophe as a rhetorical device that "manipulates the I/Thou structure of direct address in an indirect, fictionalized way," making inanimate objects "present, animate, and anthropomorphic."[2] But understanding apostrophe in this way only partially accounts for what is going on in these three poems. For, as Bill Brown suggests in his *A Sense of Things,* "the mereness of the thing, its physical presence," is nonetheless "inseparable from its metaphysical past." He continues: "Taken literally, the belief that there are ideas in things amounts to granting them an interiority, and thus something like the structure of subjectivity."[3] To imagine the sense of the material objects, as Sigourney does in these poems, is an exercise in enlarging the spiritual capacity of the structure of her subjectivity.

Sigourney's three fabric poems depict the remnants of cloth as having "something like" a richly interior subjectivity as well as a wondrous metaphysical past—mysteries that can be revealed only through the speaker's meditative interrogation. Brown refers to Vladimir Nabokov's insight that, in moments of focused concentration, objects do carry the potential to be "read . . . as transparencies" that reveal their past: "When we concentrate on a material object, whatever its situation, the very act of attention may lead to our involuntarily sinking into the history of that object."[4] But Sigourney's poetic "act[s] of attention" yield far more than object-based histories, and her lyric meditations transcend the singular act of "involuntary sinking" into past history. For in each of these fabric poems, she describes the way in which a transcendent ability to vividly experience the present sense of material existence (the "thingness" of the thing), and to imaginatively discover future possibilities result from a concentrated, contemplative focus on a lowly material object.[5] She uses direct address as part of a metaphysical conceit in which the material object undergoes an actual or projected transformative process that affects both speaker *and* object. She details the practice of meditative communion with the tangible scraps of domestic life through which the speaker renews and enlarges her own sensibility by meditating on the mysteries that an object might reveal. In these poems, the fabric of everyday life is transformed from a barrier to a medium for the culture of one's own spiritual self.

The contemplation of an ordinary physical object as a technique for developing the spiritual self has long been a distinctive feature of the Jesuit tradition, and within and against this context the spiritual, metaphysical nature of Sigourney's poems stands out. This particular form of meditative practice was widely disseminated throughout the larger Christian community after it was first codified in *The Spiritual Exercises of Ignatius of Loyola* in the early sixteenth century.[6] Sigourney, as far as we know, was not directly influenced by this Catholic tradition. Yet *The Spiritual Exercises* provide a conceptual framework for reading these poems as traces of her own Protestant (Episcopal) spiritual practice. Like the conceits of John

Donne and Edward Taylor, Sigourney's poems yoke the most ordinary of objects into contemplations of spiritual transcendence. Whether or not she had read Donne's lyric meditations—many of which feature complex literary conceits inspired by inanimate or mundane physical objects—she was likely aware of an ongoing metaphysical tradition that included his work.[7] Sigourney's fabric poems are thus part of an ongoing exploration of lowly objects as metaphorical interrogations of the spiritual self, and they demonstrate that one's relationship with material objects can serve, not oppose, the effort to enhance moral and spiritual development. Her apostrophes animate the spiritual rather than the physical nature of the objects they address. For the speaker, these objects become instructive models; for the reader, these conceits model the spiritual efficacy of making sense of the material world.

Ignatius designed the methodology of *The Spiritual Exercises* primarily for religious instructors and retreat leaders, and Sigourney's own approach in her three fabric poems, in some measure, replicates the Ignatian focus on a spiritual director's effort to guide others with instruction and moral advice. She attempts in each poem to faithfully narrate "the true groundwork of the history" involved in a given context as a way of helping others to "find something that makes the history a little clearer or more deeply felt . . . in the contemplation or meditation of a visible object.[8] And although Ignatius "does not use the terms [*contemplation* and *meditation*] with absolute consistency," the contemplation of a physical object or the act of meditating on an imagined historical scene—two exercises that feature significantly in the fabric poems—are both understood to produce a transcendent experience or at least an important moral lesson with life-altering possibilities.[9]

Significantly, in these poems, ethical guidance is infused throughout moments of object-based contemplation, for Sigourney seems acutely aware of her opportunities to posit interiority by imaging scenes from each object's history. As she turns inward toward the sense of the scrap or fragment, she simultaneously turns the poem as a whole outward providing moral instruction to a wider audience. This dual impulse, or dynamism between inward and outward, part and whole, is also consistent with *The Spiritual Exercises.* The Jesuit scholar John O'Malley confirms that the "call to interiority . . . derived from the *Exercises*" is not only a directive for the individual to move toward "heartfelt acceptance of God's action in one's life" but also a clear commitment to "persuading and teaching others how to be Christians in the fullest sense, with a special awareness of social responsibility."[10] Sigourney's own sense of social responsibility was, according to Gary Kelly, part of a "powerful religious evangelicalism" that gave her "a program for social action converging the sacred and the secular." She "was not only a teacher with a religious-social program but a tireless advocate of religious based education."[11] Sigourney clearly exhibits this "powerful religious evangelicalism" in her expressly didactic prose and poetry, where, much like a spiritual advisor, she guides others to "all methods of preparing and disposing the soul to rid itself of all inordinate affections, and after it has rid itself of them, to seek and to find the divine will in the ordering of one's life with a view to the salvation of one's soul."[12] Moreover, her autobiographical *Letters of Life* confirms that poetic process and spiritual exercise were conjoined for her: "My journals were usually made the repositories of my poems, in the order in which they were composed. Those systematic records became a sort of necessity of my existence. They seemed an adjunct in religious progress . . . consecrated [that] I may be renewed in the image of a glorious immortality."[13]

In two of Sigourney's three fabric poems, the final transformative process produces a transcendent form of the very object of contemplation—at once a base material object and a "renewed in the image of a glorious immortality." In "To a Shred of Linen," the "littering shred" of the poem's opening lines is, in the final line of the poem, "immortalize[d]" through an "apotheosis" when it is transformed from domestic rag into smooth paper upon which lines of poetry will be transcribed.[14] In "To a Fragment of Cotton," a remnant of a cravat becomes an object of spiritual homage, one ritualized by "reverent hand / And genuflection"; it may one day become a sacred text transcribed with biblical verses.[15] Even in the earliest of her metaphysical forays, "To a Fragment of Silk," the final transformation of "radiant shred" into "bank-paper" offers a moral lesson. Silk is the object of "Envy" for those who can't afford to buy it (an outward show of one of the seven deadly sins); and as paper currency, it "mak[es] the rich o'erprize the gifts of earth, / And the poor covet what God denies."[16] Sigourney pictures the process of transformation (either actual or notional) as resulting in some form of paper, an object whose purpose is to convey sense. But the ability to imagine this future results from concentrated, contemplative attention to the physical characteristics of the object as well as a consideration of its past history, before it was found in the litter of an ordinary household. This idea of animating objects with the presence of the past is foundational to object lessons that, in Brown's words, emphasize "the set of questions raised by the effort to turn matter into meaning."[17]

Silk's "Vanit[ies]"

As I have mentioned, "To a Fragment of Silk" is the earliest of Sigourney's object studies. It first appeared in print about ten years after the Connecticut-based Mansfield Silk Company was established as the center of the nation's growing silk district. Ulrich notes that "a few Connecticut towns had experimented with sericulture before the Revolution, but the real craze came in the 1820s and 1830s. Encouraged by enthusiastic reports in agricultural journals, government officials passed legislation encouraging the new enterprise."[18] Silk production as a politically encouraged enterprise would have been consistent with what Kelly sees as "Sigourney's national vision" as well as her "reinvention of earlier republican agrarian values as the national 'tradition.'"[19] In this first fabric poem, however, the history and process of silk production is only partially traced, and not in ways that support the new agrarian enterprise of sericulture. Even the diction Sigourney uses in the initial contemplation of the silk fragment seems to mark it as an object of luxury and indolence rather than one resulting from enterprising industry: "Well, radiant shred of silk, is it your choice, / Here on my carpet, thus at ease to lay?" [20] Sigourney's speaker addresses six rhetorical questions to the fragment in three of the poem's five stanzas but elicits few visionary scenes or stories of origin and change. What Brown calls the "set of questions raised by the effort to turn matter into meaning" fails in spite of the speaker's coaxing:

I've heard the veriest trifles have a voice
    Unto the musing mind; what can you say?
. . . .
Who were your ancestors?
. . . .
What was your destiny in the New World?[21]

Unlike the speakers in Sigourney's two later fabric poems, this speaker is clearly not certain of (nor interested in) the long history of silk production. She speculates only briefly on "rudiments" in Italy, where a number of the first silk makers in New England originated, and then vaguely acknowledges a "voyage o'er the boisterous ocean" for "rainbow tinted tissue."[22] Instead of following the deliberate and repeated pattern of question and contemplation depicted in the later poems, the speaker generates a series of moral lessons, first by addressing the exploitation of silkworms in the making of silk and then by exposing the ethical shortcomings of coveting silk products. In a book for children published in the same year, Sigourney warned against "carelessly destroy[ing]" insects and worms "since the Almighty has seen fit to create and adorn them. . . . Live in kindness and peace with the inferior creation. The Father of us all, hath given them for our use,—but not for the exercise of savage power, or malevolent dispositions."[23] In this poem, however, the newly endorsed enterprise of silk making is overshadowed by an account of profit making marked by neglect and indifference: "unsightly worms, with tireless maws" are prized for their "marvellous digestion," but after sacrificing their "health" for spinning wheels they are cast off as victims who "fold themselves in cone-like urns to die."[24]

Kelly notes that Sigourney "symbolized the agrarian republic through humble domestic objects, as in 'To an Ancient Rocking Chair' or 'To a Shred of Linen,'" an approach that is clearly "contrasted to products of luxury, as in 'To a Fragment of Silk.'"[25] Even the poem's focus on the process of making silk cloth is markedly void of purpose and direction: "Perchance, to reel their slight cocoons did foil / The patient skill of many a purblind dame, / While firmer nerves essayed the shuttle's toil."[26] Both patience and skill are "foil[ed]" in this domestic activity, and a "purblind" worker is at best visually impaired, at worst slow and dimwitted—lacking vision, insight, or any understanding of what Kelly calls Sigourney's focus on the "mission" of "American republican domesticity."[27] This characterization of the silk object stands in marked contrast to the process of linen making featured in Sigourney's next fabric poem, "To a Shred of Linen," where, Kelly writes, spinning and weaving are "part of a secular cultural institution . . . infuse[d] with religious patriotic purpose."[28] Clearly, the coveting of silk fabric and clothing is the primary focus of her first fabric poem. Sigourney depicts this breach of the Ten Commandments as a human weakness for all ages, yet silk, in its material nature, inspires vanity in the young and deceives and placates the elderly clinging to their waning beauty:

> What was your destiny in this New World?
>
> In dazzling robe to make young beauty vain?

Or for some waning lady pranked and curled
To hide time's ravage from the giddy train?[29]

In the next lines, the capitalization of "pale Envy" and the phrase "with outward show" seem to deliberately link the coveting of silk to one of the seven deadly sins, for the outward show of inner grace that good works were known to produce is instead an outward show of the "erring bliss" of envy.[30] Here, Sigourney echoes the Ignatian directive that the "best course to take" with spiritual advisement is in "explaining [to others] each Commandment, and in a like manner the deadly sins."[31] "To a Fragment of Silk" does not include a transcendent transformation of the object Sigourney is addressing; instead, the speaker predicts a future in which the "gaudy fragment" joins human vanity and "vile worm" in a context of greed and sinfulness:

Your history's not complete. Your second birth
Is in bank-paper, to allure the eyes,
Making the rich o'erprize the gifts of earth,
And the poor covet what God denies:
Man's vanity from a vile worm may grow,
And paper puff his pride; go, gaudy fragment, go![32]

All three fabric poems ultimately conclude with the possibility of a transformation of fabric into paper, but in "To a Fragment of Silk" the predicted future for the fragment is archetypically negative: bank paper that lures rich and poor alike becomes the moral cautionary tale for "money is the root of all evil" rather than a representation of hard work and well-earned wages. In this spiritual exercise, communion with the scrap of silk yields insight into a past of exploitation and cruelty as well as a future of possible corruption. Importantly, Sigourney's use of apostrophe forces the speaker (and the reader positioned with the speaker) to confront her own complicity in this story.

Linen's "Hallow'd Lineaments"

In contrast, Sigourney's second fabric poem, "To a Shred of Linen," celebrates the long and detailed history of linen as a rich symbol of the nation's agrarian roots as well as the basis for the virtue of the nation's vision. But this poem is also a longer and more complex spiritual exercise than Sigourney's first one. Through a clever and intricately patterned metaphysical conceit, the speaker traces the history of linen production, envisioning a long heritage of growing and harvesting flax in both ancient and more modern times and detailing the subsequent spinning and weaving of flax into cloth as one of the most enduring aspects of our cultural history. Yet instead of immediately positing a direct address of the "littering shred" after noticing that it has been "left behind" in a household sweeping, the speaker of this poem provocatively juxtaposes the domestic pursuits of "all good housewifery" with the literary pursuits of "*reading books*" and "*writing poetry.*"[33] Gendered subtexts and age and class distinctions are unmistakable; a woman devoting too much time to reading and writing could expect to be judged adversely by a "neat lady train'd in ancient times" as well as by a refined "spruce beau."[34] But the direct address that follows is free of any social commentaries, and the first and second of eight rhetorical questions directed at the shred suggest that a witty and sustained exploration of the poetics of contrasting ideas will follow this first visual assessment:

> Come forth—offender!—hast though aught to say?
> Canst though by merry thought, or quaint conceit,
> Repay this risk, that I have run for thee?
> —Begin at alpha, and resolve thyself into thine elements.[35]

Here it is the speaker of the poem (and not the shred) who begins at alpha and "resolve[s]" the elements of the object. Contemplation of the shred then gives voice to the prospect of hearing "merry thought[s]" that include the speaker's own gendered sarcasm in a later parenthetical aside: "(For men have deeper minds than women—sure!)."[36] In a clear statement of a poetics that the speaker acknowledges as old-fashioned or "quaint," she names what she is doing as a "conceit." By the end of the poem we see the metaphysical nature of this conceit as a practice through which the speaker transforms herself into a poet by recounting the sense she finds in this object and in herself. Vivid scenes from biblical and colonial history follow the first direct address of the material object, and each of these sequences is infused with a varying pattern of social commentaries, cultural critiques, philosophical insights, and the moral lessons of scripture.[37]

The vision rendered in lines 40 through 49 is augmented by the ameliorating effects of music from the classical Hygeian harp, the soothing lyre of the biblical David, and the sound of colonial spinning (a sonorous effect produced by both the song of the "ruddy damsel" and the sound of the wheel itself as it spins in the imagined scenes of the poem), all of which conjoin in the "rare fruit" of the nation's Protestant work ethic and virtuous vision.[38] At this point the speaker describes a moment of disorientation—she has briefly lost track of the chronology of her narrative—but the interruption is all part of the spiritual nature of this exercise. The literal and metaphoric "drop[ping]" of both object (the shred) and original idea (the description of the history and process of making linen) marks a recognition of the natural process of drifting concentration in any contemplative or meditative exercise.[39] This intentional digression conjoins form and meaning as well, for the speaker integrates her recognition into the theme of the poem's sustained conceit with wordplay and a clever pun:

> But come back,
> Thou shred of linen. I did let thee drop,
> In my harangue, as wiser ones have lost
> The thread of their discourse.[40]

The remaining seven questions addressed directly to the shred speculate on its point of origin as well as the "secrets" it may have heard in its "freshen'd youth" before its deterioration into a mere littering scrap.[41] But because, as Bill Brown avows, the "mereness of the thing, its physical presence," is still "inseparable from its metaphysical past," the speaker of the poem refuses to accept the shred's mute defiance in leaving all seven questions unanswered.[42]

> Still, close and mute!—
> Wilt tell no secrets, ha?—Well then, go down,
> With all thy churl-kept hoard of curious lore,
> In majesty and mystery, go down
> Into the paper-mill, and from its jaws,
> Stainless and smooth, emerge.[43]

In a clear directive, the speaker dictates the shred's final transformation, charging it to emerge newly formed as quality paper—that is, paper made with high rag content. Ulrich explains that linen and other natural fabrics were recycled repeatedly, although "few of these textiles have survived. Over time, sheets, tablecloths, towels, and napkins became bandages, menstrual rags, patches on shirts, filling for rag coverlets, or raw material for paper."[44] Paradoxically, the transformation from linen into paper at the end of Sigourney's poem is intended to last for the ages: the process may well effect an "apotheosis" if "Wisdom and truth" expressed in lines of poetry are "Trace[d] for posterity" on the paper's "stainless and smooth" surface.[45]

In an apt synthesis of a meditative spiritual exercise and the "secular cultural institution" of spinning and weaving, Sigourney's poem acknowledges both the "rare fruit" of paper "immortalize[d]" and made god-like, and the "rare fruit" of what Kelly describes as work "infuse[d] . . . with religious-patriotic purpose."[46] Spinning and weaving are part of the nation's history, purposeful work that in Sigourney's imagined scenes becomes inseparable from the "home-born, heart-felt comfort, rooted strong / In industry, and bearing such rare fruit, / As wealth might never purchase."[47] But linen making also ultimately produces paper, and the poem, with its lines "Trace[d] for posterity," is itself rare and transcendent fruit, the result of a complex spiritual exercise undertaken by a now "worthier bard" who has both contemplated a mundane material object and meditated on imagined scenes from that object's history.[48] Interspersed throughout is the "set of questions raised by the effort to turn matter into meaning," to quote Brown's earlier cited phrasing—questions that explore both "the poetics and politics of the object."[49]

Cotton's "Higher Ministr[ies]"

Sigourney's achievement in all three fabric poems—turning the matter of a base material object into transcendent meaning—is no small feat, even with the possibilities of ingenuity that metaphysical poetry allows. The material object in each poem literally begins in a state of abject rejection when the speaker begins to contemplate it. As I have noted, there is no transcendent transformation in "To a Fragment of Silk," for the "radiant" shred is no more than a "veriest trifle" languishing on a carpet. By the close of the poem (and following a didactic moral lesson), it has been lessened to a "gaudy fragment" grown from a "vile worm." But silk isn't a symbol of the agrarian republic; and as an emblem of luxury, it is clearly not a part of Sigourney's instructive evangelical vision. In her two later fabric poems, however, a mundane scrap of fabric becomes something transcendent and sublimely elevated—even deified. And in both cases, the extreme metamorphosis from the opening lines to the close of the poem is especially striking because the subject's initial rejection of the object is so pronounced.[50] The "littering shred of linen left behind" in "To a Shred of Linen" is a passive and mute "offender," a "vile reproach to all good housewifery" called out by the speaker's scolding subjectivity as the poem opens. And in Sigourney's final fabric poem, the "passive" fragment is subjected to more extreme forms of abasement and rejection as the speaker accounts for its past history in her opening direct address.

In "To a Fragment of Cotton," an "unbidden" scrap is, like the silk fragment, one of those "veriest triflers," appearing to remain passive and mute in spite of the speaker's willingness to listen, as expressed as a demand to be told. Moreover, in the poem's opening, the cotton fragment is an object that is physically alienated and accursed, first "tor[n]" by a baby, then "munched" by a dog, and finally subjected to an unceremonious "hanging" at the end of a housemaid's broom—all within the first six lines of the poem.[51] Yet this material object prevails; it is "indestructible" and somehow universal: "Yet here thou art, for all," the speaker marvels.[52] Dorothy Z. Baker speculates that the poet is "merely repeating the information whispered to her by the genius of the object"; her *genius loci* argument is similar to Brown's later assessment of "the way a *genius rei* seems to animate objects with a sense of the past."[53] But the visionary scenes from cotton's history are clearly generated by the speaker's concentrated, contemplative focus on the material object itself, a metaphysical practice aimed at transforming the spiritual self of the poet. Baker's later assessment that "the genius of the cotton quickly merges with the genius of the poet" seems more apt, for, as I have noted, "the contemplation or meditation of a visible object" is a catalyst for visionary insight in an Ignatian spiritual exercise, where the implied intent is to merge the mundane with the divine.[54] Moreover, the subsequent narration of cotton's wide sweep of history and cultural influence is infused with wonder and amazement:

> So, thou wert known in history! And thy sire
> The sounding name of Sir Gossypium bore.
> He was a younger brother of the fleece,
> And of the flax of Egypt, and the silk
> Which the poor spinning-worm doth die to make
> A present of, to those who thank her not.[55]

The manufacturing history of cotton is "younger" than that of wool, linen, or silk—an assessment that allows Sigourney to again briefly elegize the silkworm—but by the near midpoint of the nineteenth century, it was also a more versatile and far-ranging plant and fabric, one with the capacity to multiply "exceedingly" and to prosper "in every sunny zone" on the earth's surface.[56] In addition, the more contemporary process of making cotton into finished fabric causes a "clamour" heard across the world, one marked by "thundering crash[es]" of water-wheels and looms as well as by "steaming smoke" from coal-fed chimneys that blacken the skies.[57] Here, Sigourney echoes other nineteenth-century critiques on the dark side of industrialization, but her environmental concerns are only a subtext of her concerns about the smallest and most vulnerable victims of industrialization: the child laborers who are denied the intrinsic bond with nature promised by romanticism:

> . . . 'tis sad to see
> Such troops of little ones, with pallid cheek,
> Yielding their joyous birthright at thy shrine,
> And all sweet intercourse with fields and flowers,
> That glads the peasant's child.[58]

Somewhat surprisingly, the poem does not acknowledge the connection between cotton and slavery in the 1840s, except in a mention of "the planter's hand, / Well pleased," perhaps an indirect reference to a plantation owner's benefiting from slave labor to grow and harvest cotton in the antebellum South.[59] "Sigourney sympathized with the condition of slaves," Kelly notes, but she was "relatively conservative on the abolition of slavery."[60]

According to Ulrich, by the end of the first decade of the nineteenth century, there were already "112 cotton-spinning factories concentrated in southern New England," and factory sites continued to increase in the North in spite of growing social reform concerns about cotton slave labor in the South. "New Englanders . . . spun cotton," she adds, "though they were ambivalent about the region that produced it."[61]

Although Sigourney isn't morally ambivalent in "To a Fragment of Cotton," she does seem far more preoccupied with acknowledging the impressive and diverse range of cotton as both material object and cultural marker. It is "loved well" by commerce, which commands a "vassal throng of toiling artisans," and is marked by countless "transmigrations" and human dramas in which it "enact[s] the most changeful parts." It clothes laborers and gentry alike; it can be simply and "coarse[ly]" woven or fast-printed and glazed with "many color'd" decorative "chints." It marks most of life's significant rites of passage across the social strata, "veil[ing] the fair bride" at weddings and "drap[ing] the throned queen" at coronations. It also forms the universal "snowy shroud" of the dead.[62] Cotton is pervasive in life's varied dramas and countless "transmigrations"—a word Sigourney also uses in variant form in "To a Shred of Linen"—describe the extreme changeability (and commodification) of material objects.[63] In this final fabric poem, however, "transmigrations" has a deeper spiritual context, foreshadowing the "higher ministry" of cotton's ability to "commune with the soul" even after death:

> But yet thou hast a higher ministry
> Of kindliness, and, when thou well hast served
> His body's need, dost turn thy hand and touch
> The ethereal mind. Yea, when thou seem'st to die,
> Thou only dropp'st thy grosser elements
> To commune with the soul.[64]

Although the idea of revering a material scrap as a holy object may seem awkward or bemusing, in this spiritual exercise the cotton fragment inspires a devotional stance. "Mysterious Guest! I seem to fear thee," the speaker exclaims in awe as she kneels down to grasp and then lift the material object she is contemplating:

> . . . With reverent hand
> And genuflection, I do take thee up,
> And straight bespeak for thee more fitting place
> Mid thy compeers.[65]

Kelly's notes for this poem explain "the use of cotton rags in making paper, from which is made books that address the mind and spirit."[66] But unlike the paper from which linen is made in the second fabric poem, multiple uses are possible for this imagined smooth surface, derived from a scrap that Sigourney's speaker declares is wondrously "here . . . for all."[67] The next "transmigrated" form for this fragment could be anything from a child's primer, to a mariner's nautical chart, to a sage's writing tablet, to a bard's sheet music, even to a page from the Bible itself.

There is a clear pattern of forms ascending into higher forms in the listing, and Sigourney is indeed a poet in the Emersonian tradition in this final fabric poem—one who knows that "nothing in Nature is exhausted in its first use" and whose wisdom makes clear "the miraculous in the common."[68] It is the poet who "shows us all things in their right series and procession . . . and sees the flowing or metamorphosis" as a base material object becomes transcendent.[69] But in a clear departure from Emersonian poetics, Sigourney's final form in this poem—a "message from The Book of Life"—isn't an example of transcendentalist thinking as key to the reformation of Christian theology.[70] It reinforces instead a more traditional scripture-based foundation. For in the closing lines of the poem, the poet incorporates the Bible as the most pervasive symbol of the evangelism of her national vision. As the most widely published book of the nineteenth century, the Bible could be found in every New England home and was distributed by missionaries in faraway benighted lands—including those sunny climes of both hemispheres where cotton first originates in Sigourney's imagined history. In this sense, "To a Fragment of Cotton" includes a more integrated spiritual exercise, one that includes the Ignatian factors "of examination of conscience, of meditation, of contemplation, of vocal and mental prayer, and of other spiritual operations" that assist in "the salvation of one's soul."[71] Clearly this method—or more likely a Protestant version of the approach—was part of Sigourney's practice in composing what she called "a systematic record" of her poems as "an adjunct in religious progress."[72]

Ricardo Miguel-Alfonso's essay (chapter 12) addresses Sigourney's instructive approach in her teaching and writing, with its "aim . . . to reinforce a preexisting, even metaphysical, notion of goodness."[73] He rightly posits that her "educational model parallels that of Emerson and other transcendentalists in its use of history and biography as didactic tools" but that her "work as a whole differ[s] from [them not only] in its strongly religious inspiration, [but also in the] relentless (quasi-Aristotelian) confidence in the powers of emulation as an educational instrument."[74] I argue that, at least in the fabric poems, Sigourney's religious inspiration and her confidence in the powers of emulation are conjoined. The Bible as an "educational instrument" is a feature in all three poems—in brief but didactic scriptural references to Moses, David, and Saul in "To a Shred of Linen," and perhaps a more grounding reference to the commandment against coveting material goods in "To a Fragment of Silk." But in "To a Fragment of Cotton," paper into scripture as the final form possible for the fabric scrap is clearly the most pronounced example of Sigourney's biblical exempla. For the base material object in this poem has indeed aspired to a higher life within the poet's focused process of contemplation. It seems that the "aesthetic" experience itself, as Miguel-Alfonso suggests, "creates a version of the subject as a transparent medium that contemplates the world in a mystical way."[75]

Yet, Sigourney's fabric poems also illustrate a distinctly secular ability to look at an ordinary object and (to borrow Brown's phrasing) to discern within it "some record of the past, as though the past remained perpetually present, as though it could be repossessed—through an object—as affective experience."[76] In the process of "repossess[ing]" and rendering the history of mundane material objects, Sigourney confirms her status as the "worthier bard" whose genius can effect complex and seemingly improbable metaphysical transformations in lines of poetry.[77] Ulrich notes that an important transition "was already underway as women like . . . Lydia Sigourney began to contemplate the [fabric] scraps left behind by their mothers and grandmothers. In the next half century," she continues, "household textiles became the paper on which poets, novelists, centennial orators, and family chroniclers all over America wrote their stories of New England's past."[78] Sigourney's three fabric poems may be part of a critical transition in American literary history. But as objects in and of themselves they tell stories that help us to understand specific social and cultural contexts in the first half of the nineteenth century. That is, they provide insight into Sigourney's secular and spiritual undertaking in which "mere" material objects are worthy catalysts for poetic and spiritual inspiration.

"What a blessed age we live in," she marvels in her poem "The Sewing Machine" (1859), when our daily routines are enhanced by ordinary household objects that allow us to "fit ourselves and others / For a higher, better, life."[79] For her, the aspiration to a "higher, better life" was at least in part made possible by composing poems that provided "an adjunct in religious progress" for the poet herself and a didactic means of moral instruction for others. One of her self-proclaimed life-long "principles" was "to aim at being an instrument of good" through her writing, a goal that was a significant part of the "affective experience" in each of her meditative lessons.[80] Brown explains that even a "trivial thing" is capable of "dramatiz[ing] how an object that is neither a 'primitive' fetish nor a modern commodity can have 'metaphysical subtleties' that exceed its physical form—how it can [even] become something transcendent.'"[81] The poet's own deep sense of the material object is traced in the wondrous transformations of the physical forms of scraps of ordinary fabric, a process that also transforms Sigourney's sense of herself as a material—yet spiritual—object.

NOTES

1. Laurel Thatcher Ulrich, *The Age of Homespun* (New York: Vintage, 2002), 1.
2. Barbara Johnson, "Apostrophe, Animation, and Abortion" *Diacritics* 16, no. 1 (1986): 30. Sigourney's use of apostrophe seems consistent with Johnson's definition and with the presumption that these newly "animate, and anthropomorphic" objects are now capable of listening. On the ways in which apostrophe "produces a fictive, discursive event" within a "complex play of mystification and demystification," see Jonathan Culler, *The Pursuit of Signs: Semiotics, Literature, Deconstruction* (Ithaca: Cornell University Press, 1981), 153, 135–54.
3. Bill Brown, *A Sense of Things: The Object Matter of American Literature* (Chicago: University of Chicago Press, 2003), 1, 7.
4. Ibid., 7. I believe that Brown quotes from Nabokov's *Transparent Things* ([1972; reprint, New York: Vintage, 1989], 1) to foreground the potential of objects to be "read . . . as transparencies" that reveal an object's history but not necessarily its essence. In Brown's view, a great deal more than history "lies somewhere within the object materialized by human attention" (*A Sense of Things,* 7).
5. Brown, *A Sense of Things,* 7. Citing examples from Heidegger and Lacan, Brown explains that revealing the "thingness" of the thing is ultimately an act of discovery (11).
6. Saint Ignatius of Loyola was a sixteenth-century Spanish priest who used his own conversion experience and practice of contemplation to help others deepen their faith. His work, *The Spiritual Exercises,* became the basis of a meditative retreat experience for aspiring members of the Jesuit religious order he founded (known as the Society of Jesus), but for more than five centuries Christians of all denominations have used its methodology. A principle of Ignatian spirituality is the use of one's imagination in meditative prayer; retreatants are instructed to place themselves imaginatively in scenes inspired by the contemplation of scriptural passages and religious objects. I am indebted to Reverend Brian J. Cummings, S.S.E., the director of campus ministry at Saint Michael's College, for background information on Ignatius and meditative prayer. I am also indebted to Lisa M. Hastings, the director of formation programs for the Office of Ignatian Spirituality in the USA Northeast and Maryland Provinces, Society of Jesus, for her advisements that Ignatius regularly included the laity in retreat experiences; moreover, Ignatian meditation techniques have seen a marked resurgence in popularity since Vatican II.
7. Donne's biographer, Dayton Haskin, acknowledges a long history of literary scholarship that documents the poet's "great familiarity with Catholic doctrines and Jesuit practices" (*John Donne in the Nineteenth Century* [Oxford: Oxford University Press, 2007], 86). However, a number of earlier critics have argued that Donne's poetry was probably influenced more directly by *The Spiritual Exercises.* According to Thomas Van Laan, "Ignatius presented a method of meditation so well-conceived that all the succeeding important treatises adopted his fundamental procedure" ("John Donne's 'Devotions' and the Jesuit Spiritual Exercises," *Studies in Philology* 60, no. 2 [1963]: 193). Van Laan concludes that both "Louis L. Martz and Helen Gardner, working independently of each other, have demonstrated quite conclusively that Donne's poetry, especially his *Holy Sonnets,* shows evidence of his experience with a tradition of systematized meditation." His article offers detailed information on Martz's and Gardner's scholarship, especially the conclusion that the meditative "disciplines which the Anglican Church advocated . . . were identical to the disciplines practiced in the Ignatian exercise" (192).
8. Saint Ignatius of Loyola, *The Spiritual Exercises of Saint Ignatius of Loyola,* trans. W. H. Longridge, 3rd ed. (Milwaukee: Morehouse, 1930), 7, 53. I consulted Longridge's

editorial notes, but more recent scholarly editions include *The Spiritual Exercises of Saint Ignatius: A Translation and Commentary*, by George E. Ganss, S.J., (Chestnut Hill, Mass.: Jesuit Sources, 1992); and *Draw Me into Your Friendship: A Literal Translation and Contemporary Reading of the Spiritual Exercises,* by David Fleming (Chestnut Hill, Mass.: Jesuit Sources, 2013).

9. Ignatius, *Spiritual Exercises,* 250. This quotation is from the text of editorial note O, which acknowledges that the difference between meditation and contemplation is "not altogether clear" in the Ignatian primary source.
10. John O'Malley, "How the First Jesuits Became Involved in Education," *Jesuit Ratio Studiorum: 400th Anniversary Perspectives,* ed. Vincent J. Duminuco (New York: Fordham University Press, 2000), 59. O'Malley also addresses the "humanist system" of Jesuit pedagogy, with its belief in "the potential of poetry . . . to foster *pietas*—that is, good character" (66).
11. Gary Kelly, ed., *Lydia Sigourney: Selected Poetry and Prose* (Peterborough, Ont.: Broadview, 2008), 42, 43.
12. Ignatius, *Spiritual Exercises,* 4.
13. Lydia Sigourney, *Letters of Life* (New York: Appleton, 1867), 324. Here, Sigourney's understanding of poetry as a spiritual practice is expressed in language that is consistent with earlier Puritan reflections, such as those in Samuel Sewall's *Diary*, Jonathan Edwards's *Personal Narrative,* and most overtly in Edward Taylor's poem "Huswifery." It would have been impossible for Sigourney to have read Taylor (his poetry did not surface until the early twentieth century), but in my essay "Lydia Sigourney's 'To a Shred of Linen': Lineaments of the Domestic and the Sublime," I do address general similarities between her practice and Puritan spiritual life as well as the ongoing tradition of metaphysical typology that would have included domestic conceits such as those expressed in "Huswifery" (*American Transcendental Quarterly* 22 [June 2008]: 403–14).
14. Lydia Sigourney, "To a Shred of Linen," in Kelly, *Lydia Sigourney,* 171, l. 77.
15. Lydia Sigourney, "To a Fragment of Cotton," in ibid., 185, ll. 63–64.
16. Lydia Sigourney, "To a Fragment of Silk," in ibid., 108, ll. 27–28.
17. Brown, *A Sense of Things,* 84, 18. Brown's suggested queries can readily be applied to Sigourney's three fabric poems: "What ideas are imbedded in things? How does the [poet] gain access to them? What are the poetics and politics of the object?" (12).
18. Ulrich, *Age of Homespun,* 378.
19. Kelly, *Lydia Sigourney,* 34.
20. Sigourney, "To a Fragment of Silk," 107, ll. 1–2.
21. Brown, *A Sense of Things,* 124; Sigourney, "To a Fragment of Silk," 107, ll. 3–4, 7, 19. The pattern of direct address followed by musing contemplation is far more fully developed in Sigourney's other fabric poems, where vivid scenes of place and process follow a focus on the material object.
22. Sigourney, "To a Fragment of Silk," 107, ll. 6, 16, 17.
23. Lydia Sigourney, *How to Be Happy,* in Kelly, *Lydia Sigourney,* 108. Kelly's note identifies this text as "one of Sigourney's several books for children."
24. Sigourney, "To a Fragment of Silk," 107, ll. 9–12.
25. Kelly, *Lydia Sigourney,* 44.
26. Sigourney, "To a Fragment of Silk," 107, ll. 13–15.
27. Ibid., ll. 13–14; Kelly, *Lydia Sigourney,* 25.
28. Kelly, *Lydia Sigourney,* 24.
29. Sigourney, "To a Fragment of Silk," 107, ll. 19–22.
30. Ibid., ll. 23–24.
31. Ignatius, *Spiritual Exercises,* 17.
32. Sigourney, "To a Fragment of Silk," 108, ll. 25–30.
33. Sigourney, "To a Shred of Linen," 168–69, ll. 1–3, 9, 12.

34. Ibid., ll. 4–12.
35. Ibid., ll. 13–17.
36. Ibid., l. 32.
37. Ibid., 169–70, ll. 14, 17–49. In these scenes, Sigourney's efforts to faithfully narrate "the true groundwork of the history" as a way of inspiring others to "find something that makes the history a little clearer or more deeply felt" is in the spirit of an Ignatian spiritual exercise but with distinctly evangelical Protestant overtones (Ignatius, *Spiritual Exercises,* 7, 53).
38. Sigourney, "To a Shred of Linen," ll. 27, 49.
39. Ibid., 168–69, l. 51. For interesting "practical considerations" connected to engaging in meditative or contemplative exercises, see Shannon Rupp Barnes, "The Spiritual Exercises: Their Adaptation in Daily Life and the Laity," in *A New Introduction to the Spiritual Exercises of St. Ignatius,* ed. John E. Dister (Collegeville, Minn.: Liturgical Press, 1993), 88–95.
40. Sigourney, "To a Shred of Linen," 170, ll. 50–53.
41. Ibid., 170–71, ll. 68, 60.
42. Brown, *A Sense of Things,* 1.
43. Sigourney, "To a Shred of Linen," 171, ll. 68–72.
44. Ulrich, *Age of Homespun,* 139.
45. Sigourney, "To a Shred of Linen," 171, ll. 77, 74–75, 72.
46. Ibid., ll. 49, 77; Kelly, *Lydia Sigourney,* 24.
47. Sigourney, "To a Shred of Linen," 170, ll. 48–50.
48. Ibid., 171, ll. 75–76.
49. Brown, *A Sense of Things,* 84, 18.
50. Brown quotes Jean Baudrillard's assessment of "the long history of [an] object's passivity and abjection, its status as no more than the 'alienated, accursed part of the subject'" (ibid., 179). The definition of *abjection* as "the state of being cast off" does seem to be the premise for object-based contemplation in Sigourney's fabric poems. Baudrillard's words are from *Fatal Strategies* (New York: Semiotext, 1990).
51. Sigourney, "To a Fragment of Cotton," 183, ll. 3, 8, 4–6.
52. Ibid., l. 7.
53. Dorothy Z. Baker, "Ars Poetica/Ars Domestica: The Self-Reflexive Poetry of Lydia Sigourney and Emily Dickinson," *Poetics in the Poem: Critical Essays on American Self-Reflexive Poetry,* ed. Dorothy Z. Baker (New York: Lang, 1997), 72–73; Brown, *A Sense of Things,* 112–13. In an explication of Sarah Orne Jewett's story "The Foreigner," Brown similarly notes that "the past seems to reside in objects; historical *insight* seems to be graspable from *inside* the material record, from the way a *genius rei* seems to animate objects with the presence of the past. This *genius rei* [then] extends to a *genius loci*" (112–13).
54. Baker, "Ars Poetica/Ars Domestica," 73.
55. Sigourney, "To a Fragment of Cotton," 183, ll. 14–19.
56. Ibid., ll. 16, 20–21.
57. Ibid., ll. 27–30.
58. Ibid., ll. 31–34.
59. Ibid., ll. 22–23.
60. Kelly, *Lydia Sigourney,* 30.
61. Ulrich, *Age of Homespun,* 318, 289.
62. Sigourney, "To a Fragment of Cotton," 183–84, ll. 26–52.
63. In "To a Shred of Linen," the dairy commodities of "golden cheese" and "pot[s] of butter" made by the thrifty wife in Sigourney's imagined scene may be "transmigrated" into "new thanksgiving coats" for her "calculating" husband (169, ll. 33–39).
64. Sigourney, "To a Fragment of Cotton," 184, ll. 53–58.

65. Ibid., ll. 63–66.
66. Kelly, *Lydia Sigourney,* 184.
67. Sigourney, "To a Fragment of Cotton," 183, l. 7.
68. Ralph Waldo Emerson, *Essays and Lectures* (Cambridge, Mass.: Library of America, 1987), 18, 47.
69. Ibid., 456.
70. Sigourney, 185, l. 74.
71. Ignatius, *Spiritual Exercises,* 4.
72. Sigourney, *Letters of Life,* 324.
73. Ricardo Miguel-Alfonso, chap. 12.
74. Ibid.
75. Ibid.
76. Brown, *A Sense of Things,* 104.
77. Ibid., 104; Sigourney, "To a Shred of Linen," 171, l. 76.
78. Ulrich, *Age of Homespun,* 412.
79. Lydia Sigourney, "The Sewing Machine," in Kelly, *Lydia Sigourney,* 289–90, ll. 41, 47–48. This poem doesn't feature a direct address opening or a focus on transformation, but the moral lesson "use time wisely" is a significant part of the poet's celebration of domestic efficiency. Of Sigourney's other object-based poems, only "To an Ancient Rocking Chair" seems to follow a pattern of direct address similar to the one in the three fabric poems—although without an actual or projected final transformation of the object (105).
80. Ibid, 290, l. 48; Sigourney, *Letters of Life,* 324.
81. Brown, *A Sense of Things,* 42.

4

ENGAGING CONTRADICTIONS

SIGOURNEY'S *SKETCH OF CONNECTICUT, FORTY YEARS SINCE*

Sandra A. Zagarell

Lydia Sigourney's *Sketch of Connecticut, Forty Years Since,* a collection of eighteen sketches, explores aspects of New England's and the nation's past that were largely excluded from the triumphalist histories that had taken shape by 1824, when the book appeared.[1] In it, she proffers a model of community that is both more inclusive and more stable than the polity. Located in an actual place, the northern section of Sigourney's natal town of Norwich (called N___ in the text), this Connecticut community comprises the entirety of the town's economically, religiously, and ethnically diverse population and is led, compassionately and ethically, by a woman, the genteel Christian Madame L___. It does not, however, include any of the Mohegan people who continue to live on the ancestral land that was once the organic source of their culture but is now the site of N___. Sigourney's book also counters the prevailing notion that the history of the new United States is the story of the emergence and transformations of an Anglo-America by sketching the active struggles of Mohegans, as individuals and as families, to respond to the ongoing forces of dispossession. These alternative histories divide *Sketch* into two strands: both of which contradict the triumphalist version of American history while, at the same time, contradicting each other. Far from obscuring these impasses between the stories of N___, Sigourney brings them into the foreground of her *Sketch*, insisting not only that these incommensurable stories exist but also that they are mutually dependent. Committed to engaging with what America has been, is, and could become, *Sketch* emphasizes that the conflicts of interest that shape the competing histories it explores were as unresolved in the period during which the book is set (1784–85) as in her present moment of the early 1820s.

Sigourney's use of genre plays an essential part in *Sketch*'s refusal to impose a resolution on the contradictions with which it engages.[2] As a form, the sketch was so open that it is best characterized as a suite of possibilities, not a set of conventions. Unlike the novel, which was based on character, plot, and action, and in contrast to many of the other forms in which Sigourney wrote (including epic, hymn, meditative descriptive poem, and the short story), the sketch was governed by few principles except for length, the use of prose, and the presumption that it would capture facets of real life that existed independently of it. Sketches' foci ranged widely, as Washington Irving's enormously popular *Sketch-Book* (1819–20) shows. People, scenes, scenery, historical events, ways of life, visits, and conversations are among the subjects of Irving's sketches. Moreover, they unfold in a variety of ways, keeping pace with the movements, associations, musings, or observations of sketcher-narrator Geoffrey Crayon as he recounts a tale or a brief history.[3] And while some sketches are nostalgic for an idealized pastoral way of life Crayon imagines he has found in England, others, including "Rip Van Winkle" and "Philip of Pokanoket," are critical of the United States.

Whether or not Sigourney knew Irving's work, she used the form even more critically than he did, taking advantage of its flexibility to devote her sketches to suppressed histories and to kinds of people who were given little or no representation in the most visible versions of New England or the national life. She affirmed the legitimacy of her subjects' often-clashing outlooks by sequencing the sketches in ways that underscore the depth and persistence of the ethical and political issues they raise. To be sure, Irving's entertaining sketches had many imitators, and most of the village sketches that would soon be a staple of New England literature nostalgically portrayed eighteenth-century villages as idyllic communities whose homogeneous populace and traditional culture were a heritage the nation would do well to follow. But Sigourney and a few other writers composed sketches that challenged such a concept of a regional or national heritage. Eliza Buckminster Lee (*Sketch of a New England Village in the Last Century,* 1838) and Caroline Kirkland (*A New Home—Who'll Follow?,* 1839) presented villages fraught by difficulties, both local and large-scale, while a number of later sketch collections, among them Sarah Orne Jewett's *The Country of the Pointed Firs* (1896), though not critical, were self-reflective about local life and the dynamics between regional New England and the metropole.

That the feminist scholars who inaugurated *Sketch*'s recovery in the 1980s, myself included, downplayed or overlooked its contradictions is a situation that should remind us that all reconstructions of literary history have much to tell us about the historical moment of reconstruction as well as about literature. The emphasis on the coherence of literary writing that prevailed into the 1980s, along with the assumption of many feminists that "lost" women writers were worthy because they disputed the sexual politics of their day, generally made irresolvable textual contradictions or discomfiting implications. Nina Baym's brilliant "Reinventing Lydia Sigourney" did note unresolved tensions in *Sketch* and other works that feature Native Americans, but she did not center her analysis on the book's self-contradictions. Approaching it as a work of historical imagination that included an investigation into the racial-ethnic character of N___ in 1784–85, Baym was interested in how *Sketch* was pervaded by an ethos of conservative compassion, which she correlated with Sigourney's orthodox Christianity and elite class affiliation. My own early work on Sigourney sought to recover *Sketch* as a book whose coherence was part of its merit, and I superimposed unity on it by seeing N___ as a counter-historical prototype for an inclusive nation, a rebuke to the male-led Anglo-America that was actually coalescing in 1784.[4]

However, more recent scholarship recognizes that self-contradiction can reflect political and ethical integrity and carry affective and aesthetic charge. This understanding is reflected in a number of essays in this volume, including Paul Lauter's wide-ranging investigation of "Sigourney's Poetry of Death" (chapter 11). Enriching earlier commenters' recognition of Sigourney's skepticism about masculine dominion, Lauter shows that the century-plus dismissal of her work has overlooked her richly self-contradictory concept of death as both a Christian view (that casts death as the welcome precedent to the heavenly afterlife) and the specifically gendered notion of a terrifying male ravisher. Her multidimensional treatment of death, he suggests, contrasts sharply with the melancholic presentations in poetry by Poe and Whitman, while (though Lauter does not pursue this) her faith and her concern about the destructive treatment of Native Americans suggest comparisons with Catharine Maria Sedgwick and Lydia Maria Child.

Reconsidering *Sketch,* I realize how indebted I am to Baym's scholarship and how important my own earlier work has been to my thinking. Taking my cue from Sigourney herself as well as from many colleagues, I have come to regard the inclusive community led by Madame L___ as only one center of gravity in the book, not its epicenter, and the Mohegans, who originally inhabited the area which now constitutes N___ and were devastated by Anglo-American land-grabs and cultural-political expansion, as another. As I now see it, *Sketch* proffers two versions of N___: as a fairly heterogeneous community formed around the benevolent, genteel, female leadership of "the Lady" and as the homeland from which the Mohegans have been and are continuing to be displaced. Although both versions reflect critically on the newly founded nation, *Sketch*'s effectiveness, I now also see, lies in its emphasis, in both form and substance, on their incompatibility and their mutual dependence. In order to foreground how unflinchingly and effectively *Sketch* engages contradictions that are formative of Connecticut, and of the nation, this essay unfolds in three sections, each of which focuses on a central aspect of those contradictions. The first explores the two conflicting histories that *Sketch* counterposes to the triumphalist narrative of U.S. progress and to each other, that of the inclusive community of N___ and that of Mohegan devastation. The second analyzes how contradiction shapes the structure of *Sketch,* allowing it to highlight each of its alternative histories while acknowledging their incompatibility and the challenges they offer to the nation's official history. The third proposes that what allows Sigourney to entertain diverse histories and colliding worldviews is what I term *Christian empathy.* This is the capacity, sustained by her Christian faith, to inhabit and give powerful voice to positions and viewpoints that are not always her own and do not align with one another but coexist nonetheless and must be reckoned with. Never dissolving into resolution, *Sketch* thus charges its implied readers to confront the issues it presents and, ideally, to devise ethical, Christian ways of addressing them.

History as Divergent Histories

Sketch's subtitle alludes to Walter Scott's *Waverly: Or, 'Tis Sixty Years Since,* the 1814 novel that launched historical fiction as *the* genre about national origins. At the same time Sigourney's title announces her own subject: a nation that, unlike Scotland, actually did succeed in wresting independence from England. Her epigraph, taken from Scott's *Lay of the Last Minstrel,* reaffirms her affiliation with the Scottish writer while again distinguishing between the failed nation of Scotland and the successful United States: "Land of my sires!—What mortal hand / Can e'er untie the filial band / That knits me to thy rugged strand?"[5] Carrying forward the title page's invocations of Scott, the text initially appears to align itself with the triumphalist historiography that many American historians, poets, fiction writers, orators, and pamphleteers were evoking to promote the new nation as the embodiment of liberty and progress, for it is set just after the signing of the Treaty of Paris, when "the British Colonies of America [became] numbered among the nations."[6] An avid reader of history, Sigourney was familiar with the work of New England historians who embraced this historiography and were instrumental in inventing a tradition of the region's culture and history in which the pursuit of liberty and a homogenous, industrious Protestant population, gathered in utopic villages, qualified it for leadership of the new nation. Yet *Sketch* quickly establishes that its bid to participate in this shaping of regional and national history is actually a critical intervention in the prevailing narratives. It turns away from "the British colonies of America" to limn two aspects of the past that providential historiography has elided. One is a form of community that includes everyone who happens to live in any given town or village; the other concerns Native peoples who are discursively annihilated both by Anglo-American histories and by Sigourney's own vision of America's not-yet realized legacy of inclusive community. Both, *Sketch* shows, presuppose the decimation of Native peoples.

Sigourney makes no bones about presenting the diverse and harmonious community of N___ as a desirable alternative to the nation as a whole. The United States, she declares, "the first joys of tumult subsiding, discovered a government not organized, and resting upon insecure foundations," but in Connecticut, particularly in N___, a hierarchical social order has preserved stability. She writes, "The agitation which pervaded the general council of the nation, was unknown" because N___ is led by a local elite, "illustrious in virtue," and "the body of the people trusted in the wisdom of [their] heroes and sages."[7] The goodwill of both the upper class and the demos allows N___ to accommodate a heterogeneous population. This is in contrast with the restrictions on full, voting membership in the national community as well as with the homogeneity that conventional histories were ascribing to early New England.[8] N___'s residents comprise active members of several Protestant denominations (including Methodists, whose growing appeal to the "body of the people" alarmed many Congregationalists and Presbyterians), an impoverished widow and her family, Revolutionary War veterans whom the national government has neglected, a tenant farmer (not a landowner and thus not a voting citizen), formerly enslaved African Americans, and the widow of a British soldier killed in the Revolution. Full or partial sketches are devoted to members of most of these groups, often in the form of miniature autobiographies. Recounted in each speaker's own voice, they accentuate the legitimate presence of that person and the group to which she or he belongs. When the widowed Mrs. Rawson tells of her husband's decline into alcoholism and death and of her own tireless efforts to support her children and aging parents, her story partakes of a generic temperance narrative, but her tale of resolute endurance departs from that genre to feature one woman's determination. Similarly, Primus, a former slave, recounts his life from birth in "that part of Africa, which lies between the rivers Gambia and Senegal," his capture by English raiders and the harrowing experience of the middle passage, and then his purchase and conversion to Christianity by a benevolent Connecticut master who "[at] his death gave me his freedom."[9] Primus's life story bespeaks Sigourney's opposition to the slave trade but casts him as a person, not a cause—someone who mourns his separation from his natal family *and* one whose Christianity and deep knowledge of the Bible give him both spiritual strength and community standing. And in contrast to virtually every other representation of New England towns and villages, Sigourney's book presents the reigning figure of N___ as a "Lady," not a minister or another male dignitary. The leadership of genteel Madame L___ inheres in her wealth and autonomy (she is widowed), her generosity, her status, and her Christian concern for all of N___'s residents.

Yet this community is only one center of the book. Even as *Sketch* presents the former community of N___ as a legacy that could be revitalized as a model for the national life, it casts doubt on this idea by acknowledging that, like the nation, this community excludes N___'s dwindling population of Mohegans, who have been pushed to a reservation just outside the town. As it does so, *Sketch* openly contests the celebratory national history (which Sigourney's own race and class might have encouraged her to endorse) to demonstrate that the Mohegans have declined over the past 150 years because Anglo-Americans have taken their land. Her approach, and the history of the Mohegans she composes, can be seen as a form of what Dana Luciano has characterized as counter-monumentality: a disruption of the monumental American history that historians such as Frances Parkman would make a commonplace.[10] Sigourney uses three kinds of sources: regional and national written histories, the land, and Mohegans' own accounts of their past. She reads the written historical work available to her against the grain to ferret out what it unwittingly reveals about the Mohegans because she holds that it "represent[s] the natives in shades of indiscriminate blackness" ("our national annals" have been "careful to give us a reverse picture" of the heroic Mohegan chief Uncas and to suppress the crucial role played by his son Owaneco ("Oneco") in the war against King Philip," she insists).[11] For Sigourney, moreover, the native sources that most Anglo-American historians marshaled as testimony to the triumph of "American" history also provide eloquent historical evidence in idioms other than the written word on which standard U.S. histories have relied. She is alert to the traces of the Mohegans' past that are inscribed on the land in the form of monuments and memorials and is attentive to Native peoples' oral accounts of their past and present.

Using these diverse methods, Sigourney pieces together a many-dimensioned narrative that disputes the self-congratulatory providentiality of American history. It also rebukes contemporary Anglo-American images of Indians as demons or savages (images that are prominent in 1820s-era Puritan histories) and the trope of the mysteriously vanishing Indian (visible in William Cullen Bryant's "The Prairies," some of Sigourney's own poetry, and even, occasionally, *Sketch* itself). She renders Natives as bona fide peoples, with distinctive experiences, practices, and values and an abiding faith in the "Great Spirit" and that their relationship with their ancestral land has always been the foundation of their culture as well as their material well-being.[12] She assembles a century-long Mohegan history, a genealogy of tribal leaders that counterpoints and undercuts the genealogies that many Anglo-American New Englanders were constructing by the 1820s to establish their descent from the early colonists. Beginning with Uncas, an invaluable ally of the colonists in King Philip's War, this genealogy continues through his last direct descendant and includes a lateral descendant, Martha, who lives in N___ in 1785. Sigourney also lays out a history that honors the integrity and courage of most Mohegan leaders while emphasizing that the Mohegans' alliance with the colonists led to their loss of their land, and she shows that land takeovers, not providence, were responsible for the colonists' success. Repurposing Benjamin Trumbull's celebratory *A Complete History of Connecticut, Sketch* identifies Uncas's voluntary ceding of a "large tract of land" to English colonists in gratitude for their rescue of his people from the Narragansetts as the origin of the Mohegans' destruction.[13] The settlers immediately "plant" the town of Norwich, as Trumbull puts it, and, as Sigourney shows, are so greedy for "all the [patrimony] of the aborigines" that the Mohegans lament, "Soon . . . we shall not have land enough left, on which to spread our blankets."[14] Successive dispossessions, she demonstrates, have caused the crisis the Mohegans experience in 1784–85. "After a lapse of more than a hundred years" from the time of Uncas's gift, they have almost no land at all; and in 1785 most leave Connecticut, following the Reverend Samsun Occom to a refuge and a different way of life on Oneida lands in the state of New York.[15] *Sketch* does not mention their further dispossession in 1824, when the Oneida move to Wisconsin and Canada, but it lingers on the devastation that removal entails. The sketch describing the Mohegans' division ends by depicting Chief Robert Ashbow sitting in the "chair of Uncas"—the stone recess where Uncas had awaited his Anglo-American rescuers—grieving the state of the Mohegans in 1785, "diminished and dispersed" from the land that was theirs.

In juxtaposing the different histories it refers to or develops, *Sketch* offers no authoritative alternative and no workable template for America in the nineteenth century. But in problematizing heroic accounts of national origins while laying out both another history and an alternative form of civil society, each at odds with yet dependent on the other and neither in harmony with the triumphalist narrative, it spotlights the biases of official histories of origins and indicates that those left out of them, far from vanishing in 1784 or forty years thereafter, still actually counted as Americans.

Contradiction as Structure

Sketch is built around two linked strands: one comprising sketches of members of the community of N___, one comprising sketches about the area's Mohegans. Over the course of the book the patterns in which these strands are arranged reflect Sigourney's struggles to engage *Sketch*'s constitutive contradictions. The first twelve sketches alternate between the two strands, bespeaking *Sketch*'s emphasis on the presence of both groups in and around N___, the Mohegans' geographical and cultural marginalization, and the community's exclusion of Native people. While this alternation between the strands establishes a species of structural control over the disparity between the favorable depiction of the community and the critical account of the Mohegans' history and their circumstances in 1784–75, the interruption of one strand by the other suggests that the community exists at the Mohegans' expense and that the Mohegans' destruction lies at the community's door as well the nation's. We'll see that narrative integrity is also consistently undercut by other tensions Sigourney does not elide or otherwise downplay, and that when *Sketch* confronts the historical reality of the Mohegans' division in 1785, the structural equilibrium between the strands collapses. *Sketch*'s final six sketches portray N___ and the Mohegans in two extended and discrete sequences whose subjects and registers differ so sharply from the text up to this point and are so openly at odds with one another that they cast Mohegan devastation as a crisis not confined to 1784–75.

The plasticity of the sketch as a form plays a major role in Sigourney's division of *Sketch* into the two strands that reflect its constitutive contradictions, for she uses different formats for the sketches that make up each strand. Reflecting the stability of the community, the sketches that feature N___ as a community are formally similar. Each depicts one or several community members. The first two portray Madame L___ and her household. Each of the others centers on other residents of N___: one on the poor and featuring the widowed Mrs. Rawson; one on the white children of N___, whom Madame L___ entertains and educates; two on her tenant, Farmer Larken; one on a disabled Revolutionary War veteran. While these sketches capture the community's diversity, they also manage it by mobilizing forms of classification prevalent in Sigourney's era. They presume that, with the exception of Madame L___ and other members of the elite, N___ is composed of the kinds of persons who belong to discrete groups and that these groups can be represented synechdocally, by typical members. Farmer Larken is pure Yankee—an honest Congregationalist, hardworking and self-sufficient. African Americans are either virtuous (Primus) or less than fully civilized (Madame L___'s squabbling, literal-minded servants Cuff and Beulah, who anticipate figures of minstrelsy).[16] This taxonomy casts in high relief the demographic partitioning on which Sigourney's representation of N___ relies. The separation of members of groups into discrete sketches obviates the possibility of contact among them, let alone interaction. Conflict, uneasiness, cooperation, or communication among Farmer Larken, Mrs. Rawson, and the war veterans need not come up. Moreover, taken together, these sketches characterize the community as a group formed around the single governing figure of Madame L___ and consisting only of people who live in N___ or are guided by her. All but two feature community members' visits to her in her parlor to seek her aid or counsel. They create the wheel-like pattern that Elizabeth Ammons has termed radial structure: Madame L___ and her home form the wheel's hub, and the sketches depicting community members are its spokes.[17]

The exceptions to this pattern are informative about both the inclusiveness of *Sketch*'s concept of community and about its limits. One details the Lady's visit to the home of Farmer Larken; it testifies to her commitment to extending the community to Anglo-Americans living beyond N___'s borders. The other, the sketch about Primus and his daughter Flora, registers Sigourney's discomfort with free African Americans and the history of slavery in Connecticut. Though these African Americans live in N___ and are part of the community, they, alone among the community members, are not shown to interact with Madame L___. In addition to constituting structural segregation, this isolation allows Sigourney to dwell on Primus's enslavement and gruesome Atlantic crossing, to acknowledge his and his daughter's lives as free residents of N___ while cordoning them off from N___'s other residents, and to weave into his history the false assertion that Connecticut had abolished slavery in the past.[18] In fact, antislavery legislation was not passed in Connecticut until 1784, and it mandated only gradual emancipation. Slavery still existed in the state in 1784 and in 1824 (the last Connecticut slaves would die only in 1848), but Sigourney does not acknowledge this.

While radial structure tacitly testifies to N___'s exclusions and to the ongoing dispossession of the Mohegans, the sketches devoted to representing the Mohegans openly cut through the image of a self-sufficient community by inscribing the devastation of the people whose displacement has made the community possible. Not only do they differ structurally from those that depict the community members; but they also differ from one another, accommodating the fragmentation to which the Mohegans have been subject throughout the history that *Sketch* limns. The sketch that details the genealogy of the Mohegan chiefs is a chronicle of successive generations of leaders whose authority is eroded by the group's displacement. The next one underscores the Mohegans' cultural fragmentation: comprising thumbnail portraits of five Mohegan men, it highlights how differently each has responded to Anglo-American dominion. One man is a determined traditionalist; another seeks to assimilate; one, a Catholic convert, is largely isolated; two try to preserve aspects of their traditions while acceding to Anglo-American hegemony. A third sketch recounts the troubled life and death of the Catholic man, Maurice, whose religion Sigourney, like most Protestant Americans, regarded as tyrannical and a threat to American liberty. Manipulated by his priest into committing a murder, Maurice subjects himself to penitential self-punishments, eventually dying of starvation. The only sketch to depict the Mohegans visiting Madame L___ features the crisis of 1785 and centers on a debate between Chief Robert Ashbow and the Reverend Samson Occom about the self-exile of most of the tribe. The sketch that follows portrays the Mohegans' anguish when most of the tribe leaves and concludes with Ashbow's grief over what could be the end of Mohegan life.

Although *Sketch*'s alternating strands simultaneously contain contradictions and express them, as the book moves into spring 1785, when the division of the Mohegan community takes place, Sigourney's historical integrity apparently renders her unwilling or unable to continue managing contradictions as she had. After describing the departure of most of the Mohegans, she abandons both her depiction of N___ as a workable community and her history of the Mohegans. Rather, she splits *Sketch* into two discrete clusters, each comprising three chapters. One cluster is retrospective, featuring veterans who visit Madame L___ and recount Revolutionary War stories; the other, which imagines a far more inclusive community than N___'s, is set in the home of Zachary (also known as Arrowhamet) and Martha, a Mohegan couple who have remained in Connecticut. The two clusters depart so dramatically from the earlier sketches and are so discordant with each other that they fracture the book. The first cluster, chapters 13 through 15, features visitors to Madame L___ who reminisce about the fight for nationhood, not about their own lives. Stridently militant in tone and substance, their stories align so well with triumphalist American history that they seem to signal a retreat on Sigourney's part in the face of the 1785 outcome of her history of the Anglo-Americans' treatment of the Mohegans. Whereas the language of earlier sketches is often religious, the language of these celebrates war and American heroism. A wounded veteran, Anderson, describes in stirring terms the Battle of Bunker Hill. Rejecting the word "retreat," he blames the loss on "the fortune of war" and returns repeatedly to the carnage that the Americans caused. "We fought till not a cartridge was left, and then gave them a parting salute with the butt-end of our muskets, as they leaped into our entrenchments," he tells Madame L___. "My musket burst, and I snatched another from the dead hand of a comrade. The Almighty have mercy on the souls, who were sent by me to their last account."[19] The veterans recount battles in the struggle for independence and celebrate the courage of American heroes. Two former officers then detail, in comparable terms, the courage and devotion of Nathan Hale and of Champé, an American officer who attempted to foil Benedict Arnold's betrayal of the colonists. Madame L___, whose preferred idiom has hitherto been religious, becomes almost chauvinistic. She pronounces the Battle of Bunker Hill "a retreat . . . which produced the effect of victory" and terms Arnold a "solitary" "instance of treason." When she does express religious sentiments, they serve nationalism: Washington is "he, whom Heaven raised up for its own great purpose."[20]

As rousing as these war stories might have been as a freestanding unit, they are openly discordant in register and subject with the sketches which precede them and with the three that follow and end *Sketch.* The subject of this second cluster is people who have been excluded by the new nation, whose founding the veterans and the Lady commend: Zachary/Arrowhamet; Martha; their adopted daughter Oriana, who is also the British widow of a British soldier; and Oriana's minister, an Anglican whose church was shut down by colonists during the war. In terms as vivid and harrowing as Anderson's account of Bunker Hill but coming from an English perspective, Oriana describes a battle in which her husband was killed: "I heard the horrible uproar of war in [the Americans'] redoubts, the roar of cannon, the clashing of swords, and the cry of men."[21] Her Anglicanism receives as much sympathetic attention as Madame L___'s Christianity does throughout most of *Sketch;* and in contrast to the Lady's militant rhetoric in the Revolutionary War cluster, it expresses familial love for her adopted Native parents. Her minister, too, is ecumenical; he offers religious comfort to Arrowhamet and Martha as well as to Oriana. Not only do these three sketches depict bonds among different kinds of people: they emphasize likenesses among their subjects yet do not minimize difference. They honor distinctions between the Anglican church and other Protestant denominations. Martha and Zachary are faithful to their original religion *and* embrace Christianity, and *Sketch*'s own prose models this multiplicity of religions by pairing the Anglican minister's invocation of the "Holy Spirit" with Zachary's of the "Great Spirit" and the "Spirit of Truth."[22] Though *Sketch* cannot portray the community or the nation that includes Zachary, Martha, and Oriana, by placing sketches that portray them immediately after those about the veterans and the Revolution, it gestures toward a different America than the one that was coalescing in 1784: an America that embraces the common humanity of all its residents while recognizing their heterogeneity.

Christian Sentiment

Sigourney's historical integrity and use of genre underwrite her capacity to engage contradictions, but she may not have been so uncompromising in doing so were she not a devout and empathic Christian. Christianity, one of her abiding subjects, is prominent in many of her works, including "Death of an Infant," "Niagara," and other poems; hymns; the book-length *Lucy Howard's Journal;* her memoir *Letters of Life;* as well as *Sketch.* Christian faith suffuses the language and the ethos of many, including "Niagara." In *Sketch* it is a primary medium. It colors the compassion with which Sigourney represents mutually exclusive versions of history and imagines multiple, often divergent experiences, and it informs the idiom in which she writes.

As in much antebellum writing, the faith that informs *Sketch* is multifaceted. For Sigourney, as for many people in her America, Christian faith and the conditions of daily life were intimately connected. Faith was at once encouraged and challenged by the ubiquity of illness and death, which, like birth, usually took place in the home. As Lauter's essay reminds us, with infant mortality rates high and life expectancy short, the deaths of the young were commonplace and the losses difficult to bear. Religion was formalized in the church but was also part of daily life. It offered providential explanation for suffering and mortality and also, especially in the wake of the Second Great Awakening, the solace of an afterlife. The pervasiveness of religious language has particular significance for readings of Sigourney and many other antebellum writers. Whether in the form of the

Bible (usually the King James Version) or in phrasing that recalled that text, this language circulated throughout Sigourney's world. Combining authority and meaning with sound and image, it took the semantic form of household prayers and individual ones, written texts and musical ones; it was woven into everyday speech, letters and diaries, educational material, literary texts, and probably many Americans' thoughts.

In *Sketch,* Biblical passages and paraphrases meld with exposition to express loss, sorrow, and, often, acceptance and to offer consolation. Many of these expressions are likely to seem formulaic to twenty-first-century readers but would have been sustaining to Sigourney's contemporaries. In describing Madame L___'s grief at the deaths of her family members, for example, the narrator evokes the reassurances of Psalm 23: "I thank Thee, that I am not alone, for *Thou* art with me."[23] Sigourney and her readers would have been aware of the previous lines, "Yea, though I walk through the valley of the shadow of death, I will fear no evil." Similarly, the account of the early death of the Lady's mother paraphrases Peter 1:24, "*For all flesh [is] as grass, and all the glory of man as the flower of grass*"; she has been "blasted by Him who maketh all the 'glory of man, as the flower of grass.'"[24] Although this assertion is implacable in its dismissal of human importance and self-impotence and its placement of human death within a divinely ordained natural cycle, its faith comforts on the same grounds. By exemplifying faith in biblical language that is both poetic and familiar, these passages and many others like them may stir readers' grief yet offer consolation.

While religious language may speak to readers as individuals, it is complemented and extended by Sigourney's Christian empathy, a religious form of negative capability that allows her to imagine, with deep feeling, the multiple perspectives and many voices of the figures she represents even when they are odds with one another or go beyond her own class and race.[25] This is not to say that Sigourney's representation of empathy is untouched by her elitism and racial identity. Christian empathy is allied with *Sketch*'s elite, personified by genteel Madame L___, not by Farmer Larken, Mrs. Rawson, or Primus. By following Christ's injunctions and "lov[ing] the poor and the sick, as if they were unfortunate members of her own family," the Lady inscribes her social standing: her "sympathy" is directed downward to those who are socially or racially beneath her. But the sense of loss she experiences at the deaths of all her loved ones has created in her a perpetual "Sabbath of the Mind" and engenders in her a "sympathy with all who mourned," which is to say with everyone.[26] This sympathy leads her to exemplify compassion not tinged by condescension or self-focus. She recognizes the likeness between herself and others in ways that do not cast the ubiquity of suffering as a level playing field of emotion. When "those who mourn" visit her, she encourages them to speak, to describe their experiences and articulate their views in what *Sketch* presents as their own words. When they do so, she, and the text, concentrate on them, not on her emotions or other responses. *Sketch*'s Christian empathy differs substantially from what Lauren Berlant has characterized as a deep structure of antebellum sentimentality: an appeal to relatively privileged white women to conceive of themselves as members of a large counter-public united by suffering and thus to short-circuit its own potential to encourage structural change.[27] Although *Sketch* does not call for change openly, it distinguishes consistently between individual suffering caused by illness and death and the suffering of the Mohegans caused by the Anglo-Americans, implicitly asking readers to redress the latter as well as alleviating the former.

While Madame L___'s compassionate listening encourages Mrs. Rawson to tell the story of her late husband's alcoholism and the Congregationalist Farmer Larken to express discomfort at the emotional excesses of his nephew's Methodism, Christian empathy also inspires the substance and form of a number of the book's most challenging sketches. Underscoring the necessity of change that *Sketch*'s counter-history also urges, these sketches concern the book's greatest sufferers, the Mohegans, and present them all with sympathy and respect even when they take exception to the very Christianity which the text manifests. One sketch describes with compassion the different ways in which Mohegan men have adopted Christianity and Anglo-American practices or resisted them. The sketch depicting the departure of most of N___'s Mohegans conveys with equal empathy the agony of those who leave and those who stay. The one which plays out the debate between Chief Ashbow and Reverend Occom about the departure honors the integrity of both men and gives each convincing arguments that are expressed in Sigourney's own cherished idiom, the language of faith. Occom uses religious and biblical language to insist that self-removal promises the only possibility for Mohegan survival. Holding that the current state of Native peoples exhibits the workings of providence, he also maintains that, if they vanish from earth, they will find salvation in the afterlife. Quoting Lamentations 3:39, he says, "All men, all nations of men, have sinned. In this world retribution is not perfect. It becomes not us to contend with Him, who dealeth more lightly with us than our iniquities deserve. Saith not that holy book . . . 'Wherefore should a living man complain, a man for the punishment of his sins?'"[28]

Yet Ashbow, while esteeming the Christian benevolence of Madame L___, uses biblical language to contend that divine providence is not the cause of the Natives' condition. "Why," he asks, paraphrasing Psalm 85, "does the God of Christians . . . draw out his anger [against us] to the latest generations?" Echoing Psalm 83, he continues, "Are *we* sinners above all men, that we are made as driven stubble before our enemies?" He blames the Anglo-American Christians who justify Native peoples' dispossession in the name of Christianity—"Why are Christians so eager to wrest from others lands, when they profess that it is gain for them to leave all, and die"—and his expressions of sorrow, which interweave biblical language and naturalistic speech, have *Sketch*'s characteristic affective resonance. Yet they eschew the consolation of an afterlife that Occom has invoked: "Where shall the poor Indian turn in his sorrow, but to that spirit of mystery, which had led him on through darkness, all his life long? He was hungry, and his bow satisfied him. Thirsty, and drank of the brook."[29] These last two sentences, which adapt Matthew 25:35, exemplify the reach of Sigourney's Christian empathy. Confronting Christians' deeds that violate Christianity's ethos of love and charity, Ashbow's bitter repudiation of a cornerstone of Christian faith is all the more powerful because it is expressed in the language of the Bible.

By foregrounding the irreconcilability of the men's Christian arguments and the validity of both, *Sketch* underscores the historically created character of the Mohegans' circumstances. Yet it also strongly indicates that empathy is only a starting point for addressing that crisis. The sketch offers no direct comment on what Ashbow and Occom say; but after they end their debate and leave the parlor of the Lady, a final scene, a conversation between her and her nephew, demonstrates both the necessity and the limits of empathy. They discuss two other clergymen long estranged by doctrinal disputes who reconcile lovingly on the deathbed of the older man. Though this thematizes the power of acknowledging loss and death, the incommensurability between the obliteration of Native peoples and the abandonment of theological quarrels is so stark that it demonstrates the need for both empathy and active measures if that obliteration is to be halted.

The book's final sketches—those that feature Arrowhamet, Martha, Oriana, and the Anglican minister—constitute a charge to readers even more pronounced than that leveled by the debate between Ashbow and Occom: to acknowledge the distinction between the kinds of loss all humans experience and the suffering caused by their own America, and not to shirk from engaging the latter. Focusing on a cross-racial family, this cluster is a provocation: affective and urgent. Whereas the era's concept of the family was generally conservative, structured by patriarchal domesticity and cast as a ground of national sameness and unity, this family gestures toward the possibility of both a domestic and a large-scale formation along very different lines. Comprising Mohegans and a British woman who are not kin but have chosen each other, it does not adhere to the conventional roles, and its members are bound only by love. Oriana paraphrases the Sermon on the Mount in consecrating this family: "I was a stranger, and ye took me; sick and ye ministered unto me." Such affirmations of a shared home are brief—her death ends them—and they coexist with her counsel that her adopted parents focus on their heavenly home, not their earthly life with her. "In my Father's house there are many mansions," she promises.[30] Although *Sketch* does not reconcile earthly and heavenly homes and families, it asks its 1824 readers to acknowledge that, with Indian removal becoming official policy, their America is in a crisis with which they are obliged to engage, ethically and compassionately.

Oriana's final injunction, nominally to her minister but clearly to readers, makes this request explicit: to "sometimes grant a visit, and a prayer to those who were parents to her without the bonds of affinity; philanthropists, without hope of the world's applause; Christians, though proscribed as the heritors of a savage nature; and who will also, she trusts, be heirs of heaven, through faith in Him who hath promised that 'the merciful shall obtain mercy.'"[31] Her characterization of Native Americans as proscribed "heritors of a savage nature" exemplifies the capacity of the language of faith to foreground contradiction. Martha and Zachary have been "proscribed" as savages, but who proscribes? God? Christianity? Americans who profess Christianity but do not exemplify faith? Oriana's trust that Native peoples are "heirs of heaven" disputes the insistence of many contemporary Christians that they were without souls, while her directive that they be visited, another echo of the Sermon on the Mount, acknowledges them as residents of earth, of the United States. Her final words, also from the

Sermon on the Mount, again convey Native peoples' legitimate residence in the United States by extolling their mercy, an essential feature of Christianity. At the same time, she charges readers to be merciful, thickening that charge by linking human mercy with divine mercy.

Sketch cannot resolve a crisis that had only deepened in 1824, but it tasks readers to engage with the contradictions it expresses. As it lays out colliding histories and disparate standpoints, casts Native American removal as a national crisis, portrays a heterogeneous community, and valorizes the benign leadership of a woman, all in a form which eschews closure and often in language which bespeaks faith, the book asks readers to inhabit, with Christian empathy, the many positions it has represented. Taking them all into full account, these readers must devise ways to make their United States an inclusive republic, and a just one.

NOTES

1. [Lydia Sigourney,] *Sketch of Connecticut, Forty Years Since* (Hartford, Conn.: Cooke, 1824). Sigourney was not writing for economic gain or social advancement when she published *Sketch.* It was released anonymously and copyrighted by the publishers. Bound between paper boards with a plain print cover, it does not seem to have circulated widely, and I have found no evidence of a second printing, though Sigourney did reprint one sketch in her 1834 collection *Sketches.* These circumstances indicate how important it is to take into account the changing character of Sigourney's authorship and to recognize that explanatory models, which situate authorship within the soon-to-emerge commodity economy, should not be superimposed on her entire oeuvre.
2. Sigourney did not generally use such an open form. In *Traits of the Aborigines* (1822) she had used the epic form to air criticism of Anglo-American Christians' treatment of Native peoples while describing the latter with respect and sympathy, but she had also hewed to the epic's conventions to re-contain the challenges to Anglo-American hegemony that she issued. For a sustained discussion of *Traits,* see Christopher N. Phillips, *Epic in American Culture: Settlement to Reconstruction* (Baltimore: Johns Hopkins University Press, 2012), 187–219. Throughout Sigourney's long writing career, she often used other genres comparably: the poem "Indian Names," for instance, stretches but accedes to the conventions of the elegy. Its forceful rhetoric conveys Anglo-Americans' responsibility and casts the names of rivers, mountains, and other natural phenomena as ineradicable traces of Natives' long presence, yet it mourns—and thus accepts—their obliteration.
3. Irving's *The Sketch-Book* also exemplifies the different ways in which sketches might appear in print: singly in a magazine, in parts, or collected in a codex. For the complicated history of the book's publication, see Washington Irving, *The Sketch-Book of Geoffrey Crayon, Gent.,* ed. Haskell Springer (Boston: Twayne, 1978), 340–56.
4. Sandra A. Zagarell, "Expanding 'America': Lydia Sigourney's *Sketch of Connecticut,* Catharine Sedgwick's *Hope Leslie,*" *Tulsa Studies in Women's Literature* 6, no. 2 (1987): 225–45; Nina Baym, "Reinventing Lydia Sigourney," in *Redefining the Political Novel: American Women Writers, 1787–1901,* ed. Sharon M. Harris (Knoxville: University of Tennessee Press, 1995), 66–85.

5. [Sigourney,] *Sketch,* title page.
6. Ibid., 15. For a good overview of triumphalist historiography, see Lawrence Buell, *New England Literary Culture: From Revolution through Renaissance* (Ithaca: Cornell University Press, 1985), 193–201, 214–38. See also Joseph A. Conforti, *Imagining New England: Explorations of Regional Identity from the Pilgrims to the Mid-Twentieth Century* (Chapel Hill: University of North Carolina Press, 2001), 1–202.
7. [Sigourney,] *Sketch,* 15, 16.
8. U.S. Census Bureau categories, literary and historical works, and nongovernmental accounts of regions of the country offer information about what classes of people were recognized by the government. See, for instance, Timothy Dwight, *Greenfield Hill* (New York: Childs and Swaine, 1794); Timothy Dwight, *Travels in New England and New York* (New Haven: 1821); Jedediah Morse, *The American Geography, or, a View of the Present State of all Empires, Kingdoms, States, and Republics in the Known World, and of the United States of America in Particular* (Boston: Thomas and Andrews, 1796); and Benjamin Trumbull, *A Complete History of Connecticut, Civil and Ecclesiastical, from the Emigration of the First Planters from England, 1630 to 1764* (New Haven: Maltby, Goldberg, and Company/Wadsworth, 1818). The U.S. Census Bureau reports that, in 1790, the "six inquiries . . . called for the name of the head of the family and the number of persons in each household of the following descriptions: Free White males of 16 years and upward (to assess the country's industrial and military potential)[;] Free White males under 16 years[;] Free White females; all other free persons; slaves" (https://www.census.gov).
9. [Sigourney,] *Sketch,* 89.
10. Dana Luciano, "Melville's Untimely History: 'Benito Cereno' as Counter-Monumental Narrative," *Arizona Quarterly* 60, no. 3 (2004): 33–60.
11. [Sigourney,] *Sketch,* 42, 37–47.
12. Ibid., 162, 248, 258.
13. Ibid., 178–79; Trumbull, *Complete History of Connecticut,* 1:236.
14. [Sigourney,] *Sketch,* 46.
15. Ibid., 179.
16. Sigourney's depiction of Native Americans also relies on conventions of classification. They are either good (the Protestant Mohegans who live in N___) or savage (the Delaware, or Lenni-Lenape, who live elsewhere). The partial exception among the good Mohegans is the Catholic convert, Maurice.
17. Elizabeth Ammons's important "Going in Circles: The Female Geography of Jewett's *Country of the Pointed Firs*" (*Studies in the Literary Imagination* 16 [Fall 1983]: 83–92) identifies the wheel-like, or radial, structure of the best-known example of this format. For the similar concept of centric structure, see Joseph Allen Boone, *Tradition Counter Tradition* (Chicago: University of Chicago Press, 1987). Ammons's work has been indispensable to my own on narratives of community; see, for instance, Sandra A. Zagarell, "Narrative of Community: The Identification of a Genre," *Signs,* 13, no. 3 (1988): 498–527. While Sigourney may have known Irving's *The Sketch-Book*, she was most likely not aware of the first collection of sketches to feature radial structure, Mary Russell Mitford's *Our Village* (1824). She probably developed radial structure independently, and her conjoining of two structures is definitely original.
18. [Sigourney,] *Sketch,* 18–191.
19. [Sigourney,] *Sketch,* 190–91.
20. Ibid., 193, 199, 225.
21. Ibid., 266.
22. Ibid., 250, 233, 248, 275.
23. Ibid., 23.
24. Ibid., 22.

25. My thanks to Mary Louise Kete for recognizing Sigourney's Christian empathy as a form of negative capability, originally defined by John Keats as the capacity "of being in uncertainties, mysteries, doubts, without any irritable reaching after fact and reason" (letter to George and Thomas Keats, December 21, 1817) or, in the case of *Sketch,* ideological or narrative coherence (*The Complete Poetical Works and Letters of John Keats,* ed. Douglas Bush [Boston: Houghton, Mifflin, 1958], 277).
26. [Sigourney,] *Sketch,* 8, 14.
27. Debates about the effects of sentimentality have long been a central concern of feminist critics and theorists. See, for instance, Ann Douglas, *The Feminization of American Culture* (New York: Knopf, 1977), which holds that sentimentality was the special province of nineteenth-century American women and that the heightened emotions it solicited bolstered the status quo; and Jane Tompkins, *Sensational Designs: The Cultural Work of American Fiction* (New York: Oxford University Press, 1985), which analyzes sentimentality as a way in which women such as Harriet Beecher Stowe bid for radical social transformation. For works that undo the dichotomies on which the sentimentality debates turn, see Mary Louise Kete, *Sentimental Collaborations: Mourning and Middle Class Identity in Nineteenth-Century America* (Durham: Duke University Press, 2000); and June Howard, *Publishing the Family* (Durham: Duke University Press, 2001), 213–56. By historicizing sentimentality, both Kete and Howard ask what it was and how it worked in specific times, places, and circumstances. More recent debates about sentimentality continue to be informed by polarities. Lauren Berlant has been especially influential in arguing that sentimentality tapped into the potentially transformative power of affect while foreclosing on the realization of that potential (*The Female Complaint: The Unfinished Business of Sentimentality in American Culture* [Durham: Duke University Press, 2008]). Among these and many other scholars, Douglas, Tompkins, and Kete are notable for engaging the religious character of some antebellum sentimentality. I argue here that, in *Sketch,* Sigourney aligns Christian sentiment with acts; she expects her readers not only to feel right and to pray but to commit themselves to active reform.
28. [Sigourney] *Sketch,* 160–61.
29. Ibid., 161, 160, 162.
30. [Sigourney,] *Sketch,* 247–48, 232. *Sketch* misattributes the Sermon on the Mount slightly, citing "the fourteenth of John" instead of John 13. This is one of many indications that the language of the Bible was so familiar to Sigourney that she relied on memory when citing it. In parallel but less religious language, Oriana excoriates the "importance which we attach to shades of complexion, and gradations of rank," testifying to her adopted parents' equality as beings of "philanthropy [and] intellect." But in the same sentence, she also characterizes them as somewhat childlike, proclaiming that they manifest "devotion, inviolate attachment and deathless gratitude for trivial kindness" (277).
31. Ibid., 278.

5

FROM "AMERICAN HEMANS" TO GLOBAL SAVANT

THE STRUCTURE OF SENTIMENTAL COSMOPOLITANISM IN SIGOURNEY'S *PLEASANT MEMORIES OF PLEASANT LANDS*

Sean Epstein-Corbin

Martha Nussbaum's widely cited "Patriotism and Cosmopolitanism" (1994) suggests that those of us who pursue a cosmopolitan agenda "may and should devote special attention to [our special affections and identifications] in education. But we should work to make all human beings part of our community of dialogue and concern, base our political deliberations on that interlocking commonality, and give the circle that defines our humanity a special attention and respect."[1] Reading her piece, I was both pleased and dismayed to see the core of Lydia Sigourney's sentimental principles repeated more than 150 years later, as though they required such strident defense. In our era of deep xenophobia and increasing patriotic fervor, Nussbaum is right to launch such a defense of classical Enlightenment values. Yet I couldn't help wondering if any other contemporary cosmopolitan theorist—Kwame Anthony Appiah or Peter Singer, among others—would view Sigourney as a compatriot. It is my aim here to suggest that they should.

T. Gregory Garvey, in "Simular Man: Emerson and Cosmopolitan Identity," and Branka Arsić, in *On Leaving: A Reading in Emerson,* have noted a similar cosmopolitan theory at work in the writing of Sigourney's contemporary, Ralph Waldo Emerson.[2] Like them, I am using a detailed investigation of an antebellum figure to make twenty-first-century cosmopolitan theory richer while opening new paths of inquiry in nineteenth-century sentimental studies. To illustrate why antebellum figures like Sigourney can help flesh out the importance of feeling in the cosmopolitan tradition, I offer a few topic sentences from the final section of her book *Pleasant*

Memories of Pleasant Lands (1842), in which she expounds her own theory of cosmopolitan education:

> Among the advantages of travelling, it is common to allow a high place to the knowledge of human nature. A still higher accession might be mentioned, the knowledge of ourselves. . . . This increase of self-knowledge often brings an enlargement of the mind, and deepening of charity. . . . We find it possible to love those of differing creeds, and to respect every form in which the Supreme Being is worshipped with sincerity. . . . Travelling teaches the value of sympathy. . . . Travelling unfolds to us the love of home, and the length and breadth of the domestic charities.[3]

Unlike Nussbaum's model, Sigourney's has an overtly Christian register and does not focus primarily on solving common global problems. Yet the two share a common moral note within their distinct timbres: cosmopolitan education, they say, produces self-knowledge and improves human sympathy beyond the merely provincial, and these facts connect to matters of universal human importance. I do not mean to hastily conflate the two models, which diverge sharply when it comes to religion, global capitalism, and other relevant issues. Nonetheless, Nussbaum makes room in her cosmopolitanism for the deep connection between what Graham Long distinguishes as moral versus sentimental cosmopolitanism. He argues that "moral cosmopolitanism, to be truly effective as an argument for the realization of our global duties, requires support from a more sentimental approach."[4] While I think his observation is wise, I also think it is unfortunate that the modern notion of a "sentimental approach" is denuded of the moral philosophy that underwrote most sentimental writing of the nineteenth century—certainly Sigourney's. Sentimental cosmopolitanism is, by definition, a form of moral cosmopolitanism, one that emphasizes the power of sympathy in generating moral concern for others as well as the ensuing concrete duties that arise from such concern, such as hospitality and charity. As such, Sigourney contributes to a sentimental cosmopolitanism that is experiencing a renascence of sorts today, a fact perhaps related to her renewed popularity among literary critics.

On examination, Sigourney's sentimental cosmopolitanism fits Samuel Scheffler's definition of a "moderate cosmopolitanism."[5] In his characterization of different conceptions of cosmopolitanism, he argues that debates over the obligations one has toward all human beings versus the obligations one has toward one's associates can be divided into justice-based and culture-based accounts. In justice-based accounts, the norms governing claims to justice are not confined within national or communal borders. In culture-based accounts, one is obliged to both learn about and appreciate always-evolving cultural differences but against a backdrop of the fundamental moral obligations shared by all people. In this sense, Nussbaum and Sigourney are moderate cosmopolitans with regard to justice and culture insofar as they contend that one can remain devoted to friends and close associates while still attempting to develop moral and political principles that stem from an understanding of shared commonality across borders. They believe, for example, that the notion of obligation exists only so far as one's agency can be said to extend toward another. Yet they both suggest that we should actively seek out cosmopolitan experiences and connections, whether through travel or reading, so that we might widen our sphere of concern beyond the merely provincial. They believe we have such an obligation precisely because they are cultural cosmopolitans: those who insist that cultural change is ubiquitous and that individual identity is fluid. Yet, for Nussbaum, our duty rests on some fundamental conception of humanness that is, at times, poorly defined. For Sigourney, sentimentalism provides a more robust definition of the human—namely, those who experience and might cultivate sentiments, whatever they might be.

In contrast, consider Peter Singer's view of the obligation of an average citizen of a wealthy nation to a member of what he calls "the global poor," which, he argues, requires giving most of one's personal income to reliable and effective charities.[6] Scheffler characterizes views like Singer's as radical insofar as they seem to violate commonsense notions of agency and implausible insofar as they seem unlikely to lead many citizens to Singer's level of giving.[7] Sigourney's view, on the other hand, would be characterized as moderate insofar as it seems to gel with commonsense—perhaps even deeply engrained—notions of friend preference and presents a set of moral and political expectations that a large number of people might plausibly support. Such support matters because it can help build sustainable cosmopolitan institutions.

This isn't the only contribution that Sigourney offers to ongoing attempts to give "special attention and respect" to the "circle that defines our humanity." Those attempts are, I argue, the central topic of *Pleasant Memories of Pleasant Lands.* Here, by turning the narrative conventions of the travelogue to her own purposes, Sigourney posits a form of sentimental cosmopolitanism that is distinct from the more familiar and modern versions. Her model assumes that sentiments are learned—built up from experience through the process of moral imagination and reflection. Once learned, she shows us, such sentiments are more than mere principles; they are, instead, integral to one's being. Further, it is through contact with others that sentiments are cultivated, whether through travel, socializing, or reading. In contact and exchange—not simply in philosophical meditation—one learns new sentimental techniques. Lastly, Sigourney's notion of justice forms around her notion of cultural cosmopolitanism. Justice is, to a large extent, those principles of governance that foster the cultivation of sentiments—liberty, charity, and mercy chief among them. We might summarize Sigourney's sentimental cosmopolitanism, then, as a cultural cosmopolitanism organized around the intersubjective notion of sentiment and aimed toward a libertarian conception of justice.

Tropes of Travel and Sigourney's Sentimental Ethos

By focusing on *Pleasant Memories of Pleasant Lands,* a travel guide published simultaneously in Boston and London, we allow the American contours of Sigourney's cosmopolitanism to come into view.[8] This guide also attests to the anti-patriarchal nature of Sigourney's "counter-monumental" demand (to again use Dana Luciano's term) that historical memory acknowledge its own evolving nature while refusing cultural amnesia and redemptive teleologies. To this end, Sigourney adapts sentimental conventions to perform virtuous femininity. Doing so allows her to guide readers through the performance of sentimental cosmopolitanism in such a way as to educate them in proper cosmopolitan feelings and inspire them to go on their own cosmopolitan excursions. It is of historical importance that Sigourney's travel narrative sold well when a generation of young women, the era's future abolitionists and suffragists, were entering seminaries and reading *Godey's Lady's Book.* As Susan L. Roberson notes, "antebellum women travel writers used the travel narrative to claim a rhetorical space where they could locate and shape subjectivities as cultured women participating in a traditionally male activity without losing any of their femininity."[9]

Sigourney constructs herself in *Pleasant Memories of Pleasant Lands* as a cosmopolitan mother untainted by gossip or vice and thus able to speak authoritatively about Lord Nelson's military tactics and Napoleon's sexual power or to brave icebergs and foreign lands without unsexing herself. The rhetorical space she creates, tied to cultural work done by a previous generation of sentimentalists, does not resist the ideology of separate spheres; instead, it reconfigures these spheres in distinctly pro-woman terms. Near the end of her travelogue, for example, Sigourney's exhaustive description of Newgate Prison might so lull readers into illusions of normalcy that they might not notice that Sigourney—with no male chaperone and 2,000 miles from her home—is the lone aide alongside one other woman, Elizabeth Fry, as they minister to felons about to board a ship to Australia. Early in the book, Sigourney uses cultural notions of appropriate women's charity to deliberately obscure the rebellious nature of her cosmopolitanism, according to which contact with prisoners becomes yet another way to cultivate sentiment—to stretch the moral imagination to include the downtrodden and outcast in her sphere of concern.

Pleasant Memories of Pleasant Lands is a description of Sigourney's trip to Britain and France, which took place between August 1, 1840, and April 1841.[10] The book includes prose and verse along with two appended illustrations: one of Walter Scott's house at Abbotsford, the other of the Luxor obelisk. The text is predominantly an episodic narrative, with each section bearing the name of the place visited. Most sections end with a fitting piece of original verse composed by Sigourney. Her trip began in New York aboard the *Europe,* which sailed north-by-northeast along the coast of Newfoundland and then across the Atlantic to Ireland, eventually docking in Liverpool. She spent eight months touring famous historical and cultural sites in England, Wales, Scotland, and France, where she was most interested in visiting romantic poets, exemplary women, and medieval ruins. In England, she met William Wordsworth, toured Newgate with Fry, and frequently spent time with Maria Edgeworth, the well-known novelist and women's advocate who wrote *Castle Rackrent* and *Belinda.* Sigourney returned to New York aboard *The Great Western,* which was nearly wrecked on icebergs following the appearance of the aurora borealis.

The travelogue's text follows a clear but somewhat heterodox structure, one that is indebted largely to previous literary travel guides but mixes prose and verse.[11] Proceeding chronologically through geographic space in its broad outline, Sigourney initiates each account of a visit with an effusive lyric, extending the poem with either historical notes or a prose travel narrative before concluding, frequently, with another lyric or a quotation by or about the figure under discussion. Elizabeth A. Bohls notes in her anthology *Travel Writing, 1700–1830* that the travelogue genre has a robust tradition of "generic and discursive hybridity."[12] As with Mary Wollstonecraft's *Letters Written During a Short Residence in Sweden, Norway, and Denmark* (1796) and Helen Maria Williams's *Letters from France* (1790–96), the "generic and discursive hybridity" of Sigourney's book is made possible partly through the audience's familiarity with common tropes of sensibility, such as Albion and virtuous motherhood. For example, an early chapter, "Approach to England," begins with a blank verse lyric expressing the poetess's jubilation at the sight of the English shore, which she has longed to see since childhood. She uses the trope of motherland to present England as a homeland to which she is returning, a fond presence that brings her comfort, and a source of cultural authority: "O England, Mother-Land! how oft my heart / In its young musings hath gone out to thee / With filial love."[13] The section then shifts into a harrowing prose account of the ship's navigation of the foggy channel, during which Sigourney highlights a mother's love for her seasick child: "In that strange communion was the mother imparting to her nursling her own speechless weight of agony, at parting with other beloved objects in their distant home?"[14] She creates an immediate circuit channeling energy from the emotional power of her poetry to her didactic prose, which helps the reader interpret each verse. By making the different formal energies of prose and verse serve each other and the reader, Sigourney enacts a sentimental-cosmopolitan ethos while she anchors her travel narrative in the rhetoric of Christian virtue, the poetics of sympathy, and the hagiography of exemplary women.[15]

The various modes, styles, and topics of *Pleasant Memories of Pleasant Lands* interact to construct Sigourney as a feminine—maternal and soraral—authority and instruct the reader in similar cosmopolitan virtues. Picturesque chapters such as "Approach to England," "Chester," and "Corra Linn" rely heavily on landscape aesthetics to both provoke pleasant feelings in the reader and argue that Britons' have a superior appreciation for cultivated beauty as opposed to Americans' misplaced desire for gaudy show and "the expense of large rooms, seldom to be used."[16] Such admonitions are certainly not intended to prove Britons' superiority in general; instead, Sigourney uses them as arguments for ways in which America might improve itself by "transplanting" some aspects of British sensibility and countering the notion of the inevitability of national character.[17] Sigourney's metaphor of transplantation, in the context of her pervasive attention to landscape, reminds the reader that while the local landscape may be changed by the transplant, the transplant will itself be affected by its new environment. Contrarily, cemetery chapters such as "Necropolis at Glasgow," "Pere La Chaise," and "Westminster Abbey" secure their effect by calling on cultures of mourning, making each chapter a celebration of poets and exemplary women, a meditation on what Luciano calls "countermonumental" time, and an education in correct Christian attitudes toward both literature and death.[18]

Celebrity chapters such as "Lake Windermere," "To Miss Edgeworth," and "Mrs. Fry at Newgate Prison" recount Sigourney's visits with notable figures. They serve two primary functions: to substantiate her formidable literary reputation and to help her perform the virtues of sociality and friendship so important to polite society since at least the era of the bluestockings.[19] Other chapters, such as "Anne Boleyn," "Lady Jane Grey's Prison Window," and "Tomb of Josephine," borrow much from Felicia Hemans's *Records of Woman* (1830), privileging the sacrifice and genius of women who, in conventional histories, are usually overshadowed by male counterparts. Here, Sigourney uses the material, physical remains of the women to construct an imaginary visit with them that allows her to think carefully, as Nussbaum asks, about how she defines her own circle of humanity.

In her use of sentimental devices as well as through the familiar gestures of polite travel literature, Sigourney constructs herself as a cosmopolitan figure, framing her travels as a cosmopolitan education of the sort that aligns with Nussbaum's views. While conventional, the form of her travelogue gives her the flexibility to address two implied audiences at the same time: middle-class Americans and polite Britons. I have already noted that the first edition of *Pleasant Memories of Pleasant Lands* was released simultaneously in Boston and London, a decision that signaled Sigourney's intention to anticipate and adapt to dual audiences. In her case, these dual sets of readers comprised the two great branches of Protestant sentimentality. Although they were separated by their political forms and cultural histories, they were united by certain discursive formations and common interiorities. The fact that *Pleasant Memories of Pleasant Lands* underwent three successive editions—1842, 1844, and

1856—suggests that Sigourney anticipated the tastes of her audiences well.[20] American readers followed her from the familiar into the foreign; British readers followed her from the foreign into the familiar. Sigourney's cross-cultural movement enacted the sympathy and cosmopolitan hospitality that had been central to the cult of feeling since its first literary manifestations—but did so through a woman's voice and infused with her distinct reformist energy.[21]

Defining Sigourney's Cosmopolitanism

As I have argued, Sigourney constructs herself as a cosmopolitan through the tropes of travel and sympathy, but does that make the book itself an argument in favor of any specific notion of cosmopolitanism? In my view, *Pleasant Memories of Pleasant Lands* forwards a cosmopolitan theory organized around an intersubjective experience of sentiment but aimed toward a libertarian concept of justice. Sigourney accomplishes this by building an intimate public across national borders, using international figures in order to make moral claims, and positioning herself as a figure who is able to see the commonality of interests beneath superficial national differences. Here, I use the term *intimate public* as Lauren Berlant defines it in her preface to *The Female Complaint:*

> By "intimate public" I do not mean a public sphere organized by autobiographical confession and chest-baring, although there is often a significant amount of first-person narrative in an intimate public. What makes a public sphere intimate is an expectation that the consumers of its particular stuff *already* share a worldview and emotional knowledge that they have derived from a broadly common historical experience. A certain circularity structures an intimate public.[22]

In other words, Sigourney does not cause her readers to become cosmopolitans. Instead, by means of the circularity that Berlant describes, she draws on a sentimental cosmopolitan culture already available to her readers to help shape and adapt their "emotional knowledge" in useful ways—with *useful* defined by the intimate public itself. That is, her ability to perform a sentimental cosmopolitanism relies on her readers' ability to recognize the performance, albeit in a contested space in which not all critics recognize

Sigourney's credibility. This fact of intimate publics takes nothing away from Sigourney's text; on the contrary, her deft use of common tropes and devices is a powerful element of *Pleasant Memories of Pleasant Lands.*

Sigourney uses generic conventions to unsettle sentimental discourse in several other works, often as a way to critique abuses of power. As Janet Dean aptly remarks in her essay on the poem "Pocahontas" (chapter 9), her revisions "[make] possible a more penetrating interrogation of the gendered and racialized politics of conquest" by reimagining "the romance of exile to record a history of colonization and to confront its ugly legacy."[23] In "Pocahontas," Sigourney skews the trope of exile in order to denaturalize conquest, but she does so in a way that resonates with the larger cosmopolitan ethic at work in *Pleasant Memories of Pleasant Lands.* Indeed, her reversals in each text—of exile, on the one hand; of travel, on the other—suggest that they are part of a shared cosmopolitan project. Just as Sigourney urges the readers of *Pleasant Memories of Pleasant Lands* to travel beyond their native shores and sympathize with a generative, if troubled past, represented by Albion, she urges the readers of "Pocahontas" to resist erasing the history of displacement experienced by Native Americans at home. While some may claim that her relative exaltation of England and France in *Pleasant Memories of Pleasant Lands* lacks the same colonial critique, I argue that it does appear, especially in those chapters dealing explicitly with imperialism and conquest.[24]

A particularly rich example of Sigourney's performance of sentimental cosmopolitanism, including a critique of conquest, appears in two sequential chapters in the travelogue. "The Return of the Ashes of Napoleon," a firsthand account of the return of Napoleon's remains to Paris in December 1840, forms a powerful diptych with "The Tomb of Josephine," which immediately follows. Each chapter begins with a prose account followed by an original verse meant to deepen and extend the themes in the prose. In "The Return of the Ashes of Napoleon," Sigourney minimizes Napoleon's greatness, using the irony of his belated return to Paris as an opportunity to meditate on the follies of ambition and the ravages of jingoism. "The Tomb of Josephine," in contrast, credits Napoleon's wife, Josephine, with paving his way to "the emperor's throne," suggesting that fate damned him for his mistreatment of her and lifting her efforts as a philanthropist and a mother above the fleeting success of her husband's "selfish soul."

In the first of these two chapters, Sigourney begins by situating herself among the throngs of Parisians gathered to watch the festive return of Napoleon's remains:

Ho! City of the gay!
 Paris! what festal rite
Doth call thy thronging millions
 All eager for the sight?[25]

Yet slowly she reveals that this festive atmosphere is a device for undercutting his claim to immortality:

 Heads in dense masses rise,
And tower, and battlement, and tree
 Are studded thick with eyes.
Comes there some conqueror home
 In triumph from the fight,
With spoil and captives in his train
 The trophies of his might?[26]

The answer to this mocking rhetorical question is an emphatic *no.* Sigourney quickly capitalizes on her ironic charge:

A requiem for the chief,
 Whose fiat millions slew,
The soaring eagle of the Alps,
 The crushed at Waterloo;—
The banished who returned,
 The dead who rose again,
And rode in his shroud the billows proud
 To the sunny banks of Seine.[27]

Sigourney deflates Napoleon's conventional historical reputation as a great military leader beset by tragic failure, instead casting him as a disinterred corpse returned for purely ceremonial purposes.

Initially, the poem seems to undermine Sigourney's prefatory admonition that one should not focus on the negative in a foreign land, but it eventually veers into an allegorical indictment of war and civil strife. Gary Kelly interprets her poem "Carlisle" as an attempt to dissuade Americans from allowing the strife between North and South to escalate.[28] "The Return of the Ashes of Napoleon" serves a similar but more powerful function, largely allowable because neither British nor American readers were likely to take offense at

Sigourney's ironic undermining of the "eagle of the Alps"—although they might have if it had been directed at, for example, Lord Nelson.[29]

Sigourney's visit to Paris gives her an opportunity to counter the monumental rhetoric of heroic national violence embodied in the figure of Napoleon and thus establish a cosmopolitanism with greater latitude than she could have done in a description of a British or an American war hero. Potentially, she could acknowledge that any redeeming glory for Napoleon might arise from the immortality of his reputation or from some transcendent value attached to his military victories. In fact, however, as she closes the poem, she makes quick work of these possibilities while continuing to undermine any monumental energy that one might perceive in his burial:

> Mysterious One, and proud!
> In the land where shadows reign,
> Hast thou met the flocking ghosts of those,
> Who at the nod were slain?
> Oh, when the cry of that spectral host,
> Like a rushing blast shall be,
> What will thine answer be to them?
> And what thy God's to thee?[30]

Instead of separating Napoleon from the common throngs he killed, implicitly privileging his greatness and the fame that will follow him through history, Sigourney places him in a conventional scene of judgment, where he is interrogated not only by God but also by the "spectral host" of those who have died because of his pursuit of fame. Sigourney does not clarify what Napoleon might say to those souls, but she is fairly clear—again through her previous irony and the tone of her inquisition—about what God's answer will be to this man who privileged "mad Ambition" above charity or compassion.[31]

By placing "The Tomb of Josephine" directly after "The Return of the Ashes of Napoleon," Sigourney raises a series of questions designed to contrast Josephine's maternal power with Napoleon's earthly ambition. Given the sarcasm directed at Napoleon, one might expect a fanciful lampoon of his wife, especially if the author's intent were to undermine French character. Of course, however, Sigourney was making no such attempt. Rather, her depiction falls into her usual terrain: the celebration of maternal virtue and her amazement at Josephine's fidelity in the face of Napoleon's scorn. The poem begins by gesturing to the empress's erstwhile nobility—"She, who o'er earth's most polished clime / The empress-crown did wear"—but quickly shifts to her maternal function—"Beneath this turf doth rest, / Where boldly spring two clasping hands, / To guard her pulseless breath."[32] Then Sigourney returns to mocking Napoleon:

> Came he, with sweet funereal flowers
> To deck her couch of gloom,
> And like repentant Athens bless
> The guiltless martyr's tomb?[33]

The terms of the poem are thus rapidly set. Josephine is placed in a matrix of noble power, maternal goodness, and scorned love that is not diminished by the object of her devotion.

Within these terms, Sigourney sets a powerful sentimental charge:

> Still o'er the joys of earlier years,
> With tender spirit hung,
> And mourned, when sorrow o'er his path
> A blighting shadow flung;
>
> Give thanks, if victory's meteor-wreath
> His care-worn temples bound,
> And in the blessings of the poor,
> Her only solace found.[34]

Yet if Josephine does not judge Napoleon's actions, Sigourney assuredly does. She sees his greatness as a veil for his iniquity and Josephine's meekness as a guidon that signals her feminine virtue. Again, the constructed poet in *Pleasant Memories of Pleasant Lands* displays a discriminating cosmopolitan sentiment: she is able to rightly judge the past—favoring domestic virtue over ambition—and to initiate right feeling in regard to historical facts.

Beyond its formal elements and the rhetorical structure of its cosmopolitanism, Sigourney's travelogue has a larger significance in a broader cosmopolitan tradition. Her cosmopolitanism, as I read it, is more moral and aesthetic than it is overtly political; that is, while the author assumes that one has a moral duty to be charitable to the downtrodden of other lands and hospitable to strangers in one's own land, she does not appear (at least in this particular book) to be interested in the deliberative, universal, cosmopolitan justice that can, as Scheffler argues, underwrite a desire for world governments. Yet her cosmopolitanism does conflict with certain strands that suggest being a citizen of the world implies being a citizen of no one nation. Sigourney never repudiates her native land in this way, nor does she seem interested in setting aside her American allegiances. Instead, she is concerned with improving her country and its people by suggesting a cosmopolitan ideal that would allow cross-cultural exchange, minimize parochialism, and increase "self-knowledge."[35]

Sigourney's cosmopolitanism is a nineteenth-century adaptation of the version that Nicole Pohl describes in her study of Enlightenment bluestockings: a cosmopolitanism that is more cultural and aesthetic than utopian.[36] It is in many ways a secularized extension of the Christian principles of hospitality and charity, of compassion for the stranger, and of beholding the otherness of God in the foreigner's gaze. I say *secularized* not because her cosmopolitanism is faithless or shorn of Christian metaphor but because it embeds itself in primarily commercial and literary circuits of exchange instead of the evangelical context of missionary work. While Sigourney's cosmopolitanism certainly arises from the egalitarian foundations of the republic of letters (in that it privileges literary exchange and reasoned sensibility over the reinforcement of homegrown prejudices), it conforms more closely to Berlant's model of intimate publics. Constructing an intimate public out of her *Pleasant Memories of Pleasant Lands,* Sigourney expands the circle of concern beyond national borders while enlarging the historical horizon of experience to embrace the suffering and wisdom of women, such as Heloise, who lived as long ago as the Middle Ages.[37]

Sigourney's nineteenth-century Christian cosmopolitanism resonates with contemporary cosmopolitanism in ways that might make us, as postmoderns, a bit squeamish. Yet this resonance is firmly in line with Nussbaum's and Appiah's writings on moral cosmopolitanism in the context of embodied difference. Her model also reverberates with the writings of Emmanuel Levinas and Jacques Derrida, who consider the duty of hospitality and our moral obligation to respond to the other.[38] Nussbaum, in *Cultivating Humanity,* and Appiah, in *Cosmopolitanism,* approach the concept in a similar way by suggesting a set of cross-cultural norms built on robust imagination and frequent points of contact.[39] Further, each posits a simple directive: that it is both practically valuable and morally preferable to imagine the world as composed of human beings alike in their ethical standing and basic needs. Derrida and Levinas, without quite disagreeing with Nussbaum and Appiah, nonetheless choose to emphasize the value of confrontation with difference—and a refusal to assimilate. While Derrida's implicit theory of imagination is different from Nussbaum's and Appiah's, he is, at times, sympathetic to the Christian Enlightenment tradition of which Sigourney is a part:

> St. Paul says that we are all brothers, that is sons of God, so we are not foreigners, we belong to the world as citizens of the world; and it is this tradition that we could follow up until Kant for instance, in whose concept of cosmopolitanism we find the conditions for hospitality. But in the concept of the cosmopolitical in Kant there are a number of conditions: first of all you should of course welcome the stranger, the foreigner, to the extent that he is a citizen of another country, that you grant him the right to visit and not to stay, and there are a number of other conditions that I can't summarise here quickly, but this concept of the cosmopolitical which is very novel, very worthy of respect (and I think cosmopolitanism is a very good thing), is a very limited concept.[40]

While Derrida is correct about Kant, the archive of nineteenth-century sentimental cosmopolitanism does not locate the foreigner's worth in citizenship but in brotherhood: that is, in his or her status as an "atom . . . in the mighty creation of God," as Sigourney put it, regardless of creed.[41]

Interestingly, Sigourney attaches value to *being* the foreigner during one's travels. She implies that, in subduing oneself to the hospitality of others (Derrida reminds us that hospitality itself is predicated on a certain kind of control and acquiescence), one learns to both trust in God and extend hospitality unconditionally to others. The experience is, in no uncertain terms, an enactment of Leviticus 19:34: "You shall treat the stranger who sojourns with you as the native among you, and you shall love him as yourself, for you were strangers in the land of Egypt." In Sigourney's words:

> Travelling teaches the value of sympathy. . . . If from the coldly rendered service, meted out by the expectation of reward, you were transferred to the care of those, who, though born under a foreign sky, had been taught by the spirit of a Christian's faith to "be pitiful, be courteous," then in those periods of convalescence when the events of a whole life sweep in vision through the soul, did you not resolve . . . to obey more faithfully his precepts, to "use hospitality without grudging," and to "love the stranger," since you had thus learned to know the heart and the solace of a stranger?[42]

Here, she explicitly celebrates the redeeming power of otherness, figuring it as both an enactment of God's commandments and a demonstration of sympathy's bonding force. While other Enlightenment traditions, such as natural law theory, might root hospitality in natural rights encoded through national citizenship, the sentimental tradition roots hospitality in both a natural (though cultivated) sympathetic drive and a reciprocal bond closely related to friendship but born from the mere fact of sharing in God's creation.

Like Nussbaum and Appiah, Sigourney acknowledges and values difference, placing this difference in the context of a larger affinity. Aside from her receptivity to foreign lands, her preface announces the intentional style of her travelogue; she demonstrates hospitality in her circulated text as a gesture toward the larger importance of universal sympathy:

> [The journal's] writer has not sought to dwell upon the dark shades of the countries that it was her privilege to visit. It might have been easy to fix the eye upon the blemishes that appertain to each, as it is to discern foibles in the most exalted character. Yet it is but a losing office to quit your own quiet fireside, and throw ourselves upon the stormy billows, for the sake of finding fault. This we might do with less fatigue and peril at home. . . . It would seem that an obligation was laid on him not to use the knowledge thus acquired, to embarrass and embroil God's creatures, but to bright the bands of the nations with a wreath of love.[43]

Here, Sigourney frames her reader's expectations according to the cosmopolitan ethic that echoes throughout her travelogue. We might use Appiah's words and say along with her that "a cosmopolitan should—etymologically, at least—be someone who thinks that the world is, so to speak, our *shared hometown,* reproducing something very like the self-conscious oxymoron of the 'global village.'" Indeed, Appiah could be channeling a passage from *Pleasant Memories of Pleasant Lands* when he writes, "Liberal cosmopolitans should acknowledge the ethical salience of not just the state but the county, the town, the street, the business, the craft, the profession, the family *as* communities." Though there are vast differences between Appiah's "rooted cosmopolitanism" and Sigourney's universal hospitality, they share far more than they differ.[44] Certainly, Sigourney would have approved of more vigorous missionary work than most contemporary cosmopolitans might, but in her role as foreigner and a reformed native, she neither proselytizes nor minimizes her Christian faith. Instead, she enacts a sympathetic confrontation with the other, including him or her in her circle of concern at both the individual and the abstract level.

NOTES

1. Martha Nussbaum, "Patriotism and Cosmopolitanism," in *The Cosmopolitan Reader,* ed. Garrett W. Brown and David Held (Cambridge, U.K.: Polity, 1994), 155–62.
2. T. Gregory Garvey, "Simular Man: Emerson and Cosmopolitan Identity," in *Emerson for the Twenty-First Century: Global Perspectives on an American Icon,* ed. Barry Tharaud (Newark: University of Delaware Press, 2010), 513–32; Branka Arsić, *On Leaving: A Reading in Emerson* (Cambridge: Harvard University Press, 2010).
3. Lydia Sigourney, *Pleasant Memories of Pleasant Lands* (Boston: Munroe, 1842), 364–68.
4. Graham Long, "Moral and Sentimental Cosmopolitanism," *Journal of Social Philosophy* 40, no. 3 (2009): 317.
5. Samuel Scheffler, *Boundaries and Allegiances: Problems of Justice and Responsibility in Liberal Thought* (Oxford: Oxford University Press, 2001), 112.
6. Peter Singer, *The Most Good You Can Do: How Effective Altruism Is Changing Ideas about Living Ethically* (New Haven: Yale University Press, 2015), 118.
7. Scheffler, *Boundaries and Allegiances,* 101.
8. Gary Kelly, ed., *Lydia Sigourney: Selected Poetry and Prose* (Peterborough, Ont.: Broadview, 2008), 28.
9. Susan L. Roberson, *Antebellum American Women Writers and the Road: American Mobilities* (New York: Routledge, 2012), 131.
10. Sigourney, *Pleasant Memories of Pleasant Lands,* 27.
11. For a full treatment of the cultural politics of scenic tourism among Sigourney's transatlantic contemporaries, see Elizabeth A. Bohls, *Women Travel Writers and the Language of Aesthetics, 1716–1818* (Cambridge: Cambridge University Press, 1995), 170–208.
12. Elizabeth A. Bohls and Ian Duncan, eds., *Travel Writing, 1700–1830: An Anthology* (Oxford: Oxford University Press, 2008), xxii.
13. Sigourney, *Pleasant Memories of Pleasant Lands,*14.
14. Ibid., 20.
15. For a relevant examination of sentimental rhetoric, compare Paul Goring, "Sentimental Fiction and the Performance of Response," in *The Rhetoric of Sensibility in Eighteenth-Century Culture* (Cambridge: Cambridge University Press, 2005), chap. 5; and Brycchan Carey, "The Rhetoric of Sensibility," in *British Abolitionism and the Rhetoric of Sensibility: Writing, Sentiment, and Slavery, 1760–1807* (New York: Palgrave Macmillan, 2005), chap 1. On dominant theorizations of the poetics of sensibility and sentiment, see Jerome McGann, *The Poetics of Sensibility: A Revolution in Literary Style* (Oxford: Oxford University Press, 1998), intro. For an overview of the American context, see Paula Bernat Bennett, *Poets in the Public Sphere: The Emancipatory Project of American Women's Poetry, 1800–1900* (Princeton: Princeton University Press, 2003), intro.
16. Sigourney, *Pleasant Memories of Pleasant Lands,* 34. "Chester" documents Sigourney's visits to two sites in Cheshire: Chester Castle, built in 1070 by the First Earl of Chester, and Chester Cathedral, whose major construction dates to the late eleventh and early sixteenth centuries. "Corra Linn" records her visit to Corra Linn, part of the upper section of the Falls of Clyde in South Lanarkshire, Scotland. The poem also mentions Corra Castle, dating to the sixteenth century.
17. Ibid., 298.
18. Dana Luciano, "Melville's Untimely History: 'Benito Cereno' as Counter-Monumental Narrative," *Arizona Quarterly* 60, no. 3 (2004): 33–60. The term *counter-monumental* suggests the fluid nature of historical memory, a resistance to cultural amnesia or redemptive teleology, and the adaptation of monuments to anti-patriarchal purposes. In other words, Sigourney does not create an alternative narrative of history so much as a collage of sentimental types, using each to marshal historical memory to her sentimental cosmopolitan ends.

19. See Elizabeth Eger and Lucy Peltz, *Brilliant Women: 18th-Century Bluestockings* (New Haven: Yale University Press, 2008). For a range of studies on women's poetry in the long eighteenth century, see Anne Mellor, *Romanticism and Gender* (New York: Routledge, 1993); Jerome J. McGann, *The Poetics of Sensibility: A Revolution in Literary Style* (Oxford: Clarendon, 1996); and Adriana Craciun, *Fatal Women of Romanticism* (Cambridge: Cambridge University Press, 2003).
20. Sigourney, *Pleasant Memories of Pleasant Lands,* 28.
21. Mary Suzanne Schriber notes that only twenty-seven travel books were written by American women abroad before the Civil War (*Writing Home: American Women Abroad, 1830–1920* [Charlottesville: University of Virginia Press, 1997], 2).
22. Lauren Berlant, *The Female Complaint: The Unfinished Business of Sentimentality in American Culture* (Durham: Duke University Press, 2008), vii.
23. Janet Dean, chapter 9.
24. See, in particular, the chapters "Clifton" and "The Return of Napoleon" (Sigourney, *Pleasant Memories of Pleasant Lands,* 344–49, 245–52). Time spent in Clifton, Sigourney's site of departure back to the United States, becomes an occasion for meditating on the first British trip to America, what Sigourney views as Britons' un-Christian treatment of Native Americans, and their unethical attempt to tyrannize Americans during the Revolution and the War of 1812.
25. Ibid., 245.
26. Ibid.
27. Ibid., 247.
28. Gary Kelly, ed., *Lydia Sigourney: Selected Poetry and Prose* (Peterborough, Ont.: Broadview, 2008), 48–49.
29. In fact, Sigourney treats Lord Nelson in a rather off-handed and cursory way, without any counter-monumental charge, in the prose accompaniment to her chapter "Divine Service" (*Pleasant Memories of Pleasant Lands,* 28).
30. Ibid., 249.
31. Ibid., 254.
32. Ibid., 253. Here, Sigourney describes the tomb itself, as commissioned by her children: "Two hands, sculptured in marble, and grasping each other, appear as the symbols of their united, filial love" (255).
33. Ibid., 253.
34. Ibid., 254.
35. Ibid., 365.
36. For a discussion of bluestocking cosmopolitanism, see Nicole Pohl, "Cosmopolitan Bluestockings," in *Bluestockings Now! The Evolution of a Social Role,* ed. Deborah Heller (Oxford: Ashgate, 2015), 71–90.
37. Heloise is a well-known twelfth-century Frenchwoman whose affair with the scholar Peter Abelard is recorded in their correspondence. See Peggy Kamuf, *Fictions of Feminine Desire: Disclosures of Heloise* (Lincoln: University of Nebraska Press, 1987); and Berlant, *The Female Complaint,* vii.
38. For their representative writings on hospitality, see Emmanuel Levinas, *Time and the Other,* trans. Richard A. Cohen (Pittsburgh: Duquesne University Press, 1987); Emmanuel Levinas, *Totality and Infinity: An Essay on Exteriority,* trans. Alphonso Lingis (Pittsburgh: Duquesne University Press, 1964); Jacques Derrida, *The Politics of Friendship,* trans. George Collins (New York: Verso, 2006); and Jacques Derrida, *Adieu to Emmanuel Levinas,* trans. Pascale-Anne Brault and Michael Naas (Stanford: Stanford University Press, 1999).
39. For robust contemporary treatments of feeling and cosmopolitanism, see Martha Nussbaum, *Cultivating Humanity: A Classical Defense of Reform in Liberal Education*

(Cambridge: Harvard University Press, 1998); and Kwame Anthony Appiah, *Ethics in a World of Strangers* (New York: Norton, 2007).

40. Geoffrey Bennington, "Politics and Friendship: A Discussion with Jacques Derrida," Center for Modern French Thought, February 13, 2009, http://hydra.humanities.uci.edu/derrida/pol+fr.html.
41. Sigourney, *Pleasant Memories of Pleasant Lands,* 365.
42. Ibid., 366–67.
43. Ibid., iv–v.
44. Kwame Anthony Appiah, *The Ethics of Identity* (Princeton: Princeton University Press, 2010), 217, 246, 213.

6

"you sink the woman, & the wife, in the writer"

SIGOURNEY AND THE FEMINIST LITERARY ATLANTIC

Gary Kelly

In her posthumously published memoir *Letters of Life* (1866), Lydia Sigourney declared, perhaps both proudly and defiantly, "If there is any kitchen in Parnassus, my Muse has surely officiated there as a woman of all work, and an aproned waiter."[1] The kitchen was literally in Hartford, Connecticut, and synecdochically in the world of women's work, while Parnassus here symbolized the home of modern rather than classical muses, located not in ancient Greece but in the modern American segment of Sigourney's contemporary Atlantic world. It was a world in which she and many contemporary American women writers consciously situated themselves.[2] Here, they sought "the right to call [themselves] famous."[3] Sigourney herself purposefully fashioned a distinctive literary persona, work, and career that was in, for, and, at times, against that world. She emulated transatlantic models, circulated her work as widely as she could in the United States and Britain, and was recognized by many commentators as the leading American woman poet in the Atlantic world. Yet as I will show, she found, in the very birth of that fame, that its pursuit could be dangerous and costly

Sigourney's Atlantic world was engaged, at the onset of modernity, in a complex and contested process of economic, social, cultural, political, and technological transformation. This process accelerated and was accelerated by wars of commercial and political rivalry between the Atlantic states and by economic-cultural competition for both national prestige and market advantage. Among the most contested issues in this period, and ones that Sigourney addressed in her literary persona, writing, and career, were the character and role of women.

Many regarded the emergence and encouragement of women intellectuals and artists as an important, even essential, aspect of modernization. Beginning in the 1760s, British women writers and intellectuals in the bluestocking circle and beyond asserted and demonstrated their roles in the development of arts and manufacturing, humanitarianism and social philanthropy. In the 1790s, Mary Wollstonecraft argued that the French revolutionary government, like modernizing regimes elsewhere, had vitiated their enterprise by failing to provide females with an equality of education that would make them self-reflexive modern subjects and hence partners with men in modern domestic, professional, and civic life. In the aftermath of the French Revolution and the Napoleonic era, women writers and intellectuals critiqued the persistence of destructive masculinism across history and promoted the feminization of modernity in various ways. The French writer Germaine de Staël criticized Napoleonic absolutism, militarism, and imperialism and in the eponymous heroine of her transatlantic bestseller *Corinne* (1807) created instead the figure of a female national bard as the exemplar and voice of a modern, liberal, constitutional nation-state. Likewise, in her verse collections *Tales and Historic Scenes* (1819) and *Records of Woman* (1828), the English writer Felicia Hemans portrayed a wide range of historic and fictional women resisting masculine militarism and imperialism. The Scottish feminist, novelist, and dramatist Frances Wright and her sister Camilla traveled back and forth between Britain and the United States promoting Owenite socialism and a broad range of reform causes, and in 1825 they established a utopian community on the American frontier to demonstrate the superiority of free labor over slavery and the benefits of education and social equality.

Yet some people treated the growing prominence of women intellectuals and artists and their claims for greater gender and sexual equality as either a vestige of aristocratic and courtly libertinage or a dangerously destabilizing excess that threatened modernization by encouraging women to interfere beyond their so-called "proper" and "natural" sphere of domestic life. Critics of the bluestockings and their successors, the learned lady and the literary lady, claimed that such women would spurn men who were less learned or talented and would either remain unmarried and thus be a drain on their families or, if married, neglect the domestic management, sexual relations, childbearing and -rearing, and sociability that were necessary to men's professional and commercial success.[4] Further, some claimed, by engaging in the commerce of the arts, such women would transgress middle-class social propriety, making themselves public figures and selling themselves like actresses and prostitutes. The scandalous private lives of Wollstonecraft, de Staël, Wright, and others were cited as confirmation. Thus, alternative roles were envisioned for women in modernity. Notably, by the late 1780s, the prolific English writer and energetic religious and social campaigner Hannah More, herself a member of the bluestocking circle, was promoting a dual role for middle-class women as modernizers. Within the domestic sphere they were to educate and discipline men to modernize the public-political sphere in certain interests, and within the social sphere they were to organize in the same interests the modernization of what were seen as lower orders or problem social groups by taking part in charitable and educational work, undertaking domestic and foreign religious evangelization, founding and supporting asylums and prisons, and so on. By the 1820s such views were dominant among the Atlantic world social elites to which Sigourney belonged.

This was the context of the Atlantic feminisms in which Sigourney forged her literary identity, work, and career, as indicated by an episode in October 1827, which took place just as she was becoming a figure of national and potentially Atlantic literary prominence. In a draft of an appeal to her (which may have been unsent or sent in a different form), her husband, Charles, addressed a crisis in their marriage, explicitly placing her literary ambition in the context of the transatlantic controversy over literary feminism and doing so in a way that indicated that she and their Hartford circle would understand this context. He rejected what he termed her "fourth" request for a separation and exhorted her to limit her writing, control her desire for literary celebrity, and resume her duties as wife and mother.[5] He recalled that in the "first years of our marriage . . . I took a pride in admiring the talents with which your mind was adorned, & the efforts, then only occasional, of your poetical imagination." He noted that he had even helped her by providing learned notes for her poem *Traits of the Aborigines of America* (1822), though he had opposed her desire for publication. After the book appeared, however, he observed in her a "great susceptibility of praise" and increasing "passion for literary distinction." As he complained elsewhere in this appeal, "you sink the <u>woman</u>, & the <u>wife</u>, in <u>the writer</u>." Doing so, he contended, led her "into conduct I could not reconcile with my ideas of the delicate propriety which should ever mark the female character" and to neglect her "conjugal affections, & domestick habits" and "to make advances to, to solicit the notice, & correspondence, or in another word the praise of, literary men"—one unnamed man in particular.

Charles asked how his wife could "be surprised that I am displeased if, when returning at night, weary from my customary place of labor, I find you with * * *, whose visits are too pointedly exclusive *for me* to appropriate any part of the compliment of them to myself," or at his "being displeased at your carrying on a private, I might almost say a clandestine correspondence with him (I say *clandestine,* for both your notes, & his answers are carefully kept from all other eyes)—applying to him for trifling services, seemingly as an excuse for writing, which your husband could perform with equal facility,—writing him notes which he pronounces 'delightful,' & then either concealing, or destroying his replies?" Charles denied that he suspected sexual infidelity but warned, "There may be a spiritual seduction, as well as a corporeal one,—a seduction of the mind & affections, as well as of the person. And the publick may be the seducer, as well as an individual." He added, "Who wants, or would value, a wife, who is to be the publick property of the whole community?" Already, he complained, her name was

> bandied about in the newspapers, & magazines;—the burthen of paragraphs, & the praise of the witling;—in the mouths of printers, & publishers, artists, & shop boys;—subjected to the levities, & freedoms it's [*sic*] conspicuous situation invites;—exposing you to be pointed out in the streets, like a stage player or artist [that is, a public entertainer], like a Percival [a seventeenth-century actress] or a Madame de Stael [*sic*], with a kind of meretricious distinction, as Mrs Sigourney, the poetess.

Later in his appeal, he clearly set his wife's alleged conduct in terms of the Atlantic controversy over women as writers, intellectuals, and feminists, adding, "As if the example of the Miss Wrights, or the Mary Wollstonecrafts were worthier of imitation *by you* than that of Cornelia, mother of the Gracchi [heroes of the ancient Roman republic], or Milton's beautiful pattern of feminine, & conjugal excellence [Eve as consort of Adam before she sinned]."

The man Charles suspected of seducing his wife's "mind & affections" if not her "person" and of encouraging her to follow the "example of the Miss

Wrights, or the Mary Wollstonecrafts" rather than Cornelia or prelapsarian Eve was probably the Reverend George Washington Doane (1799–1859). Doane was seven years younger than Lydia Sigourney and unmarried. He had arrived in Hartford from New York in 1824 as a freshly minted, Protestant Episcopal clergyman to become the first professor of belles-lettres and oratory at the city's new Washington College. The college had been founded at the instigation of Doane's patron, Thomas Brownell, the first bishop of Connecticut in the resurgent and modernizing Protestant Episcopal church, to take advantage of the 1818 disestablishment of the Congregational church as Connecticut's state religious institution.[6] The predecessor of the Protestant Episcopal church, before American independence, was a branch of the Anglican church, the established state church of England, headed by the ruling monarch. Many American Anglicans had remained loyal to Britain and the crown during the American Revolution. Some had emigrated after independence, and those who stayed were suspected by many of disloyalty to the United States. Thus, by calling itself "Protestant," the U.S. Episcopal church both associated itself with Protestant sects such as Congregationalists, Unitarians, and others, who constituted the great majority of believers in the United States, and distinguished itself from its historic rival in the Atlantic world, the Episcopalian Roman Catholic church. When Brownell and his agents toured England raising funds for Washington College, they claimed that the school would not only advance the American and Atlantic Episcopal church but also strengthen bonds between Britain and the United States, a claim that local non-Episcopalian opponents exploited. Proponents and opponents had different ideas of how the Atlantic ecclesiastical and cultural world was and should be composed.

According to its state charter, Washington College had to accept non-Episcopalians, but the school was created primarily so that American Episcopalians could rival Congregationalist-dominated Yale and Unitarian-dominated Harvard. Like those colleges, Washington provided a combined classical and modern education for both future clergymen and the sons of the national commercial, professional, and administrative elites; a shortened curriculum served sons of predominantly local petty merchants and professionals. In the Atlantic context, the college's curriculum resembled that of the modern-minded Scottish universities and English dissenting academies that served Protestant non-Episcopalians rather than that of the

Anglican-Episcopalian English universities of Oxford and Cambridge. In fact, Bishop Brownell had intended to modernize Washington College's curriculum further, and Charles Sigourney wrote to his friend Thomas Jefferson, the founder of the University of Virginia, to this purpose. Washington College was renamed Trinity College in 1842. Whereas "Washington," like Doane's own first names, emphasized Episcopalian loyalty to the American republic and Episcopalians claimed George Washington as one of themselves, "Trinity" emphasized a central theological difference between Episcopalians and their main rivals that had arisen by the 1840s as Trinity battled for influence among the New England elites. For now, the Unitarians were in the ascendant, led by figures such as Andrews Norton and Ralph Waldo Emerson.

Doane, his associates, and Washington College were engaged in a complex struggle for religious, intellectual, social, and cultural leadership of modernity in the Atlantic world, and the Sigourneys were heavily involved in the founding and the life of the college. Charles was an Episcopalian and a leading figure in Hartford. A prominent banker and hardware merchant, he was instrumental in fundraising for the college, one of three men who donated $1,000, and the first president of its board of trustees.[7] The elegant and grand Sigourney mansion was near the newly constructed college buildings. Professors and students seem to have frequented the Sigourney house: in his appeal to his wife, Charles complained that she was "running after" the college "professors," while in another version of this document she complained that his daughter was "running after" the college students. Doane was not only a major figure at the college but also an up-and-coming activist in the Episcopalian church. His son later described him as "vehement, impulsive, quick; his thoughts upon his lips, as soon as they were in his mind."[8] In addition to holding a professorship, he was a college bursar and traveled along the American Atlantic seaboard raising funds and recruiting students. (As was true elsewhere in New England, many of Washington College's students were sent up from the South.) Doane was also a published poet, and his writings show familiarity with both classical literature and the modern literature of the Atlantic world. He instigated Washington College's energetic student literary society, and from his office at the school he and his close friend William Croswell edited and largely wrote the early issues of the *Episcopal Watchman,* a literary weekly first published on March 26, 1827.

Charles's suspicion of a dangerous literary-intellectual intimacy between his wife and the professor may have been confirmed for him in the pages of the *Watchman,* which promoted a modernized American Episcopalian culture in an Atlantic context—including a role for women writers—and published a large number of Sigourney's poems. In format, it was a three-column, eight-page weekly miscellany. Its editor, Doane, claimed that it started with fewer than 400 subscribers and eight months later had almost 1,200.[9] The weekly was published at $2 per annum by H. Huntington, Jr., who was located two doors away from the Phoenix Bank (known locally as the Episcopal bank), whose president since 1821 had been Charles Sigourney.[10] The proximity may have been useful: the bank enjoyed considerable confidence well beyond Connecticut, and perhaps copies of the *Watchman* were able to follow the paths of its financial communications. Within a few months of its founding, the weekly had agents in New Haven and Middletown, Connecticut; Portland, Maine; Portsmouth, New Hampshire; Newburyport, Boston, Springfield, and Greenfield, Massachusetts; Manhattan, Lansingburgh, Albany, Troy, and Schenectady, New York; Trenton, New Jersey; Edenton, North Carolina; and Charleston, South Carolina. A volume title page with a wood engraving of Washington College was included with the year's last issue.

A typical early issue opened with "The Ritualist," a commentary (in effect, a sermon) on the upcoming Sunday and its meaning in the Episcopalian-Anglican year as set out in the Atlantic church's Book of Common Prayer. A variety of matter followed, some original but most reprinted, dealing with church history and affairs, including ecclesiastical biographies. This section of the periodical reflected Doane's evangelizing, high-church, anti-Catholic, neo-traditionalist perspective, often celebrating and citing seventeenth-century English Anglican churchmen, who were enjoying a revival of interest on both sides of the Atlantic. These first four or so pages were followed by a regular one- or two-column poetry section, some reprinted from other sources, some noted as "For the Episcopal Watchman." Here during Doane's first year of editorship Lydia Sigourney appeared more often than any other American poet. Another frequent American contributor was "Asaph," the penname of Doane's assistant Croswell. Often reprinted were prominent contemporary British poets, notably Felicia Hemans, as well as those who were Anglicans or associated with the English church, such as Robert Southey, Henry Hart

Milman, and William Wordsworth. In other words, most of the poetic contributions to the *Watchman* were from Atlantic Episcopalians, though Hemans was most ardently taken up in the United States by Unitarians, who likely found reflections of their theology in such poems as "The Forest Sanctuary" (1825).

A literary section contained reviews of current books and snippets of information of various kinds, including news of literature "Domestic" and "Foreign"—yet another indication that the *Watchman*'s perspective and circulation were transatlantic. A subsequent section was labeled "Miscellany," and during the *Watchman*'s first year it provided a clear indication of the magazine's American vision within an Atlantic one, in the form of a serial titled "Notes of a Traveler in England, in 1823 and 1824." These anonymous notes were actually the observations of the Reverend Nathaniel Wheaton, who had compiled them into journal form while fundraising for Washington College. Typically, the editorial section followed "Miscellany," offering a variety of news and comments, including those relating to Washington College and an occasional letter to the editor, often by Doane himself under another name. Next was usually a section of news on church matters in the United States and around the world. A summary often gave snippets of local and other news, and it was followed by a short section reporting deaths and marriages. Early issues closed with an advertisement for Mrs. Kinneer's "Seminary for Young Ladies" in Hartford, under the inspection of the Episcopal church.

Lydia Sigourney's writings appeared frequently in the *Watchman* during the first year of its existence. A portion of that work was prose, but most was poetry—some reprinted from elsewhere, some expressly "For the Episcopal Watchman." One poem appeared as early as the second issue (April 2, 1827), in suggestive collocation: the poetry section opened with "Lent" by Asaph, followed by "Wild Birds" "By the Rev. George W. Doane," followed by "'Wherefore I praised the dead more than the living,'" signed "H.," the first letter of Sigourney's birth name, Huntley.[11] In the issue's literature section, Doane printed (and probably wrote) "Poetry." This was followed by the first part of a laudatory review, likely by Doane, of two early American editions of Hemans's poems and dramas, which had already been promoted by the Unitarian Andrews Norton; further installments of the review appeared in the *Watchman*'s third and fourth issues. This first installment praised Hemans lavishly as a poet of Atlantic importance.

"Associated, as widely as the English language is read, with whatever is pure and elevated in poetry, beautiful in virtue, or touching in piety," her poetry owed its "immense and striking popularity" in America to its own characteristics and "to the prodigious effectiveness of the periodical press" in disseminating it. Its traits were "unrivalled *purity and tenderness,*" especially when contrasted to Lord Byron's poetry; "*simplicity,* and *truth to nature*"; and a "*uniform tendency . . . to virtue and piety.*" The reviewer also celebrated Hemans's characters and incidents, "Wherever the voice of freedom has been lifted up" and "Wherever the precious Cross has found a witness"; and the article's melancholy tone reflected Hemans's own "*peculiar character, and situation*"—an oblique reference to the fact that her husband had abandoned her with five children.[12] Just weeks earlier, in a letter to her brother-in-law's wife, Sigourney had praised these same editions of Hemans, probably obtained from Doane, comparing her to Scott in revolutionizing modern poetry and enthusiastically recalling poems by Hemans that she had encountered over the years in American periodicals.[13]

Connecting to Atlantic feminisms in a different direction, the *Watchman*'s third issue reprinted a biographical sketch of Hannah More signed "L. H. S." Elsewhere in the issue, the sketch was attributed to a two-volume American edition of More's works that the Boston publisher Samuel Goodrich had released with Sigourney's essay in 1827. Goodrich soon provided another connection between Sigourney and Atlantic literary feminisms. Some poems by "H." that appeared in the *Watchman*'s early issues were collected in Sigourney's barely anonymous *Poems: By the Author of "Moral Pieces in Prose and Verse,"* published simultaneously in July 1827 by both Goodrich and the Huntingtons, the Hartford publishers of the *Watchman.* By keeping her name off the book's title page Sigourney was observing the agreement that, according to her husband's appeal, the couple had made in which she had promised only to publish anonymously. Soon, a highly laudatory four-column review of *Poems,* likely by Doane, appeared in the *Watchman,* using terms and topics similar to those in the review of Hemans.[14]

The review of Sigourney's *Poems* opened with a boast: the author claimed that the weekly had begun publishing the author in its second issue, professed embarrassment at praising one of its own, asserted the author's steady improvement and the extension of her reputation since the publication of *Moral Pieces, in Prose and Verse* in 1815, and noted, "Writing much for the various periodicals, she is frequently before the public; and we know of no author, Mrs. Hemans excepted, whose contributions are so uniformly, and so widely copied by our numerous journals." The article added, "This, in the present day, is the surest evidence of popularity." The reviewer declared that, apart from the age of classical epic and the age of Milton, "there has been no period of greater poetical talent than the present, so there has been none in which true poetry was ever so generally admired and enjoyed, or exerted so effectually its power, to warm, refine, and elevate the soul." The article continued, "The characteristics of our author's poetry, are delicacy and tenderness,—its tendencies are all to virtue and piety. None, we are persuaded, can read it and not be improved in mind and heart—made happier and better."[15] The *Watchman*'s review of Hemans had attributed these same qualities to her.

The review next observed that "almost every style of versification has been attempted, and all with success" and that the "style is endowed with an ease and gracefulness,—a '*curiosa felicitas*' pervading and giving life, and beauty, and sweetness, alike to its imagery, its expression, and its melody." Praised next was "the ingenuity which is displayed in the selection of subjects so numerous and yet so diversified, and in giving to them all the peculiar interest and charm which is appropriate to them." A similar and purposeful "ingenuity" was notable in Hemans's poetic production. After listing some examples of Sigourney's ingenuity, the review quoted "The Pilgrims," thus at once linking and differentiating between England and the United States, and praised its last paragraph for "a moral sublimity—an expression of fearlessness and utter self devotion, which the power of the Gospel alone could sustain."[16] By contrast, the reviewer declared, her poem "To an Absent Child" (reprinted in the July 16 issue from the *Connecticut Observer*) was "instinct with domestic beauty, and maternal love." Likewise, there were "several instances of narrative in the ballad style" that were "eminently successful attempts to revive that ancient and delightful species of poetry."[17] The ballad form was also prominent in Hemans's many versions of what was known as *"national song."*

The review invoked Hemans again when noting that *Poems* contained several "specimens of that sort of fugitive poetry, which consists in the development of some trait of character, or striking incident, to which Mrs. Hemans has made so many beautiful contributions, and in which our author has adventured with no unskilful, or unsuccessful hand." It also noted poems such as "To a Wasp" and "To an Ancient Rocking Chair," which, "though . . . fraught with a moral, are pleasing instances of a light and playful style, seeking to clothe some sober truth in the fantastic drapery of fancy." Hemans herself avoided such subjects and tone, but lest such subjects and style in *Poems* be considered frivolous or unfeminine, the review quickly added, "Though indulging slightly in a humorous vein, it is a humour tempered and refined by female delicacy and propriety." The author seemed "most at home," however, "in serious, and especially in funereal subjects": "She loves to seize some incident in sacred or profane history, or some event, of daily life, and make it the vehicle of those pure and pious sentiments, and that eminently practical wisdom, with which her mind and heart seem so deeply imbued." This was the variety of Hemans's poetry most often reprinted in the United States. The review closed, as had the review of Hemans, by commending the book's "neat and beautiful appearance," tacitly excepting it from the common complaint that American books, in contrast to British, were shoddy: "It is one of the fairest specimens of American typography, as it is one of the most valuable additions to the stock of American poetry."[18]

The connection with Hemans that was stated or implied in the review was reinforced by Goodrich's March 1829 publication of Samuel Kettell's three-volume *Specimens of American Poetry,* in which both Doane and Sigourney (more fully) were represented, and where she was called, in what would become a commonplace in the Atlantic literary world, "the American Hemans."[19] *Specimens* had been advertised in the issue of the *Watchman* that first published "H.," alongside a printed notice about Goodrich's publication of More's and a forthcoming "volume of 'Unconnected Poetry,' by the author of 'Moral Pieces.'"[20]

A review of Sigourney's *Poems* appeared in the August 13 *Watchman,* but the Sigourneys may have been out of town for a period, for the weekly's October 1 issue contained, as the first item in its editorial section, the notice "'H' is welcome *home.*"[21] This cryptic, prominent, and unusually personal message, combined with Sigourney's frequent appearance in the *Watchman* and its enthusiastic review of her *Poems,* may have precipitated her husband's complaint in his October appeal, that her name was being "bandied about in the newspapers, & magazines;—the burthen of paragraphs, & the praise of the witling;—in the mouths of printers, & publishers." Two weeks later, in fact, the *Watchman*'s October 15 issue carried a poem signed "H.":

WEALTH.

Canst thou the *treasures of the mind* forego,
The etherial flight that mark'd thee from the throng,
The prompting impulse, and the gems of heaven,
For sordid dross?—Rememberest thou who sold
His birthright for the surfeit of an hour,
And found too late his penitence and tears?—
Barter'st thou *life* for gold,—in burning climes,
Far from thy home, and every kindred heart,
Consum'd by care, yet pleas'd each night to add
A shekel to thy hoard?—The insatiate grave,
The grasping avarice of stranger hands,
And the cold ridicule of ghastly death
Decry thy choice.—Giv'st thou thy *love* for gold,
Its cankering rust shall eat thy flesh like fire,
And on thy couch, sleepless, or curs'd with dreams,
Distorted, shalt thou wail thy wretchedness;
Light-hearted peace, and thrilling fair-ey'd Hope,
Undoubting confidence, and Eden's joy
Forever forfeit.—Giv'st thou *Virtue's wealth,*
Integrity's pure armour, and the key
Of Honour's casket, for the mine's low gain?—
Go!—wrap thee in close shades, where day's broad eye
May ne'er reproach thee, and with ceaseless prayers
Win from Remorse her scourge. Sell'st thou thy *soul*
In mad exchange for gold?—Ah! will it spread
A table for thee, where the eternal gulph
Divides the rain-drop from the parching tongue?—
Will it thy revel aid, or trick thy robes,
Or bid the lute, and sprightly viol sound,
Where the worm dieth not, and the dire flame
Is never quench'd?[22]

In lines 4 and 5, the speaker of "Wealth" invokes the biblical figure of Esau as the standard against which the reader should judge him or herself.

Thus, the poem asks to be read against multiple contexts at the same time. In Old Testament, Esau sold his birthright to his brother Jacob to satisfy his immediate bodily appetites, but in the New Testament's Epistle to the Hebrews, Esau became a symbol of those who succumb to fleshly desire and so lose their spiritual and eternal birthright. In a religious context, then, the poem underscores the Christian injunction, reiterated in much of the era's religiously oriented literature in the Atlantic world, to reject fleshly and material desires or forfeit salvation. At the same time, read within the context of the debate over modernity, "Wealth" restates the commonplace notion that pursuit of commercial and material interest can endanger one's intellectual, affective, and spiritual integrity.

If we consider the poem in terms of Sigourney's awareness of the cost of fame, we can read it as an expression of her conflict between a preference for intellectual and emotional over material wealth and a fear that choosing the former over the latter would mean moral, material, and social ruin. More privately, in the context of the Sigourneys' marital crisis, the poem works as a response to Charles's worry that his wife had committed intellectual and affective—if not sexual—adultery. We can read also it as an acknowledgment of a remorseful desire to emulate intellectually, politically, socially, and sexually transgressive feminists such as Wollstonecraft, de Staël, and the Wrights. The convergence of these multiple contexts in one seemingly conventional poem was a typical characteristic of Sigourney's purposeful use of poetry for personal and professional but also political and cultural ends in national and Atlantic scope.

In any case, the relationship between "H." and Doane continued in the pages of the *Episcopal Watchman,* if nowhere else, for some months. Reading this relationship is complicated by the fact that, as she would soon have known, Sigourney became pregnant, probably in the second half of October 1827. The birth of a daughter, Mary, on August 3, 1828, fulfilled at least one of the requests her husband had made in his appeal: to try again, after a stillbirth and two short-lived premature children, to consolidate their marriage with a child. Meanwhile, in the *Watchman*'s October 22 issue, "H." contributed a verse, "Appeal for Missions," a cause the *Watchman* often supported; and the first entry of the issue's editorial section singled out that poem for praise. In the same issue a melancholy meditative prose piece, "Twilight," also appeared, the first of a series signed "Evelyn," one of Doane's pen names. At that time, the seventeenth-century English diarist

John Evelyn was known as an anti-Catholic writer, which made him an especially suitable persona for Doane, who also prided himself on such opposition. In the next issue a poem, "To Evelyn," by "Miriam" urged consolation. The author's pseudonym referred to the biblical figure of Miriam, who saved her infant brother Moses from death so he could later fulfill his divinely appointed mission to lead his people from bondage in Egypt to the Promised Land. The *Watchman*'s November 12 issue reported a motion by Doane at the Connecticut Episcopal diocese's convocation to formally lament the recent death of Bishop Kemp. In the November 19 issue, an unsigned poem, "On the Death of Bishop Kemp," appeared. In the January 7, 1828, issue the *Watchman*'s editor identified the author as "H." after a New York paper had attributed it to the "Rev. Prof. Doane."

More suggestively, on December 3, the *Watchman* had reprinted "From the Token for 1828" an unsigned poem titled "Penitence" that echoes some themes of "Wealth":

> *Aye, look to Heaven!*—Earth may not lend
> Refuge or ray thy steps to guide,
> Suspicion will with friendship blend,
> Or slander chills compassion's tide.
>
> We will not ask what thorn hath found
> Keen entrance to thy bosom fair.—
> If love hath dealt a deathless wound,
> Or deeper folly woke despair.
>
> We only say, *that* sinless clime
> On which is bent thy streaming eye,
> Hath pardon for the darkest crime,
> Though erring man the boon deny;
>
> We only say, the prayerful breast,
> The crystal tear of contrite pain,
> Have power to ope that portal blest
> Where pride and pomp have toiled in vain.

The Token was a gift annual published by Goodrich, and the version of "Penitence" in that volume, like the *Watchman*'s reprint, was unsigned. However, in *The Token* it was attached to an engraving, also titled "Penitence," ostensibly after a painting by Antonio da Correggio but more likely after Guido Reni's *The Penitent Magdalene,* which shows a weeping woman looking heavenward. Mary Magdalene was an early and notable disciple of Christ; and though she was known as a reformed "fallen woman," she was regarded as a saint and woman religious leader in both the Catholic and the Anglican-Episcopalian churches. Goodrich's *Token* was avowedly an imitation of similar souvenir books published in London, many of which had a religious orientation. Presumably, Doane made the decision to republish "Penitence" in the *Episcopal Watchman*, which the editorial section in the same issue distinguished for praise. Its authorship was disclosed only when it was revised and republished, titled as "On a Picture of Penitence" and with numerous variations, in Sigourney's *Poems* (1834). Like many of her other poems, it expresses a widespread moral view of divine compassion for faltering humanity, perhaps especially women. Privately, the poem may have addressed Doane or Charles Sigourney or even both, disclosing consciousness and rejection of erring (or of having been perceived to err) as well as the temptations and dangers of emulating women of transatlantic literary fame.

Such oblique back-and-forth persisted within the poetry columns of the *Episcopal Watchman* throughout that winter but with diminishing frequency and pertinence. Still, someone connected with the periodical, probably Doane or a close associate, seems to have taken steps to give the weekly, and Sigourney, wider circulation in the Atlantic world. In the London-based *Christian Observer*'s February 1828 issue, a letter from "Cosmopolite" titled "American Sacred Poetry" declared that the United States was producing poetry of literary quality and religious significance and offered five unsigned specimens: "The Cemetery of Pere La Chaise," "'As Thy Day, So Shall Thy Strength Be,'" "Remember the Dead," "A Dirge," and "To a Young Lady."[23] All had previously appeared in the *Episcopal Watchman,* the first three signed "H." The *Christian Observer,* "Conducted by Members of the Established Church," had been founded in 1802 by prominent Anglican Evangelical clergy and commercial magnates and had run issues until 1874. It had grown from the 1790s crisis in Britain and the Atlantic world, responding, on the one hand, to activist religious dissenters' demands for religious equality and the disestablishment of the Anglican church, inspired partly by the U.S. Constitution, and, on the other hand, to lower- and middle-class reformists' irreligion and anticlericalism, inspired partly by the French Revolution. The *Watchman*'s connection with the *Christian Observer* was likely established when Washington College fundraisers toured England in the mid-1820s on a mission to strengthen Atlantic Episcopalianism. Only two months before the appearance of Cosmopolite's letter, the *Observer* had complained that the college was barely doing its part.[24] Perhaps Cosmopolite—a name probably signifying "one who is above national prejudices"—had quickly paraded American sacred poetry to demonstrate an Atlantic Episcopalianism that was transcending national differences in the church.

Whatever Doane and Sigourney's relationship, it was likely winding down as winter turned to spring. In March 1828 Doane renewed his position as editor of the *Watchman,* with Croswell again assisting, but in May he took up a clergy appointment in Boston and the editing devolved onto Croswell. "H." appeared only eight times in the following year. At the end of the second volume in March 1829, Doane and Croswell relinquished the *Watchman* to others. Doane married later in 1829 and went on to become the bishop of New Jersey in 1832. He enjoyed a long career as an energetic promoter of, and prolific writer about, Episcopalianism.

The 1830s economic depression damaged Charles Sigourney's business interests, and his wife's literary income assumed greater importance in their affairs. In 1834 she published, with her name on the title page, the edition of her shorter poems that, with periodic alterations, would sustain her Atlantic character for the rest of her life. The *Episcopal Watchman* had helped establish this character by promoting her not as a Wollstonecraft or a de Staël but as "the American Hemans." Like Hemans, she became known mainly as a religious poet of what were called at that time *the domestic affections,* despite her experiments with the long poem and other modes. Yet in turning out an extraordinary variety of religious and didactic prose, educational literature, and poetry and prose for everyday use, she became—in effect, if not by reputation—less an American Hemans than an American Hannah More. Charles Sigourney's fear in October 1827, however well or ill founded, that his wife would become a Wollstonecraft, a de Staël, or a Wright went unrealized, if it was ever Sigourney's aim at all. Rather than sinking "the woman, & the wife, in the writer," rather than assuming a solely domestic character or following the examples of Atlantic literary feminism that her husband decried, she did something more original and more difficult. She created a complex literary persona that Charles could hardly recognize and that still poses a challenge to some: the writer as woman and wife.

NOTES

1. Lydia Sigourney, *Letters of Life* (New York: Appleton, 1866), 376. For another reading of Sigourney's "kitchen in Parnassus," see Jennifer Putzi's essay (chap. 2).
2. For a mention of Sigourney, see Lucinda L. Damon-Bach, Brigitte Bailey, and Beth Lynne Lueck, eds., *Transatlantic Women: Nineteenth-Century American Women Writers and Great Britain* (Durham: University of New Hampshire Press, 2012).
3. Though Sigourney is not mentioned, see Brenda R. Weber, *Women and Literary Celebrity in the Nineteenth Century: The Transatlantic Production of Fame and Gender* (Burlington, Vt.: Ashgate, 2012).
4. See Gary Kelly, "Bluestocking Work: Learning, Literature, and Lore in the Onset of Modernity," in *Bluestockings Now! The Evolution of a Social Role,* ed. Deborah Heller (Burlington, Vt.: Ashgate, 2015), 175–208.
5. Gary Kelly, ed., *Lydia Sigourney: Selected Poetry and Prose* (Peterborough, Ont.: Broadview, 2008), 310–16. All quotations of this document are from these pages.
6. Information about Washington College from Glenn Weaver, *The History of Trinity College,* vol. 1 (Hartford, Conn.: Trinity College Press, 1967).
7. Weaver, *History of Trinity College,* 26.
8. William Croswell Doane, *The Life and Writings of George Washington Doane* (New York: Appleton, 1860), 90.
9. "Our Own Affairs," *Episcopal Watchman,* November 19, 1827, 279.
10. Charles W. Burpee, *The Phoenix National Bank of Hartford, Covering the Span between the Federal Banking Epochs of 1814 and 1914* (Hartford, Conn.: Board of Directors for the Centennial Anniversary, 1914), 8.
11. Unacknowledged republication from the *New York Review and Atheneum Magazine,* 1 (August 1825): 245, signed "Digamma"; "H.," "'Wherefore I praised the dead more than the living,'" *Episcopal Watchman,* April 2, 1827, 12.
12. Reviews, *Episcopal Watchman,* April 2, 1827, 13; April 9, 1827, 20; April 16, 1827, 28.
13. Lydia Sigourney, letter to Jane C. Sigourney, March 10, 1827, in Kelly, *Lydia Sigourney,* 308–10.
14. Review, *Episcopal Watchman,* August 13, 1827, 164–65.
15. Ibid., 164.
16. Ibid.
17. Ibid., 165.
18. Ibid.
19. Samuel Kettell, ed., *Specimens of American Poetry, with Critical and Biographical Notices* (Boston: Goodrich, 1829), 2:207.
20. "Domestic Literature," *Episcopal Watchman,* April 2, 1827, 13.
21. [Untitled,] *Episcopal Watchman,* October 1, 1829, 222.
22. "H.," "Wealth," *Episcopal Watchman,* October 15, 236.
23. "American Sacred Poetry," *Christian Observer* 28 (February 1828): 98–100.
24. "Washington College, Connecticutt," *Christian Observer* 27 (December 1827): 765–66.

7

BABY TO BABY

SIGOURNEY AND THE ORIGINS OF CUTENESS

Angela Sorby

Lydia Sigourney's work for and about children has long been understood as sentimental, even as the term *sentimental* has been recovered, historicized, and debated by generations of scholars from Ann Douglas to Claudia Stokes.[1] Sigourney was too versatile to be pigeonholed, as the essays in this volume illustrate. However, even as she explored nature, politics, and world history, her allegiances to the entwined ideologies of republican motherhood and Protestant Christianity lent her work on domestic themes a certain consistency: a Sigourney child elegy circa 1827, such as "Death of an Infant," closely resembles a Sigourney child elegy circa 1855, such as "Requiescat in Pace."[2] Indeed, it is hardly an exaggeration to claim that she embodied sentimentalism during its culturally dominant period, when antebellum Americans of both sexes were churning out texts rooted in the veneration of suffering, the elevation and circulation of deep feelings, and the idealization of women and children. At the same time, Sigourney was sensitive to the Zeitgeist, and over her lifetime American culture was changing radically. During the antebellum era a competing aesthetic was slowly emerging directly from, but also in opposition to, the conventional sentimental worldview. This aesthetic, which by the 1850s could already be called "cute," does not dominate Sigourney's oeuvre, but it does enliven some of her work, including a scrap of juvenilia, "Concerning ye Catte" (undated but published posthumously in 1866); her baby-letter series from *Poems for Children* (1836); and her *Sayings of the Little Ones, and Poems for Their Mothers* (1855).[3] These texts suggest that, although cuteness is sometimes discursively linked to sentimentalism, it operates very differently, undermining the sentimental values of generic suffering, emotional management, and domestic privacy while advancing an ethos of novelty, emotional release, and public entertainment. However, while the inner workings of sentimentalism have been extensively described, cuteness remains underarticulated. What did it mean to be cute in Sigourney's America?

Cuteness, like sexiness, has a biological basis. As Charles Darwin observed in 1872, and as Karl Lorenz established in the twentieth century, it is an adaptive trait that helps babies survive by eliciting affective responses from their elders.[4] From an evolutionary perspective, cuteness involves infantilism: wide-set eyes, big heads, awkward forms (but not distressing deformity), pliability, sporadic ineptitude (but not stupidity), precocity, and of course smallness. Lorenz calls cuteness an "innate releasing mechanism" that sparks attentiveness, tenderness, openness, and playfulness.[5] Moreover—and this is a key point—although it originates in babies, the cuteness response can also be triggered by pets, food, objects, and even linguistic scripts and tropes. Studies have shown that adults can find cats, ice-cream scoops, and even staplers cute—and indeed, the capacious Japanese phenomenon of *kawaii* (cute) culture was first manifested in the stylized pictorial handwriting of schoolgirls.[6]

Like most natural human traits, cuteness is always mediated by culture, as Sianne Ngai has shown in her work on cuteness and modernity.[7] Lori Merish locates the origins of cuteness in nineteenth-century American freak shows, identifying Tom Thumb's 1863 wedding as one of the first cute mass-mediated spectacles.[8] Women, in particular, were mesmerized by the two freakish tiny adults whose wedding transformed them from "transgressive subjects into beloved objects."[9] While Merish's pioneering work is indispensable, I think her focus on commercial manipulation obscures an older and more complex story. In the decades prior to Tom Thumb's wedding, antebellum women like Lydia Sigourney (and her readers) were enjoying mediated forms of cuteness that circulated as written texts. Often adopting a comical tone, cute texts functioned as cheeky anti-epics that privileged the small, the lyrical, and the amusing. Sigourney occasionally embraced the new aesthetic of cuteness even as she propagated a worldview—Christian sentimentalism—that reflected older structures of feeling. In other words, to use Raymond Williams's terms, in Sigourney, sentimentalism is dominant but cuteness is emergent.[10] For Sigourney, cuteness is a way to play: with hierarchies, with ideas of gender and childhood, and even with the sentimental conventions that she herself helped to establish.

Cat-People

In her 1866 autobiography, *Letters of Life,* Sigourney looks back on her childhood fondness for cats, remarking, "I studied cat-nature like a philosopher. I believed that the world had never done justice to its capacities, and that a fostering tenderness would elicit new powers; whereupon I made my cat my favorite and prime minister."[11] Here, she adorably casts her cat as prime minister and her childhood self as a philosopher. However, her tone matters: she is denigrating neither her childhood self nor her lifelong fondness for cats. Rather, she is validating cuteness by embodying it (as a child-philosopher) and practicing it (as a consumer of cat-cuteness): "Large and fat grew my cat-people, with a lustrous velvet fur, and I exulted in their superiority."[12] Daniel Harris relates cuteness to deficiency, arguing that consumers are narcissistically attracted to anthropomorphic animals and objects because they need to feel needed: "Something becomes cute not necessarily because of a quality it has but because of a quality it lacks."[13] For Sigourney, though, cat-cuteness refigures domestic caretaking as a site of power; it does not connote an oppressive relationship. Cats deserve respect, not through suffering (as with sentimental animals) but through fatness and touchable fur. The cat and the girl exchange strokes, and their pleasure not only uses cuteness as a social releaser but also extends the circuit to include susceptible readers. Sigourney is not inviting vacant consumerism; she is modeling productive play.

In a recent essay on twenty-first-century digital culture, the philosopher D. E. Wittkower asks "why, when given access to the means of mass communication, it seems that a very significant portion of the online community is interested in creating, sharing, and enjoying cute pictures of animals, particularly cats."[14] Wittkower then speculates that, as the internet became more gender balanced, the result was an uptick in appeals to the cuteness response because women are socialized to seek these images.[15] Likewise, in the early nineteenth century, as women gained access to written mass communication, Sigourney and others seized the opportunity to cater to and value women's tastes and to insist that what happened in the domestic sphere mattered. This was an implicitly (if ambivalently) political stance because, then as now, aesthetic categories embraced primarily by women got scant respect from the mostly male arbiters of highbrow culture. Yet as Ann Beebe argues in chapter 8, Sigourney consistently depicted the domestic sphere as a rich source of creativity. In "Concerning ye Catte," Sigourney advances her own quirky version of the cat-lady hypothesis: "Ye dogge hath many admirers, ye catte but few. He followeth manne, and is praised by him. She stayeth in-doors with the women, who have not much to do with the penne, so her good deeds have little chance of being written down."[16] It turns out, then, that cats do not necessarily have fewer admirers than dogs; rather, they are simply less publicly valued because women have traditionally had limited access to print technology. Moreover, in Sigourney's approving formulation, neither cats nor women "followeth man, and are praised by him."[17] This enables women and cats to set their own rules; and if Sigourney's logic echoes the separate spheres ideology that she sometimes promoted, it also introduces an intriguing note of wildness and willfulness into the domestic space.

To flip the hierarchy of cats (gendered female) and dogs (gendered male), Sigourney uses cute strategies. On the level of content, "Concerning ye Catte" frames the cat as entertaining, "accomplished," with a "natural taste for musicke, and great compass of voice," displaying its novel tricks through Barnum-esque theatrical images. The cat is further anthropomorphized as a little mother who "doth not neglecte" her kittens' education and "boxeth their small ears with a wide-spread paw, if they disobey or displease her." Surprising capacities collide with physical limitations to produce a cute object—"ye catte"—that invites attention and play. Sentimental depictions of cats frame them among God's pitiable creatures, but by making "ye catte" cute, Sigourney gives it new powers of attraction that have more to do with the cat's innate capacities and relative limitations than with God's (or man's) approval.[18] The case should not be overstated; to display a cat singing and schooling her kittens is hardly to overturn the patriarchy. But in this moment of play, Sigourney helps her readers imagine an order that privileges female pleasure and desire. Cute cats would proliferate over the course of the nineteenth century—a trend perhaps epitomized by Eliza Lee Follen's enduringly popular "Three Little Kittens," first published in 1832.[19] Sigourney's "catte" represents an unusually early manifestation of feline mania, reflecting her tendency to anticipate and respond to new forms of middle-class pleasure.

Sigourney, in her dominant sentimental mode, helped invent a world of perfect children; in *Letters to Mothers,* she calls the child's body a "temple, where the ethereal spirit is a lodger."[20] The code of cuteness, however, hinges on embodied asymmetry. By reprinting "Concerning ye Catte," she represents her childhood self through the body of charmingly clumsy text characterized by misspellings and archaisms that prefigure Emily Dickinson's extensive use of the cute aesthetic.[21] In these ways, "Concerning ye Catte" is something of an anomaly. Elsewhere in *Letters of Life,* Sigourney represents her younger self as seriously spiritual, stressing the virtues of toil and self-abnegation. Immediately following "Concerning ye Catte," she reprints a sermon that she wrote in childhood in which the stars inspire "self-abasement" to a "law of order" enforced by God.[22] Needless to say, the sense of smallness in this passage is not cute; it echoes the language and authority of the Bible. As with the many pious children Sigourney would depict as an adult writer, her young sermonic voice is powerful insofar as it channels a divine will that transcends the individual in the context of a vast universe ruled by forces (God, the stars) that are gendered male.

By contrast, "ye catte" abjures humility: "Ye catte cometh of a high familie. This is wont to have weight with mannekine, and womankind also. To be only a cousin of my Lord Duke, causeth ye stupide to be runne after. But look you, ye catte hath ye greate, grande tiger, and ye kingly lion, for her neare relations. She boasteth not of her royal ancestry, neither is puffed up." Even the claim that the cat is not "puffed up" is a bit of a joke because earlier Sigourney observes that the cat "draweth up her bodie like a ball, and enlargeth her tail marvelously." The affective circuit of the girl and the cute cat—or the reader and the cute text—is tight and physicalized, excluding the "lofty expanse" of heavens and the "law of order enforced at their creation" to allow a moment of unruly but contained release.[23] The circuit of cuteness thus uses smallness, not as part of a transcendental microcosm-macrocosm dyad but as an end in itself: in small domestic spaces, girls and even cats are legitimated by their own self-satisfying (and perhaps self-satisfied) emotional responses. The model is not Christ the lamb but "ye greate, grande tiger," miniaturized but not entirely defanged. In this early text, then, the youthful Sigourney celebrates a small, soft predator whose positive qualities are secular and appetitive, reflecting a feminine aesthetic that rejects what Marianne Noble has called the "masochistic pleasures" of the sentimental aesthetic. To regard cute objects from a feminine subject-position is to own "the gaze" that, in erotic exchanges, was traditionally claimed by men. If, as Noble argues, sentimentalism gave women only partial and painful access to bodily pleasure, then cute texts such as "Concerning ye Catte" offered them a temporary escape from abasement to "the heavenly bodies" into a more fulfilling fleshly (but not overtly sexual) space of quaint texts, playful cats, and verbally precocious little girls.[24]

Writing Cute

In her collection *Poems for Children* (1836), Sigourney includes a series of epistolary poems supposedly penned by babies whose charm (like Tom Thumb's) stems from their blend of small and grand—child and adult—forms: "Baby's note to a Baby, with a pair of coral bracelets," "Baby to a Baby, with a New-Year's Present," "Baby of six months old, to her neighbor on his second birthday," "Child of sixteen months old to a Cousin in Boston," and "Little Girl two years old, to a little Boy on his removal to New-York."[25] In these poems, cuteness is an aesthetic that engages with a range of questions concerning bodily and poetic form, spirituality, and agency. This more nuanced use of cuteness is a function, in part, of how it is mediated: cuteness for Sigourney is not primarily specular, but verbal, linked to quaint or incongruous uses of language.

In *Poems for Children,* Sigourney's baby-letter poems stand in sharp contrast to the material flanking them, which is conventionally sentimental. For instance, the poem immediately preceding "Baby's Note to a Baby" is titled "The Grave of a Child." It begins:

> Come, see the little grassy bed
> Where our companion lies
> And 'mid your tears, remember well,
> His buried dust shall rise.[26]

Written in hymn meter and spoken in a gently didactic older voice, this poem conflates an unnamed child's death with the suffering and resurrection of Christ, counseling self-control through pious resignation. By way of generic imagery, the poem performs the cultural work of sentimental mourning; as Mary Louise Kete writes, it is interested "not in autonomy or liberation but in the restoration of constitutive bonds that make subjectivity possible."[27] The isolation of the "little grassy bed" is mitigated by the shared tears of the mourners, who are linked to each other and to Sigourney's implied readers through conventions that comfort precisely because they are familiar and expected. The dead child himself is emptied of particularity; his will has been subsumed into the will of God.

If "The Grave of a Child" consoles readers by meeting their generic and theological expectations, the first baby-letter poem, "Baby's note to a Baby with a pair of coral bracelets," traffics in the novelty of an unfamiliar genre: the baby-authored letter. The baby's voice asserts itself:

> Dear little Ann,
> I hope you can
> These bracelets wear,
> And that you will
> Remember still
> Whose gift they are.
>
> They're very plain,
> For to be vain
> I don't approve,
> Proud babies sure
> Few could endure,
> And fewer love.[28]

Sigourney, who is of course capable of highly disciplined metrical forms, situates these small and awkward verses between two huge white margins, inviting the reader's attention and amused forbearance. On the level of prosody the poem has tiny feet—just two per line—and trips along in broken dimeter, never achieving a pattern of regular stresses. The writer is also freakishly precocious, given that she is less than six weeks old. We are asked to picture an absurd scene, akin in many ways to Tom Thumb's wedding, whereby a tiny person dips pen in ink and writes, with great seriousness, words that readers cannot take seriously. This is not the transparent versification of a perfect angel-child; rather, it calls attention to its incongruities and flaws.

Cuteness in nature is adaptive because it sparks an exchange: the chubby-cheeked baby provides a rush of pleasure to the doting adult, who in turn gives the baby attention and caretaking labor. Mediated cuteness is different because it offers pleasure without necessarily demanding labor;

through figures like "dear little Ann" or Tom Thumb, the female consumer can enjoy the payoff without the work. In *Letters to Mothers,* Sigourney meditates on the pleasures of parenting young infants: "The first months of infancy are a spot of brightness to a faithful and affectionate mother, a dream of bliss, from which she wakes to more complicated duties; a payment for past suffering; a preparation for future toil. I heard a lady, who had brought up a large family, say it was 'the only period of a mother's perfect enjoyment.' At its expiration, comes dentition, with a host of physical ills."[29] In the nineteenth century, coral bracelets were used as teething-rings, so "dear little Ann" is likely on the verge of dentition. But "Baby's Note to a Baby" gives readers the blissful rush of the cuteness-response minus the "complicated duties" and fussing that come with cutting teeth. It functions as a gift with no strings attached.

Unlike sentimental beauty, cuteness is primarily a secular aesthetic, and in her baby-letter poems Sigourney floats a version of the charmingly flawed or even naughty child that would become a dominant figure after the Civil War, epitomized by work such as Thomas Aldrich's *Story of a Bad Boy* (1869).[30] Antebellum Americans, Sigourney included, remained largely enmeshed in debates about whether children were born good (trailing clouds of glory) or evil (sinners in the hands of an angry God). The child's body was figured as the site of an ongoing spiritual emergency, and the best child was, to quote the title of Elizabeth Oakes Smith's best-selling poem, a sinless child. But what if naughtiness is neither good nor evil but simply developmentally necessary? Or—even more radically—what if it is sometimes *funny*? In another baby-letter poem, "Baby's Note to a Baby, with a New-Year's Present," the child opines with a mix of pomposity, slyness, and egotism:

When thought asleep,
I sometimes peep
  My cradle o'er,
And slily turn
My ear and learn
  Some curious lore.

A doctor grave,
Who lives can save,
  I thus espied;
And when Nurse blam'd

And loudly sham'd
  All babes who cried,

He said 't was better
To lay no fetter
  Upon the lungs,
To expand the chest
Was surely best
  By use of tongues.[31]

The baby appropriates and ventriloquizes the doctor's authority, declaring, "Such precepts rare / I locked with care / Close in my breast." But the joke is precisely that this baby, like all babies, will cry anyway, precepts be damned. Indeed her aim, as she reveals in a later stanza is not to be *good* but to be *gratified:*

If chains that bind
The free-born mind
  Make men rebel,
Can strict restraint
On all complaint
  Please *babies* well?[32]

The free-born mind is a self-interested mind, well suited to the demands of the emerging capitalist marketplace.[33] Poems such as Sigourney's "Death of an Infant" teach Christ-like surrender (and never ask the infant to speak), but "Baby's Letter to a Baby" is about the development of an individual voice that can question the status quo—even if (or precisely because) she cannot change it. Her cuteness is key because this means that, even as the child "rebels," she invites the indulgence of caretakers and readers.

From the cute object-position, the speaker can feign ignorance while performing precocity; for instance, in another poem, a girl baby writes to a boy:

Six months have shed
Upon my head
  But little knowledge,
While you are fit
In sense and wit
  To enter college.[34]

Marah Gubar has pointed out that nineteenth-century child performers appealed to viewers though an extreme precocity: "Their prematurely developed skills . . . enabled them to blur the line between child and adult, innocence and experience."[35] Gubar does not call such child actors cute, but they do contrast starkly with sentimental figures such as Lucretia Davidson, who were celebrated as frail flowers marked for an early grave. In the baby-letter series (although certainly not elsewhere), Sigourney's speakers use their lungs and tongues, not just to speak up but to act out their agency. Here, the writer coyly asserts "but little knowledge," giving lip service to a gender norm that the image of a literate six-month-old girl undercuts.

In Sigourney's baby letters, an invitation to play is an invitation to ludic excess. To be a cute child in a sentimental domestic space—or a cute poem in a sentimental poetry book—is to disrupt the established order. Thus, when Sigourney's fictive six-month-old addresses her two-year-old neighbor, she speculates that he might grow up to be like Locke, Bacon, or Franklin, musing playfully:

> Our sex I'm told
> Are formed to hold
>   A lower place,
> Our powers of mind
> Being far behind
>   Your lordly race.
>
> I've understood
> That "household-good"
>   Was our employment,
> To cook and mend,
> And babies tend,
>   Our chief enjoyment.
>
> Tis very well,
> I shan't rebel,
>   And when I grow,
> Shall like to make
> Nice pies and cake,
>   And share also.[36]

The pleasure that the speaker offers is predicated on her blithe assertion of her own excessive appetites. Even as she announces "I shan't rebel," she entertains, and invites the reader to entertain, the notion that rebellion might be warranted. This baby is cute *because* she expresses a will to power that is incongruous and unthreatening; what might count as serious flaws in an adult woman (overconfidence, pointing out gender disparities, lecturing males, owning appetites) are coded as amusing in a baby. No original sins are depicted—only "original" blunders—and these require no punishment or absolution. This and other baby letters reflect a world that was barely emergent in 1834: a market-driven world of cakes and competition, in which children's individual traits were to be cultivated. Through the visceral power of cuteness, a little two-footed poem voiced by a baby can suspend the reader's moralizing and disciplinary impulses while appealing to her desire for what Sigourney calls "perfect enjoyment." To write a baby letter is not just to depict play but to engage in play—with the rules of etiquette, with gender roles, and with questions of agency. In light of the crushing responsibilities that Sigourney's didactic, sentimental vision of domesticity typically entailed, these ludic moments offer her readers a respite as they advance a less perfect vision of domesticity. The speakers in the baby letters are hardly temples, "where the ethereal spirit is a lodger"—but because they are cute, all is forgiven.

Naming Cuteness

Like many colloquialisms, the word *cute* carried varying connotations as it emerged as part of the popular lexicon. In antebellum America, *cute* as a contraction of *acute* was often associated specifically with Yankees, suggesting the sharpness of a trickster figure. But already by midcentury the word's meaning was shifting. The first wave of children explicitly described as cute appeared in the 1850s, via a medium that Sigourney helped to popularize: the comic domestic anecdote. Such anecdotes were beloved by readers, not least because parents were eager to collect and share their own children's precocious remarks. One of Sigourney's regular outlets, the *Ladies Repository,* declared in 1857:

> SAYINGS AND DOINGS OF THE LITTLE ONES. We must enlarge our Sideboard for Children. The interest this department has awakened demands it. The material constantly accumulating requires it. At the same time we

> shall give to it a little wider range, retaining the "cute sayings" and the "wise doings;" but also, as we shall have room, such other matter as may relate to childhood[.][37]

From its earliest incarnations, then, mediated cuteness was dependent on feedback loops generated by popular media.[38] Readers came to expect these small jolts of pleasure, which also taught them to see their own children in new ways. A *Knickerbocker* correspondent captured this dynamic in 1856: "It always seems to me that the month commences wrong—that something is missing—if the Knickerbocker does not come to hand as usual at the 1st. In the 'Table' I have found some 'cute' sayings of the 'Little Folks;' but I do not now recollect any thing more original than the manner in which my little five-year-old Hattie. . . ."[39] The writer goes on to recount Hattie's adorable misapprehensions, having learned not only how to appreciate her foibles but also how to share them in public.

Cute children were clever (like cute Yankees), but they also tended to blunder, suggesting paradoxically that mistakes might be cute—and perhaps even developmentally necessary. Sigourney collected her own anecdotes in *Sayings of the Little Ones, and Poems for Their Mothers* (1855). The first section, "Humorous, or Peculiar Uses of Language," records the missteps of children for laughs. Here, her usual moral didacticism is temporarily suspended—for instance, when a child's unchecked appetites get him into mischief:

> A little boy was fond of exploring secret hoards, with a restless curiosity. When pursuing these impulses in his grandmother's room, she sometimes locked her bureau, and put the key in her pocket. On one such occasion, he said:
>
> "Grandmother, are you not very old? "
>
> "Oh, no."
>
> "Do you not wish you were young?"
>
> "I cannot say that I do."
>
> "Well, how long do you expect to live?"
>
> "That is not for me to say. Why do you ask?"
>
> "Why, I thought if you were not here, I should have much better times in rummaging."[40]

Unlike a sentimental child, the rummaging little boy doesn't teach or embody Christian virtue, but neither is he figured as sinful. Rather, he moves beyond Christian binaries—beyond good and evil—by virtue of a quality that Sigourney struggles to name and to help her readers appreciate: "The mixture of naiveté and simplicity, and the uncommon beauty of the young speaker, as well as the skill with which his good-humored questions were arranged, made their effect both unique and amusing."[41] Self-centered like "y catte," the boy's egotism cannot be taken seriously as a moral failing, as Sigourney teaches her readers to understand.

In another anecdote, Sigourney focuses on the familiar tableau of the child's sickbed; a boy, injured by a carriage, makes an appeal:

> "Big doctor! what's your name? Can't you be gentle? O dear! How savage you are!"
>
> He then besought sympathy, and addressing the family around his bed, said:
>
> "Are you sorry for me? Are all of you sorry for Sandy?"
>
> On being assured they were, he still rejoined, "Why don't you cry then? Can't you cry when Sandy is hurt? Cry, every one of you. Cry loud."[42]

Sandy lacks the sentimental moral authority of God's overpowering will precisely because he insists on retaining his own agency. This makes him more material than allegorical: he is requesting (and receiving) attention, not because he represents conventional Christian virtues but because his misunderstanding of convention gives him a certain appeal. Thus, like the rummaging boy who wishes his grandmother dead, Sandy overrides larger-scale questions of suffering and mortality ("Big doctor! what's your name? Can't you be gentle?") with small-scale quips. In this way, the cute child indexes the values of an emerging secular marketplace that favors originality in children while offering instant gratification to the adults who are amused by novelty.

At the same time, even as Sandy asserts his will ("Are all of you sorry for Sandy?"), he loses control of the discourse. Just when he expects everyone to cry, they laugh, and he is, to some degree, objectified as a figure of fun. Moreover, because he isn't actually going to die, what he says doesn't *really matter* in a theological sense. His story and his words are valued, but their value is trivial and transitory, like the form of an anecdote meant to be skimmed in a monthly magazine. Cuteness is thus a double-edged sword: Sandy's charm threatens to turn him from an agent to an object—of mirth, of attention, and perhaps of parental pride.

In her work on Charles Dickens, Lauren Byler observes that "signifying both charm and cleverness, cuteness appears most familiarly in the eccentricity of Dickens's characters: their distinguishing quirks, thingly quality, and general misshapen quaintness."[43] By performing what Byler calls "divided rhetorical labor," cuteness "blurs the difference between subject and object, active and passive, creator and creation."[44] Dickens was, of course, wildly popular in America, often in serialized form, and his memorably magnetic little characters surely hastened the spread of the cute aesthetic on both sides of the Atlantic.

Byler's analysis also indirectly suggests why Americans like Sigourney waded only gingerly into the market for cuteness. Evangelical Christian women, who played a larger role in American popular culture than in British culture of the same period, were deeply invested the moral seriousness of children and mothers. *Sayings of Little Ones* begins humorously, but by the second half Sigourney repairs to the juvenile deathbed. The imps from part I are replaced by pathetic evangels. A boy's last hours are described: "The work of death was lingering and severe, but he was patient and lamb-like. He seemed to have no will of his own. All that troubled him was, to see the grief of his parents. 'Oh, sir, my good father—dear mother, don't cry, don't cry. It is all light over head. The Saviour will save me.'"[45] Although he seems to "have no will of his own," this child is not in danger of being objectified as an adorable thing; he is leaving the material world, and the lessons he shares are not unique or original but conventional, steeped in the work of mourning that is central to Sigourney's aesthetic. *Sayings of Our Little Ones* thus rebalances the emerging secular appeal of the cute child with the dominant power of Christian allegory. In Sigourney, cuteness is permissible, but it remains an indulgence to be carefully managed.

Barnum's Baby Show

In her autobiography *Letters of Life,* Sigourney notes wryly that she was invited "to be *umpire* of a *baby-show* in the city of New York," an offer that was also extended to several other prominent women, including her close friend Elizabeth Oakes Smith.[46] Sigourney apparently either refused or ignored the request (no record exists of her response), but Smith did not decline quickly enough because in 1855 her name began to appear in publicity materials for P. T. Barnum's first Grand New York Baby-Show at the American Museum. An incensed Smith fired off a letter to the *New York Tribune:* "The harmonious woman to whom has been delegated the fostering culture of a beautiful miniature of the Creator, will hold herself as one made holy thereby, and she will profane neither herself nor child by any unseemly or ostentatious display of either. . . . I do hope and trust our women will have the taste, the decency and dignity to utterly ignore the projected baby show."[47] Barnum's baby show was a smashing success, netting $11,000 in three days, but Smith's letter captures the repugnance that many middle-class women of Sigourney's generation, steeped in sentimental "separate spheres" ideology, felt when confronted with one hundred babies on display: it was too public, too indulgent, and too commercialized.

The historian Susan J. Pearson has argued that baby shows "transformed nineteenth-century Americans' relationship to objectification, exhibition, and domestic ideology" because baby-show babies were emphatically not freaks.[48] Observers thrilled to the novelty of their ordinariness—the way that babies in public could elicit visceral responses formerly reserved for family members. The *New York Times* attempted to articulate the show's pull: "One hundred little angels! Look at them, and doubt it if you can, sneerer. . . . Thousands were there to see them, fine as they were, but each had better at home. Each little Charlie or Lulu at home far surpassed these prize specimens, the choice of the flock."[49] The attraction, then, was not just that Barnum's babies were cute but that they taught observers to see their own little Charlie or Lulu as cute in the same way—to wit, as sources of pleasure and entertainment. Unique qualities were ascribed to each baby for the purposes of a grand national competition (whose child is best?) that would eventually extend far beyond the walls of the baby show and beyond the nineteenth century. As Pearson argues, "*being shown* was transformed from a mark of difference, as it was in the dime museum and allied institutions, to a form of esteem and a goal of selfhood, as in a consumer culture devoted to fashion and self-display."[50] The child's ordinary body becomes special, marked by particularly fat thighs or a charming head of hair, and thus capable of eliciting affective "yearnings and impulses" that give adults a rush of physical pleasure.

Barnum offended because he made the link between display and commerce so uneasily obvious. As *Godey's Lady's Book*—a publication to which Sigourney lent her name as an editor—asserted, "What we would reprobate in the strongest terms is the playing upon the natural and holy feeling of *maternal pride* simply and solely for mercenary views in the getter-up of the exhibitions."[51] But *Godey's* was fighting an uphill battle because if Barnum aimed to line his own pockets, he did so by catering to, and capturing, a middle-class female audience that was ready to see babyhood, on paper and in the flesh, as "a source of entertainment and interest."

I have argued that Sigourney's occasional depictions of cute cats and babies constructed a feminine aesthetic that enabled readers to play, escape, and experience moments of pleasure without responsibility. I have also focused on what I see as the productive and positive functions of cuteness, in support of the premise that the ability to read, view, and appreciate cuteness is a competency, not a deficit. Of course, as critics from Elizabeth Oakes Smith to Sianne Ngai have noted, this aesthetic can be manipulative, especially in the hands of profiteers. But cuteness can also be liberating—especially in the context of a culture that often pressured women to act as selfless beacons of purity.[52] When Sigourney gets cute, she is not deliberately undermining sentimentalism or Christianity, but she is positing different relationships between women and their children, people and their pets, subjects and objects. Texts such as the "Concerning ye Catte," the baby-letter poems, and *Sayings of Little Ones* registered—if only inadvertently—an emerging cultural mindset that would gradually cease to exalt children as temples of the holy spirit as it learned to value them as spectacles. When Barnum began showing babies, he was not working in a cultural vacuum; the tone had been set by Sigourney and others, who whetted the public appetite for cuteness.

NOTES

1. Ann Douglas, *The Feminization of American Culture* (New York: Avon, 1978); and Claudia Stokes, *The Altar at Home: Sentimental Literature and 19th Century American Religion* (Philadelphia: University of Pennsylvania Press, 2014).
2. Lydia Sigourney, "Death of an Infant," in *Poems* (Boston: Goodrich, 1827), 86–87; Lydia Sigourney, "Requiescat in Pace," in *Sayings of the Little Ones, and Poems for Their Mothers* (Buffalo, N.Y.: Phinney, 1855), 191–92.
3. Lydia Sigourney, "Concerning ye Catte," in *Letters of Life* (New York: Appleton, 1866), 165–69; the baby poems appear in Lydia Sigourney, *Poems for Children* (Hartford, Conn.: Canfield and Robins, 1836), 26–44.
4. See Charles Darwin, *The Expression of the Emotions in Man and Animals* (London: Murray, 1872). Darwin's legacy for cuteness studies is discussed at length in Stephen Jay Gould, *The Panda's Thumb* (New York: Norton, 1980), 95–107. Also see Karl Lorenz, *Studies in Animal and Human Behavior,* vol. 2 (Cambridge: Harvard University Press, 1971).
5. Lorenz, *Studies in Animal and Human Behavior,* 115–16.

6. On cats, see Anthony C. Little, "Manipulation of Infant-Like Traits Affects Perceived Cuteness of Infant, Adult and Cat Faces," *Ethology* 118 (2012): 775–82. On ice-cream scoops and staplers, see Gergana Y. Nenkov and Maura L. Scott, "So Cute I Could Eat It Up: Priming Effects of Cute Products on Indulgent Consumption," *Journal of Consumer Research* 41 (August 2014): 326–41. On *kawaii* handwriting, see Shunya Yoshimi, "Consuming America: From Symbol to System," in *Consumption in Asia: Lifestyle and Identities*, ed. Beng-Huat Chua (New York: Routledge, 2002), 202–24.
7. Sianne Ngai, *Our Aesthetic Categories: Zany, Cute, Interesting* (Cambridge: Harvard University Press, 2012).
8. Lori Merish, "Cuteness and Commodity Aesthetics," in *Freakery: Cultural Spectacles of the Extraordinary Body*, ed. Rosemary Garland Thomson (New York: New York University Press, 1996), 185–203.
9. Ibid., 194.
10. Raymond Williams, *Marxism and Literature* (Oxford: Oxford University Press, 1977).
11. Sigourney, *Letters of Life*, 30.
12. Ibid., 30.
13. Daniel Harris, *Cute, Quaint, Hungry and Romantic: The Aesthetics of Consumerism* (New York: De Capo, 2001), 4.
14. D. H. Wittkower, "On the Origins of Cuteness as a Dominant Aesthetic Category," in *Putting Knowledge to Work and Letting Information Play*, ed. Timothy Luke and Jeremy Hunsinger (Rotterdam: Sense, 2012), 215.
15. As Wittkower notes, as of 2015 the label *cat lady* remains problematic, although cat ladies are increasingly appropriating the term with bemused self-awareness (ibid.).
16. Sigourney, *Letters of Life*, 165.
17. Ibid.
18. Ibid., 166–67.
19. Eliza Lee Follen, "Three Little Kittens," in *Little Songs* (1833; reprint, Boston: Lee and Shepard, 1856), 92. This poem was Follen's rendering of a British rhyme from the oral tradition, although it was often attributed to her in reprints.
20. Lydia Sigourney, *Letters to Mothers* (Hartford, Conn.: Hudson and Skinner, 1838), 27.
21. See Suzanne Juhasz, Cristanne Miller, and Martha Nell Smith, *Comic Power in Emily Dickinson* (Austin: University of Texas Press, 1993), 15. For a specific reading of Dickinson's cuteness in "Bees are black, with gilt surcingles," see Michael Snediker, "Fuzzy Thinking," in *Staying Alive: A Survival Manual for the Liberal Arts*, ed. L. O. Aranye Fradenburg (New York: punctum, 2013), 287–95.
22. Sigourney, *Letters of Life*, 169.
23. Ibid., 166–67, 165, 169.
24. Marianne Noble, *The Masochistic Pleasures of Sentimental Literature* (Princeton: Princeton University Press, 2000); Sigourney, *Letters of Life*, 169.
25. Lydia Sigourney, *Poems for Children* (Hartford, Conn.: Canfield and Robins, 1836), 25.
26. Ibid., 25–26.
27. Mary Louise Kete, *Sentimental Collaborations: Mourning and Middle Class Identity in Nineteenth-Century America* (Durham: Duke University Press, 2000), 62.
28. Sigourney, *Poems for Children*, 26–27.
29. Sigourney, *Letters to Mothers*, 29.
30. Many scholars have described this shift; see, for instance, Stephen Mintz, *Huck's Raft: A History of American Childhood* (Cambridge: Harvard University Press, 2004).
31. Sigourney, *Poems for Children*, 29–30.
32. Ibid., 31.
33. On the problem of being "born free," see Karen Sanchez-Eppler, *Touching Liberty: Abolition, Feminism, and the Politics of the Body* (Berkeley: University of California Press, 1993), 2–3.

34. Sigourney, *Poems for Children,* 33.
35. Marah Gubar, "The Drama of Precocity: Child Performers on the Victorian Stage," in *The Nineteenth-Century Child and Consumer Culture,* ed. Dennis Denishoff (Burlington, Vt.: Ashgate, 2008), 64.
36. Sigourney, *Poems for Children,* 34–35.
37. "Sideboard for Children," *Ladies' Repository* 17, no. 1 (1857): 62.
38. Thierry Smolderen, *The Origins of Comics: From William Hogarth to Winsor McCay* (Jackson: University Press of Mississippi, 2014), 108.
39. Letter to the editor, *Knickerbocker* 47 (May 1856): 538.
40. Lydia Sigourney, *Saying of Little Ones* (New York: Blakeman and Mason, 1864), 20. This later edition of the 1855 volume, with the poems excluded, suggests there was an audience for anecdotes specifically.
41. Ibid., 21.
42. Ibid., 39–40.
43. Lauren Byler, "Dickens's Little Women; or Cute as the Dickens," *Victorian Literature and Culture* 41 (2013): 223.
44. Ibid.
45. Sigourney, *Sayings,* 136–37.
46. Sigourney, *Letters of Life,* 374.
47. Elizabeth Oakes Smith, "Barnum's Baby Show—A Protest," *New York Herald,* May, 12 1855. Smith's letter and other artifacts are preserved in an archive maintained by George Mason University, http://chnm.gmu.edu.
48. Susan J. Pearson, "'Infantile Specimens': Showing Babies in Nineteenth-Century America," *Journal of Social History* 42, no. 2 (2008): 341–70.
49. "The Baby Show—Prodigious Jam and a Hot Time," *New York Times,* June 7, 1855.
50. Pearson, "Infantile Specimens," 348.
51. "Baby Shows," *Godey's Lady's Book* (December 1855): 569.
52. More recently, scholars have understood cuteness as a tool that can both demean and empower women who occupy, or are forced into, feminine subject positions. See Christine Yano, *Pink Globalization: Hello Kitty's Trek across the Pacific* (Durham: Duke University Press, 2013).

PART TWO
THE WORK OF SIGOURNEY

8

COMMON GROUND

THE FIGURE OF THE FEMALE POET IN SIGOURNEY'S *LUCY HOWARD'S JOURNAL* AND E.D.E.N. SOUTHWORTH'S *THE BRIDAL EVE*

Ann Beebe

The poet Lydia Sigourney (1791–1865) and the novelist E.D.E.N. Southworth (1819–99) were the most popular female writers in nineteenth-century America. Their work ethic, demonstrated through some key statistics, is humbling. In her autobiography, *Letters of Life,* Sigourney estimates that her published poems "amounted to more than two thousand . . . divided among nearly three hundred different publications."[1] Her books, which include dozens of poetry collections along with her various prose publications, numbered fifty-six when she died.[2] Southworth's statistics are equally impressive—probably more than forty-five multivolume novels—although, given her penchant for retitling her serial novels for bound publication in the United States and Great Britain, the definitive number is elusive.[3] At one time, almost every literate American would have read a Sigourney poem or skimmed a Southworth novel.

There are some compelling parallels in the women's biographies—their first careers as teachers, their unhappy marriages, their trips abroad to escape persecution from their husbands, their impressive proliferation in the face of critical disparagement, their financial success as authors, their association with Robert Bonner and the *New York Ledger,* and their shared circle of literary friends. Both Southworth and Sigourney took pride in their professional identities as published authors and valued the regard of their readers. Gary Kelly's description of Sigourney's approach to the role of author might also apply to Southworth:

> She achieved this career by self-discipline and hard work, assistance of socially prominent patrons, astute management of social networks, deft handling of the cultural and social discourses of femininity and

> domesticity, persistent practice of literary trends and tastes of the reading public, steady attention to the physical features of books and the operations of the book trade, aggressive marketing and distribution of her books, and careful management of her public identity.[4]

For both women, the assiduous self-promotion that produced their soaring popularity led many contemporary and modern critics to sneer at their work. While her publishers heavily advertised Southworth's books with lengthy and flattering blurbs, the periodical assessments could be biting. The *Southern Literary Messenger* attacked her novel *Shannondale* as "flat, stupid and absurd" in 1851, while in 1852 the *Southern Quarterly Review* critiqued her talent: "Her themes and scenes are monotonous; her tastes are reckless; her tone is unwholesome."[5] An 1860 editorial about her novel *The Haunted Homestead* went so far as to call her work "nothing but trash."[6] Likewise, Sigourney's reputation was egregiously damaged by her first literary biographer, Gordon S. Haight. His 1930 work issues the verdict that, by the time of her death, "her poems were 'classics' in the sense that everyone talked of them, but few read them."[7]

In a pair of midcentury novels, Sigourney and Southworth both addressed the question of what it means to be a woman and a poet.[8] Sigourney wrote *Lucy Howard's Journal* toward the end of her career in 1858, and Southworth wrote *The Bridal Eve* as her career was blossoming in 1860. The novels are speculative biographies of the kind of woman who could best exist in fiction: the female poet. Yet while both authors were inspired to explore the same character type, there are multiple differences between these novels. Sigourney attempted to create a semblance of nonfiction by structuring her novel as the first-person journal of a young American woman who lives in a bucolic small town.[9] Southworth's novel is representative of many of her works: she used the tools of sensationalism and elements of the gothic to create a historical romance about a young British woman raised as an aristocrat who loses her fortune and her status. Both of these young women become poets. Thus, in perhaps their most self-reflective works, the authors explore what it means to be a woman and a writer.[10]

The Worlds Created by Sigourney and Southworth

It is significant that Sigourney and Southworth elected to characterize the figure of the female poet in works published at the height of their popularity, when their reputations could withstand any charges of vanity. By 1858, when Sigourney released *Lucy Howard's Journal,* she was a best-selling poet with an international reputation.[11] Thanks to her status, several popular periodicals took notice of the new book, including *Harper's Weekly* and the *Ladies' Repository* as well as the *Southern Literary Messenger.* The majority of the reviews commended her for producing a didactic text that "suffers no errors of thought or ethics."[12] Many editors urged women of all ages to purchase the book, praising its "simple, unaffected pathos" and its "useful direction for household management."[13] Southworth, on the other hand, had just published in 1859 what was to be her most popular novel, *The Hidden Hand; or, Capitola, the Mad-cap,* in the pages of Robert E. Bonner's *New York Ledger.*[14] Although widely promoted by Bonner's innovative publicity department, her 1860 serial novel, *The Bridal Eve; or, Rose Elmer* (alternate title: *Laura Etheridge*), received few notices when it was first published.[15] *Godey's Lady's Book,* noting the reissuing of several of her novels in the 1880s, allowed it to be "one of the most sensational of Mrs. Southworth's works."[16] Neither the *Boston Daily Advertiser* nor the *National Tribune* could deny the "amusement" to be found in the tale or the fact that her "numerous romances have been read with delight by thousands."[17] But both reviewers managed snide asides about Southworth's "untiring pen" and the value of the entire genre (she "has but few equals in her line").

By focusing on the religious and household lessons learned by the "chaste sweet heart" in *Lucy Howard's Journal* and the sensational plot lines of *The Bridal Eve,* contemporary reviewers missed the relevance of these female poet characters.[18] Even a reviewer for the *Southern Literary Messenger,* on the alert for any hint of the subversive, overlooked the implications of Sigourney's creation for the literary marketplace. This critic, with patronizing benevolence, conceded that "Lucy Howard does not weary us with theories concerning the sphere of women, nor project fantastical schemes of reform."[19] When reading works by female authors, many nineteenth-century critics revealed a patriarchal obliviousness of an approach that integrated literary creativity into the domestic lives of women.[20] In the world Sigourney created for her teenage Lucy, domestic chores are not drudgery, nor are they inherently separate from the development of the mind. Instead, the sixteen-year-old challenges the attitude of those who "say that female domestic occupations are unfavorable to mental improvement."[21] Rather, female household chores and intellectual scholarship "may be so mingled as to help each other."[22] This creative partnership evokes a connection to the power of cuteness explored by Angela Sorby in chapter 7. Specifically, "cat-cuteness refigures domestic caretaking as a site of power; it does not connote an oppressive relationship. . . . Sigourney . . . is modeling productive play." The domestic duties that Lucy Howard fulfills are not allowed to oppress; they become a powerful tool for creative expression.

Moreover, husbands in this idealized world do not jealously hinder female creativity. In a move evocative of Margaret Fuller's contemporary vision of the exemplary marriage, they foster it.[23] The *Southern Literary Messenger*'s critic claimed not to have seen any "theory concerning the sphere of women" in the text. Technically, he is correct. There is no single theory propounded in the novel because the world created by Sigourney embodies the application of an unstated theory wherein the female poet uses domesticity as a tool for self-improvement and creative expression. In the reality imagined by Sigourney, Lucy's husband Henry shows concern that their marriage might have "checked [her] taste for writing poetry."[24] In his view of the proper sphere for men, a husband should cultivate his wife's creative genius: "he could not forgive himself should he be the means of destroying any gifts or attainment [she] might have possessed."[25] Is Henry's stance idealized? Yes, of course. Sigourney's own experience with a jealous husband who resented her artistic and professional success is just one of many examples of how nineteenth-century female writers were curtailed by marriage.[26] The mutual supportiveness in Lucy Howard's world that promotes female intellectual pursuits and creative productivity manages to challenge social and cultural norms in such a subtle way that readers aren't made to feel defensive.

The world that Southworth created in *The Bridal Eve* is just as implausible but in a much more obvious way. While both works are set at the beginning of the nineteenth century, Laura Elmer, this novel's female poet, is raised and educated as the heir to a barony. Most nineteenth-century critics targeted with spiteful superiority the great shell game of a plot that includes a popular nineteenth-century trope—babies switched at birth (Laura and Rose)—as well as accusations of bigamy leveled against the new Duchess of Beresleigh (Rose), and a false conviction for murder of the novel's hero (Ferdinand). Southworth's plots do not lack sensationalism.

Yet just as the sweet idealism of Lucy Howard's world covers a disruptive vision of a society that fosters female creativity, Southworth's novel employs sensationalism to camouflage the professional success of her female poet. The truly rebellious element of the world she created is not the sensational revelation of Laura's identity as the true daughter of the baron's nurserymaid but Laura's empowering plans to stop being a governess to "take some quiet, pleasant lodgings, and maintain myself by my goose quill, which already brings me an income sufficient for my few wants."[27] Neither the narrator nor the protagonist draw attention to the fact that Laura's professional plans are not mentioned after the arrest of her fiancé, Ferdinand, for a murder he did not commit. Instead, Southworth delivered a breathtaking dénouement of this sensational murder plot. Yet details of the actual implementation of Laura's planned writing projects are unnecessary. Laura, the other characters, and the narrator all believe in the probability of their success. Hidden under all the frothy layers of sensationalism is a world in which women, with education, talent, and motivation, can support themselves comfortably from the income derived from publishing poetry and essays.

The Birth of Two Female Poets

Lucy Howard's Journal opens when the title character is ten years old and ends with her death at age twenty-two after her delivery of twins. It is possible that the character of Lucy began to germinate with Sigourney's 1847 poem, "The Lost Poet," which memorializes an unnamed young woman called up to heaven with "the unfinished song / Still on thy lip, the breathing lyre / Warm in thy skillful hand."[28] The novel depicts the narrator's transformation from a bright young girl with a talent for memorization to a mature young woman with a unique poetic voice. Within the first ten pages, Sigourney emphasized the importance of a scholarly education for girls, moving Lucy from a female seminary to a coeducational institution with a rigorous male teacher. Nicknamed "Preceptor" by the students, he instructs the boys and girls together and holds then all to the same high standards. Young Lucy praises him for his "excellent system. . . . He tries to improve our conduct and character, as well as make us recite well."[29] For this fictional poet (and, coincidentally, for Emily Dickinson, who addressed Thomas Wentworth Higginson as her "Preceptor"), the teacher's emphasis on correct spelling, an appreciation of the language of the Bible, and a minute study of every "page in the Dictionary, with the orthography, meaning, and grammatical character of each word," provides the perfect training.[30] Because Lucy's description of her daily lessons and her understanding of the Preceptor's teaching philosophy is so matter of fact, casual readers or sexist reviewers might have overlooked the significance of permitting a young girl to receive an education equal to the one that university-bound boys were also receiving.

Because Sigourney wanted to create a female poetic voice enriched, not constrained, by the domestic world, she had Lucy's mother withdraw her from school at age fourteen and begin an equally systematic study of housekeeping. Lucy is intrigued by the possibilities of creative expression in the household. She notices that an elderly neighbor sits on a hard wooden chair at home and expresses concern to her mother. Mrs. Howard reminds Lucy that "ingenuity and economy were very interesting features of charity, and that this might be a good opportunity to practice them."[31] Feelings of goodwill prompt Lucy's creativity, and she designs and builds a padded chair out of an old flour barrel for the old woman. Lucy learns the power of invention, whether for the practical purpose of assuaging the discomforts of the elderly or for the creation of poems to uplift loved ones. Only by merging her love and appreciation of the power of words, as she learned from the Preceptor, with the rich imagery and themes of her domestic life does she discover her unique poetic voice.

Southworth's heroine, Laura Elmer, has a markedly different biography. As a product of the British aristocracy, not of American democracy, she has received an education in all the "polite branches . . . [in] every art and science that is deemed necessary to the training of a young lady of quality."[32] Yet she must jettison this education and endure rough trials. Only after she has lost her fortune, her social position, and her duplicitous fiancé can she gain the insight into human nature she needs to be an authentic poet. To forestall despair, Laura reminds herself, "I have lost wealth, position, and my false love; but I have left youth, health, intellect, and much acquired knowledge, with many accomplishments. These will enable me to lead a useful life."[33] Before losing her status, she had been a benevolent if somewhat emotionally removed lady of property. It is the loss of her aristocratic identity and its concomitant privileges that creates a compulsion to lead a socially useful life, which in turn gives birth to the poet. In this respect Laura appears to be a fictional descendant of female writers like Mary Wollstonecraft (*A Vindication of the Rights of Woman,* 1792) and Lydia Maria Child (*An Appeal in Favor of That Class of Americans Called Africans,* 1833) who found their vocations when exposing political and social injustice.[34] Unsurprisingly, the long poem that Laura publishes, "Woman," takes as its subject the educational and economic challenges that women face in the nineteenth century.

The Impulse to Write

What sparked the poetic imaginations of these two fictional poets? In creating Lucy Howard, Sigourney emphasized the positive influence of the intimate relationship the character develops with her journal. This daily written conversation starts as a ten-year-old's required assignment: "The schoolmistress says we must all keep journals."[35] The first entries are short and constrained; young Lucy is unaccustomed to the concentrated mindfulness that a journal requires. But her transfer to the new coeducational school and her work with a teacher who demands both extensive memorization and analytical thinking give new life to the journal. Lucy's entries become more developed, and she tentatively begins to muse on teaching styles, male critics, parenting techniques, and parties for children.[36]

In Lucy's creative process the journal fulfills multiple functions. Sigourney had long been a proponent of journal keeping for the aspiring writer, explaining in *Letters to Young Ladies* that it is a "useful adjunct in this work of self-introspection . . . [as] it seems like the visible presence of a friend, whose frown makes folly ashamed, and whose smile gives confidence to virtue."[37] In *Lucy Howard's Journal,* Lucy realizes that "a journal is an assistant to intellectual improvement," for it bears witness to any intellectual laziness or stagnation.[38] It also serves as a location for the subconscious to reveal what might have been missed: "Every line that is written recalls events and feelings that cluster about it, and might else have been forgotten. It strings the pearls that otherwise, lying loose, might be trodden upon and swept away."[39] The journal is a repository of images and topics as well as a practice ground for phrasing. It is not only a practical essential for Lucy's success as a poet, but it also fulfills certain emotional needs. Lucy remarks on the "pleasure" she derives from keeping a journal and cherishes the companionship of the project.[40] Without some level of creative or intellectual exchange, her poetry is in danger of stagnation. More than once she expresses gratitude for the intimacy and friendship a journal can supply: "It seems as a living friend. It is always ready for us, and has no occupation but our concerns. As soon as we have formed the habit of resorting to its society, it gets a strange sort of power over us. It remembers for us, and gives new life to scenes and emblems which might else have been forgotten. It never speaks a word, yet it has a reproving power, so that we respect it."[41]

Lucy sharpens her poetic voice in her entries and gains the confidence to share her finished poems with friends and family. In the journal she acknowledges and defies societal bias against female authorship: "Some wise people say that it is a waste of time. . . . But when any thought keeps singing in my ear, just like a bee, I do write it down and it comes in rhyme. If I try to drive it away, it flies round my head, as if it meant to sting me."[42] Her compulsion to write is confided to and eventually sanctioned by her journal.

Lucy is an American poet of domestic life who chiefly needs permission to devote precious time to creative production and approval to share her work with others. In contrast, Laura, the British poet, does not lack self-confidence or pride. Southworth's first description of her closes with a nod to her regal bearing: "In the carriage of her head and neck, and in her stately footsteps, there was a certain natural majesty that, even in peasant's dress, would have proved her one of Nature's queens."[43] Laura has no need of a journal to authorize her actions; her identity as a poet is stymied by the lack of a poetic subject. Without the loss of her fortune, she would never have become a poet. For Laura, the themes that can be expressed in a poem are preeminent. Because a well-crafted poem has the ability to touch the hearts of readers, it has the potential to inspire change when it confronts contentious issues such as women's educational and economic opportunities. The loss of her aristocratic status opens Laura's eyes to the disparities faced by the majority of women in the nineteenth century. Her temperament demands that she act, and poetry is a weapon she can wield to educate the public and provoke those in power to remedy the inequities.

The reader learns of Laura's poetic vocation in a letter from the current Baroness Etheridge, Rose. Rose writes to commend an anonymously published poem, "Woman," and urges Laura to obtain a copy. For, as Rose explains, "all the principal journals of the day" recommend it, as does the duke, Rose's future husband.[44] Laura reads the letter and murmurs to herself, "It is understood; it has reached one heart and soul at least; one, too, through whom its influence for good may flow to benefit a thousand others."[45] At this point in the novel, Laura has been reduced to working as a governess for a social-climbing family; and she has experienced the awakening of her social conscience and gained the topic for her poetry. Although her birth mother is guilty of the physical act of exchanging her for the true daughter of the Baron Etheridge, her crime is mitigated by a righteous anger over the social status quo, and she elects to express this wrath in poetry. Once Laura finds her poetic subject, her fury fuels her poetry. There is nothing private about her verse; it is composed for a select audience of powerful and wealthy upper-class Britons in the hopes of sparking debate and legal changes.

Readers, Critics, and Publication

The very different factors that provided the impetus for writing these two novels led to dissimilar approaches to publication. In Sigourney's book, the merging of academic studies with a domestic life gives birth to Lucy's unique poetic voice. Writing the poems becomes another act of personal service for those she loves. For example, Lucy writes a poem to honor George Washington for her grandfather, a Revolutionary War veteran; she composes a poem to celebrate Christmas as a gift for her mother; she meditates on the summer moon to calm her fiancé, who is weary of his banking job; and she creates a mourning poem on the death of their child, Willie, to soothe her husband's wild grief.[46] Perhaps most interesting are two poems written for her best friend, Mary Ann, and the young girls in town. Impressed by Lucy's homemade jellies and preserved apples, the women ask her "to give the recipe, and, write it in poetry."[47] In response, Lucy composes a gift poem that begins:

> Have you any Greening apples?
> If you have not, take some Pippins;
> Mark: I don't say they're equal
> To the Greenings, for they are not.
> Pare and core them very neatly;
> Mind you do not waste their substance,
> Nor impair their fair properties.[48]

This poem is inspired by a common female household chore and authorized by the communal responsibilities of being a friend. The poet herself does not attempt to commodify her verse; its publication is predicated, disturbingly, on the her death. For despite the empowering model of poetic creativity that Sigourney imagined in the novel, she did not envision a world in which Lucy Howard might professionalize her writing with publication and retain her domestic credentials. The novel ends with the strong sense that the grief-stricken husband will turn to his deceased wife's journal and manuscript poems for solace and eventually publish them as a memorial.

Southworth's Laura Elmer, like Elizabeth Barrett Browning's Aurora Leigh, fashions herself as a public poet. The anonymous publication of the first edition of her long poem, "Woman," is in part a publicity gambit. After weeks of speculation over the author's identity, the dowager Duchess of Beresleigh is almost overwrought in her desire to introduce the poet to society when she learns her name: "I will call on her myself to-day. . . . I really must secure this new literary star for our party."[49] The competition to discover the poet's identity sparks, as Laura had hoped, a close reading of her poem. The duchess correctly assesses the unknown poet when she describes her as a "clear-visioned, large-souled woman, one who has loved deeply, suffered greatly, and thought strongly."[50]

Laura's topics and themes require her readers to identify with the author. To that end, the reviews the anonymous poem receives are crucial. Without knowing the author's identity, Ferdinand publishes a glowing commendation of the poem in a journal explicitly intended for male readers, *Gentleman's Magazine*.[51] Men must read Laura's poems, for only they can affect the changes she advocates. Moreover, for Laura the sight of the second edition of her poem, bound expensively, gives her a sense of fulfillment. She returns to her servant's room after another humiliating moment in the Lester household and sees a box that "call[s] a smile to her lips. She cut[s] the cords, and several handsomely bound volumes [are] revealed to her eyes. Sitting down, she examine[s] one after another."[52] The physical products of her imagination, and the binding that highlights its socially recognized value, achieve the demands she places on her poetry.[53]

Ramifications for the Aesthetics of Poetry

Both novelists established their poet characters' standing through their familiarity with the work of the most influential poets of the past two hundred years. Sigourney has Lucy Howard refer to and occasionally challenge the titans of the British literary tradition. She integrates lines from Alexander Pope, Thomas Gray, Oliver Goldsmith, Walter Scott, William Shakespeare, and others into her journal.[54] She enjoys their works but is not intimidated by their stature. As an eleven-year-old, she gushes with sly humor in her journal, "I do love to parse in Milton. It is so entertaining to have to chase after a nominative for your verb, back and back through so many lines, like a needle in a hay-mow."[55] Lucy approaches his work as an equal, able to tease the famously rigid poet for his occasional poetic meandering. From youth she learns to read for enjoyment and intellectual exercise in preparation for the development of her personal poetic voice.

Southworth adopted the tradition of quotations at the start of every chapter, partially to prove her familiarity with the literary tradition. Foreshadowing a revised aesthetic for poetry, she selected both a range of authors for quotations and provocatively paired classical epigrams with sensational plot developments. The thirty-five chapters include passages from acknowledged standards by John Dryden, Shakespeare, William Wordsworth, and Lord Byron.[56] Quotations from minor authors such as Richard Henry Stoddard, Thomas Pringle, Robert Pollok, and William Havard receive equal treatment.[57] In this way Southworth relegated all past texts to the same common library, allowing them to earn contemporary value by her use of them in the novel. The Dryden lines appear at the beginning of the chapter that details the plot of Colonel Hastings and his son to defraud the Etheridge estate, while one of the Shakespeare quotations precedes the murder of a lecherous baron and another leads into a duchess's indictment for bigamy. In their own ways, Sigourney's and Southworth's references to great literary works authorized their entry into the literary tradition. They were then able to move forward and propose two variations of a new poetic aesthetic.

Lucy Howard's aesthetic is prompted by an unusual reading choice. Just as Anne Bradstreet acknowledged her debt as an apprentice poet to Guillaume Du Bartas (1544–90), Sigourney's female poet adopts a rather obscure French poet, François Fénelon (1651–1715), as her poetic model. Fénelon, a Catholic archbishop of the Enlightenment era, is not widely read in the United States today, but his works have been available since 1829, when Eliza Follen published *Selections from the Writings of Fenelon with a Memoir of His Life.* Sigourney would have been familiar with Fénelon's unexpected connection to Quakerism and quietism as well as his influence on the theology of some abolitionists. For nineteenth-century writers, he "represented those qualities of Christianity that were universal religious traits to be imitated," despite his Catholicism.[58] Sigourney's fifteen-year-old heroine, still endeavoring to meld her academic training with her domestic identity, confides to her journal her admiration for this sixteenth-century figure, who was pushed to reconcile two seemingly competitive vocations—priest and poet. Instead of assigning separate territories to the two fields in his psyche, he found their common ground and built his poetic identity on it. Lucy follows his model and refuses to let labels (*woman, wife, mother*) limit her development as a poet. The simplicity of this relatively unknown poet's work may be dismissed by the current arbiters of literary tastes, but this small girl refuses to let others dictate the route of her poetic evolution. She experiences a writer's epiphany in her sixteenth year: "It is so much easier to write poetry than prose. I don't mean that high poetical thoughts would be easy to find; but for such thoughts as you happen to have, rhyme is a great help. It hovers like music around you, and beguiles the toil."[59] She adds in a later entry, "This writing of rhymes is fascinating, and may be a useful thing."[60] This last statement leads us to one of the cornerstones of Lucy poetic aesthetic: domestic usefulness. To write verses that speak to and for readers, the poet must be involved in the daily lives of those she loves.

Toward the end of the journal, Lucy declares her full poetic aesthetic. She begins, "The poetical element, like the religious one, is a source of happiness."[61] Taking her cue from Fénelon and Bradstreet, she associates poetry with religion. For Bradstreet and the fictional Lucy, all poetry "on any subject . . . was an act of faith"; therefore, "her work made her an artist in service to God."[62] Both poetry and faith are concerned with the human spirit, and the true poet should not deny the happiness that her calling can provide. In this respect, Lucy shames the popular character of the poet as a tortured atheist who suffers away from loved ones and simple domestic comforts for the sake of his art. Such a selfish and indulgent attitude directly contradicts the aesthetic Lucy espouses. She continues, "It may be cultivated as to soothe suffering, to refine enjoyment, and to sublimate our whole nature."[63] This sentence, in its identification of the therapeutic function of poetry, might be compared to Ralph Waldo Emerson's more forcefully phrased claim for the American scholar. In an 1837 essay he declares that "the office of the scholar is to cheer, to raise, and to guide men by showing them facts amidst appearances."[64] The implications of Emerson's vision for the intellectual American changed generations of thinkers. Sigourney's vision was as potentially groundbreaking; it is simply phrased with more humility. Lucy follows her definition with this self-deprecating line: "I speak of only the very limited measure in which I have been enabled to taste it. Those who have taken deeper draughts can better set forth its Bethesda properties."[65] This rhetorical move overtly concedes the supremacy of those in patriarchal power while demonstrating the superiority of her own vision. In the aesthetic so demurely proposed, poetry is an act of cultivation. Its best creations are the works of study and determination, not the result of capricious inspiration. The first goal of the poet in this school is a domestic one: to soothe suffering. The highest service a poet can render is to ease the mental or emotional pain of a reader; thus, many of Lucy's poems fall within the genre of consolatory verse, a poetic type at which Sigourney excelled.[66]

Moreover, the true poet is not subject to unrestrained physical abandon. Lucy's vision rejects the Byron- or Shelley-like poetic figure, impaired by alcohol or drugs, who ruins the lives around him for the sake of his art.[67] Like Emerson, who disavowed this frenzied version of the poet in "Circles" ("the use of opium and alcohol are the semblance and counterfeit of this oracular genius"), Lucy, using the domestic culinary image of refining, takes the rough potential of elements and refines them into useful objects of beauty.[68] While Sorby's reading of cuteness in Sigourney's poems argues that these depictions create "a feminine aesthetic that enables readers to play, to escape, and to experience moments of pleasure without responsibility," the aesthetic embodied by Lucy Howard embraces responsibility and usefulness. The last section of this concentrated statement, "to sublimate our whole nature," is the most radical. The individual poetic voice, no matter how unique or valuable, must eventually be silenced or sublimated within the context of *Lucy Howard's Journal*. The poet must become invisible for the poem to thrive. Consequently, this entry ends with Lucy's poem to the spirit of poetry:

> I bring a broken spirit. Make it whole
> With the sweet balm of song.
>   To her I spake
> Who rules the spirit's inborn harmonies.

And not in vain; for as she struck her harp
Of varied symphony, and claimed response,
Forthwith the brooding sadness fled away,
And, sitting at her feet, I was made whole.[69]

Evoking religious imagery reminiscent of Psalm 51, she looks to poetry to soothe a spirit broken by the vicissitudes of life.[70]

Southworth's vision of the female poet promotes a contrasting poetic aesthetic. The roots of this contrast might be found in the stake the authors held in two distinct genres. While Sigourney, the "sweet singer of Hartford," identified herself as a poet, Southworth was an unapologetic writer of sprawling and sensational novels. In a neat point of contact, Sigourney has Lucy Howard refuse to participate in this overtly commercial enterprise. As Lucy understands it, all she would need to do is "take some Earls and Countesses, and several Singular people, and beauty and love, and daggers and escapes, and perils and quarrels, and shake all up together, and the end would be matrimony."[71] She decides against it upon reflection; if her mother does not approve of her reading novels, even Scott's or Goldsmith's, she would certainly object to her writing them. Sigourney's indirect disparagement of Southworth's novels is an indication that the two authors held contradictory aesthetic views. And while the aesthetic Sigourney pushes in *Lucy Howard's Journal* centers on the spirit of poetry and its ability to soothe, refine, and sublimate, the aesthetic Southworth fosters in *The Bridal Eve* abjures the very idea of the author's sublimation. In fact, by providing only the title of the poem written by Laura Etheridge, but no lines, Southworth forces all attention on the literal figure of the poet. Moreover, Laura refuses to act as someone else's silent muse. She is not waiting for a Petrarch to appear and use her as a male fantasy of idealized womanhood. This Laura invents herself, and the laurels embedded in her very name will be claimed by her, not appropriated by another.

Before such a potential can be realized, the poet must conquer and then exploit the residual atmosphere of literary patronage. Laura takes control of her public persona by organizing the ploy of publishing her first edition anonymously and providing just enough biographical hints in the poem to intrigue the public. When the richly bound second edition comes out, she dedicates it to "Rosamund, Baroness Etheridge, with the love of Laura Elmer," guaranteeing another explosion of publicity by associating the work with the aristocratic scandal of the mixed babies.[72] She agrees to be presented by the Duchess of Beresleigh at her literary salon, despite Rose's warning that the duchess "thinks that the whole of a poet is public property, [that] not only his works, but his presence and conversation belong of right to the world."[73] Laura deflects and dismisses all of the duchess's attempts at benevolent patronage. In this aesthetic, the figure of the biographical poet takes precedence over readers of all social ranks and critics. They are made to serve the ambitions of the poet, who in turn serves society by illuminating injustices and proposing solutions. The actual body of the poet and the literary celebrity she can generate to promote the work's social and economic themes obfuscate the verse. Poetry is merely the means of entry into the ranks of those with the power to effect change. Laura may have lost her aristocratic title and fortune, but she can still enter the drawing room of a duchess as the "Queen of Poetry," the "lioness of the evening."[74] The physical description of Laura at the height of the second edition's success is the embodiment of her poem, "Woman." The duchess worries that the poet will appear in shabby or outlandish clothes, but Laura's "graceful form was arrayed in a rich black velvet robe, made low in the bosom and short in the sleeves; her beautiful neck and arms were veiled with white point lace, fine as cobwebs, and adorned with circlets of pearls; a fillet of pearls bound her raven black hair away from her broad forehead, so that it fell in a glittering cascade of ringlets at the back of her neck."[75] She prowls the literary salon, the poem made physical. The verse and the body of the poet unite to argue against the social and economic injustices faced by multitudes of powerless women.

My focus in this chapter, the comparison of the figure of the female poet in Sigourney's *Lucy Howard's Journal* and Southworth's *The Bridal Eve,* raises the possibility of two distinct poetic aesthetics. Both authors created improbable worlds for their young poets in order to propose a radical agenda: the natural integration of the female author into daily life. Sigourney's creation is enriched by domestic life and imagery, while Southworth's is energized by social and political concerns. Lucy Howard demonstrates a poetic aesthetic that "soothe[s] suffering, . . . refine[s] enjoyment, and . . . sublimate[s]" human nature. This triad of poetical objectives conceives of authorship as a form of religious service wherein the dedication of the poet is venerated long after death. Laura Elmer's aesthetic is ruthlessly practical. For this descendant of Madame de Staël's Corinne, poetry is still an act of service but is written to achieve social and political ends. Moreover, the written word is subservient to the physical figure of the poet in a manner that foreshadows twentieth-century literary celebrity. The aesthetics embodied in Lucy Howard and Laura Elmer are dissimilar in significant ways, but with their creations Lydia Sigourney and E.D.E.N. Southworth boldly asserted the relevance of the female poet in nineteenth-century American literature.

NOTES

1. Lydia Sigourney, *Life of Letters* (New York: Appleton, 1867), 366.
2. Melissa Ladd Teed, "A Passion for Distinction: Lydia Huntley Sigourney and the Creation of a Literary Reputation," *New England Quarterly* 77 (March 2004): 52.
3. Melissa J. Homestead and Vicki L. Martin, "A Chronological Bibliography of E.D.E.N. Southworth's Works Privileging Periodical Publications," in *E.D.E.N. Southworth: Recovering a Nineteenth-Century Popular Novelist,* ed. Melissa J. Homestead and Pamela T. Washington (Knoxville: University of Tennessee, 2012), 294–306.
4. Gary Kelly, ed., *Lydia Sigourney: Selected Poetry and Prose* (Peterborough, Ont.: Broadview, 2008), 12.
5. "Review of *Shannondale,*" *Southern Literary Messenger* 17 (February 1851): 128; "Review of *Virginia and Magdalene,*" *Southern Quarterly Review* 6 (October 1852): 541.
6. "Editorial," *Warrenton Flag of '98,* April 19, 1860. For an exploration of contrasting evaluations of Southworth's novels, see Dale Bauer, "Why Read E.D.E.N. Southworth?" *Arizona Quarterly* 69, no. 1 (2013): 1–22.
7. Gordon S. Haight, *Mrs. Sigourney: The Sweet Singer of Hartford* (New Haven: Yale University Press, 1930), 173.
8. My topic in this chapter aligns with but does not overlap current critical assessment of the poetess tradition in the nineteenth century. For more on the poetess debate, see Paula Bernat Bennett, "Was Sigourney a Poetess? The Aesthetics of Victorian Plentitude in Lydia Sigourney's Poetry," *Comparative American Studies* 5, no. 3 (2007): 265–89; Karen L. Kilcup, "Scarlet Experiments: Dickinson's New English and the Critics," *Emily Dickinson Journal* 24, no. 1 (2015): 22–51; and Laura C. Wendorff, "'The Vivid Dreamings of an Unsatisfied Heart': Gender Ideology, Literary Aesthetics, and the 'Poetess' in Nineteenth-Century America," *American Transcendental Quarterly* 15, no. 2 (2001); 109–29.
9. British and American literature have welcomed genre hybridity, especially in the novel tradition. Many early novels incorporated traits from letters and journals. See Elizabeth Heckendom Cook, *Epistolary Bodies: Gender and Genre in the Eighteenth-Century Republic of Letters* (Stanford: Stanford University Press, 1996); Daniel Diez Couch, "Eliza Wharton's Scraps of Writing: Dissipation and Fragmentation in *The Coquette,*" *Early American Literature* 49, no. 3 (2014): 683–705; Victoria Joule, "'She Did but Take Up Old Stories': Generic Fluidity and Women's Life Writing of the Early Eighteenth Century," *Bulletin of the John Rylands Library* 90 (Autumn 2014): 47–66; Sonia Villegas Lopez, "'The Conscious Grove': Generic Experimentation in Aphra Behn's *Love-Letters between a Nobleman and His Sister* (1684–87)," *Women's Writing* 22 (February 2015): 69–83; and Miriam Nandi, "Writing Selves: Early Modern Diaries and the Genesis of the Novel," in *Narrative Developments from Chaucer to Defoe,* ed. Gerd Bayer and Ebbe Klitgard (New York: Routledge, 2011), 60–76.

10. These two novels, rarely found on recommended reading lists or syllabi, deserve to be added to the list of eighteen- and nineteenth-century poems, short stories, and novels that examine the development of the female-writer protagonist. Other examples of this subgenre include Unca Eliza Winkfield, pseud., *The Female American* (1767); Catharine Sedgwick, "Cacoethes Scribendi" (1830); Fanny Fern, *Ruth Hall* (1855); Elizabeth Barrett Browning, *Aurora Leigh* (1856); Louisa May Alcott, *Little Women* (1868); and Rebecca Harding Davis, "Marcia" (1876).
11. Kelly, *Lydia Sigourney,* 27–33; Melissa Ladd Teed, "A Passion for Distinction: Lydia Huntley Sigourney and the Creation of a Literary Reputation," *New England Quarterly* 77 (March 2004): 51–69.
12. "Literary: *Lucy Howard's Journal,*" *Harper's Weekly,* January 16, 1858, 48.
13. "Review of *Lucy Howard's Journal,*" *Harper's Weekly,* January 16, 1858, 48; "Editor's Table: *Lucy Howard's Journal,*" *Maine Farmer,* February 4, 1858, 2.
14. Christopher Looby, "Southworth and Seriality: *The Hidden Hand* in the *New York Ledger,*" *Nineteenth-Century Literature* 59 (September 2004): 179–211.
15. The novel appeared serially under the title *Rose Elmer, or, A Divided Heart and a Divided Life* in the *New York Ledger* (May 19–October 13, 1860). The *London Journal* published it serially as *Laura Etheridge* (May 26–September 29, 1860). T. B. Peterson and Brothers published the first book edition in 1864 (Homestead and Martin, "Chronological Bibliography," 299).
16. "Our Book Table: *The Bridal Eve,*" *Godey's Lady's Book* 103 (November 1881): 477.
17. "Publications of the Day: *The Bridal Eve,*" *Boston Daily Advertiser,* June 15, 1864, 6; "Review of *The Bridal Eve; or Rose Elmer,*" *National Tribune,* May 10, 1883, 4.
18. "Belles Lettres: *Lucy Howard's Journal,*" *Methodist Quarterly Review* 10 (April 1858): 337.
19. "Review of *Lucy Howard's Journal,*" *Southern Literary Messenger* 26 (March 1858): 239.
20. Sigourney's Lucy, whose name can be defined as "light" or "the dawn," might evoke associations for some readers with William Wordsworth's Lucy in the *Lyrical Ballads* (1798), Eva in Elizabeth Oakes Smith's "The Sinless Child" (1843), or Lucy Snowe in Charlotte Bronte's *Villette* (1853).
21. Lydia Sigourney, *Lucy Howard's Journal* (New York: Harper, 1858), 115.
22. Ibid.
23. Margaret Fuller, *Woman in the Nineteenth Century,* ed. Larry J. Reynolds (New York: Norton, 1998), 39–48.
24. Sigourney, *Lucy Howard's Journal,* 226.
25. Ibid.
26. Kelly, *Lydia Sigourney,* 19–27.
27. E.D.E.N. Southworth, *The Bridal Eve* (Philadelphia: Peterson, 1864), 228.
28. Lydia Sigourney, "The Lost Poet," in *The Weeping Willow* (Hartford, Conn.: Parsons, 1847), 112.
29. Sigourney, *Lucy Howard's Journal,* 13–14.
30. Brenda Wineapple, *White Heat: The Friendship of Emily Dickinson and Thomas Wentworth Higginson* (New York: Anchor, 2008), 13; Sigourney, *Lucy Howard's Journal,* 24, 27, 41.
31. Sigourney, *Lucy Howard's Journal,* 89.
32. Southworth, *The Bridal Eve,* 59.
33. Ibid., 140.
34. Mary Wollstonecraft, *A Vindication of the Rights of Woman,* in *"A Vindication of the Rights of Woman" and "A Vindication of the Rights of Men,"* ed. Janet Todd (Oxford: Oxford University Press, 2009); Lydia Maria Child, *An Appeal in Favor of That Class of Americans Called Africans* (Amherst: University of Massachusetts Press, 2012).
35. Sigourney, *Lucy Howard's Journal,* 5. Mary Loeffelholz explores the influence Sigourney's background as a teacher had on her poetry. She reads the novel as Sigourney's

"elegy for mute inglorious Lucy Howard [who] becomes the ideal-typical history of Lydia Sigourney, famous poetess on the verge of becoming the matter of tradition" (*From School to Salon: Reading Nineteenth-Century American Women's Poetry* [Princeton: Princeton University Press, 2004], 64).

36. Sigourney, *Lucy Howard's Journal,* 9–48.
37. Lydia Sigourney, *Letters to Young Ladies* (New York: Harper, 1837), 25.
38. Sigourney, *Lucy Howard's Journal,* 86.
39. Ibid.
40. Ibid., 211.
41. Ibid., 133–34.
42. Ibid., 14–15.
43. Southworth, *The Bridal Eve,* 27.
44. Ibid., 175.
45. Ibid.
46. Sigourney, *Lucy Howard's Journal,* 110–11, 138–39, 165, 307.
47. Ibid., 87, 100.
48. Ibid., 100, ll. 1–7.
49. Southworth, *The Bridal Eve,* 220.
50. Ibid., 204.
51. Ibid., 210.
52. Ibid., 218.
53. Patricia Pulham's essay on gift books and annuals expands on this connection between the opulent exterior of gift books and the physical body of the female author ("'Jewels-Delights-Perfect Loves': Victorian Women Poets and the Annuals," in *Victorian Women Poets,* ed. Alison Chapman [Woodbridge, U.K.: Brewer, 2003], 9–31).
54. Sigourney, *Lucy Howard's Journal,* 21, 29, 106, 167, 184.
55. Ibid., 12.
56. Southworth, *The Bridal Eve,* 100, 112, 218, 285, 292, 345, 393, 186, 208, 229.
57. Ibid., 49, 149, 306, 414.
58. Patricia Ward, *Experimental Theology in America: Madame Guyon, Fénelon, and Their Readers* (Waco, Tex.: Baylor University Press, 2009), 120.
59. Sigourney, *Lucy Howard's Journal,* 111.
60. Ibid., 139.
61. Ibid., 317.
62. Paula Kopacz, "'Man can doe best, and Women know it well': Anne Bradstreet and Feminist Aesthetics," *Kentucky Philological Review* 2 (1987): 28.
63. Sigourney, *Lucy Howard's Journal,* 317.
64. Ralph Waldo Emerson, "The American Scholar," in *Emerson's Prose and Poetry,* ed. Joel Porte and Saundra Morris (New York: Norton, 2001), 63.
65. Sigourney, *Lucy Howard's Journal,* 317.
66. Elizabeth A. Petrino, "'Feet so Precious Charged': Dickinson, Sigourney, and the Child Elegy," *Tulsa Studies in Women's Literature* 13 (Autumn 1994): 323.
67. Anya Taylor, *Bacchus in Romantic England: Writers and Drink, 1780–1830* (New York: Palgrave Macmillan, 1998).
68. Ralph Waldo Emerson, "Circles," in Porte and Morris, *Emerson's Prose and Poetry,* 182.
69. Sigourney, *Lucy Howard's Journal,* 317.
70. "The sacrifices of God are a broken spirit; a broken and contrite heart" (Psalm 51:17, King James Version).
71. Sigourney, *Lucy Howard's Journal,* 76.
72. Southworth, *The Bridal Eve,* 220.
73. Ibid., 212.
74. Ibid., 224, 226.
75. Ibid., 225.

9

"EXIL'D MURMURINGS"

"THE AMERICAN HEMANS" AND THE POLITICS OF DISPLACEMENT

Janet Dean

When Lydia Sigourney heard herself called "the American Hemans," she must have felt pleased and vexed in equal measure.[1] Sigourney admired Felicia Hemans, producing two biographies of the British poet and publishing a monody on her death in 1835. She was also eager to match Hemans's success and savvy enough to appreciate the currency of association with a literary luminary. As Wendy Dasler Johnson points out, even having one of her poems mistakenly attributed to Hemans, as happened in an 1828 American edition of the British poet's work, might have seemed to be a stroke of good fortune.[2] But Sigourney would have recognized, too, that the label "the American Hemans" was not entirely complimentary, and not only because it cast her as a colonial spin-off. Some used it to suggest she had crossed a line between emulation and impersonation. Edgar Allan Poe put the matter bluntly in an unsigned 1836 review in the *Southern Literary Messenger*: "Mrs. S. cannot conceal from her own discernment that she has acquired this title *solely by imitation.* The very phrase 'American Hemans' speaks loudly in accusation."[3] Sigourney felt the sting of Poe's criticism and gracefully but firmly defended herself against the charge that she was a "determined imitator." "I would not for a moment admit the idea that there is ought of equality between my writings, and that of the most gifted poet of the age," she demurred in a letter to Poe, before pointing out that she had already published two volumes of poetry and written much of a third before she had even heard of Hemans.[4] Her modesty giving way to an assertion of literary accomplishment, Sigourney insisted she was not a version of Hemans but an important American poetic voice in her own right.

Still, the indictment stuck well into the twentieth century, when Gordon S. Haight reiterated it in his patronizing biography: "While it is not impossible to choose from Mrs. Hemans' poems a stanza here and there that can be matched foot by foot with one by Mrs. Sigourney, let us say . . . that 'the American Hemans' *drew her inspiration* from her English prototype."[5]

Today's critics are kinder to Sigourney, but there remains disagreement about the extent to which she adhered to "prototype." Dasler Johnson argues that Sigourney's association with Hemans was strategic, part of the American's self-making as a professional writer.[6] More generally, recuperating Sigourney has often meant finding value in her capacity to reproduce recognizable tropes and forms, including those imported from England. In Eliza Richards's view, Sigourney's "generic sentimentality . . . is arguably a great accomplishment."[7] Some scholars, however, have begun to consider the complexity of Sigourney's engagement with literary conventions and other writers in light of her political convictions, and in so doing they invite us to rethink the notion that she merely imported and recirculated literary modes from abroad. Paula Bernat Bennett reads Sigourney's "The Lost Lily," a poem in which a white woman adopted by Native Americans refuses to return to white society, as an expression of the poet's ambivalence about conventional structures of Christianity, patriarchy, and sympathy, the very cornerstones of the literary sentimentalism that made her (and Hemans) famous.[8] Bryan Sinche locates in Sigourney's poems about sailors a "marked skepticism in the unifying power of sentimental writing."[9] And Tricia Lootens complicates Sigourney's position as one of Hemans's "American heirs" by showing how she redirects and localizes her predecessor's themes, employing them in response to American political crises like slavery and the treatment of Native Americans.[10] These important reassessments expand our understanding of the ways in which Sigourney departs from standards to craft a distinct poetry.

If it is true, as Cindy Weinstein argues, that some sentimental texts "have the capacity to interrogate their generic foundations," we need a more thorough assessment of Sigourney's position as "the American Hemans."[11] In what follows, I extend Lootens's analysis in a comparison of two long narrative poems, Hemans's *The Forest Sanctuary* (1825) and Sigourney's "Pocahontas" (1841). The volume in which Sigourney's poem appeared includes a reprint of her essay on Hemans, and at first glance "Pocahontas," which in addition to sharing the theme of exile features the same stanza form as *The*

Forest Sanctuary, might be read as an echo of one of the British writer's most celebrated works. Yet the poems are very different, as Poe apparently recognized. Sigourney sent him the volume that includes "Pocahontas," wishing, in Haight's retelling, "to see if she ha[d] improved."[12] The unsigned review of *Pocahontas, and Other Poems* that Poe published in *Graham's Lady's and Gentleman's Magazine* responds by overturning the earlier verdict: "We had accused her of imitation of Mrs. Hemans—but this imitation is no longer apparent."[13] Both Sigourney and Poe saw "Pocahontas" as evidence that the American poet had broken out of Hemans's path to create something new.

But what? In what ways did Sigourney depart from or transform Hemans's tropes and themes to address American concerns? And to what extent did she assess the literary protocols she adopted from Hemans? Careful comparison suggests Sigourney did not simply duplicate the themes and styles she encountered in Hemans's work. Rather, she revised them to address a pressing political crisis. In doing so she deliberated on the ethics of literary conventions in the context of what she called "one of our greatest national sins," the systematized oppression and dislocation of Native Americans.[14]

To show how Sigourney revised Hemans's model, I focus on preoccupations with exile in the two poems. Both recount dramatic crossings between Europe and North America, and both address the consequences of their central figures' displacements. *The Forest Sanctuary* tells the story of a sixteenth-century conquistador driven by religious intolerance to a North American wilderness. "Pocahontas" relates the famous Powhatan woman's rescue of John Smith, her conversion to Christianity, and her marriage to another Englishman, John Rolfe, but the last third of the poem focuses on her journey to England, where she died at Gravesend in 1617. While not exiled in the sense of being barred from her native land, Sigourney's Pocahontas experiences a transatlantic displacement rooted, like the Spaniard's, in broader political conflicts. Yet "Pocahontas" reroutes the exile's direction of travel and changes the subject position of the heroic figure, from colonizer to colonized, from European to North American indigene, and from male to female. This revision makes possible a more penetrating interrogation of the gendered and racialized politics of conquest. Reading "Pocahontas" against *The Forest Sanctuary* allows for a reflection on the nineteenth-century significance of dislocation on individual and mass scales.[15] In a historical moment when the U.S. government was forcing thousands of Native Americans from their homes, Sigourney reimagined the romance of exile to record a history of colonization and to confront its ugly legacy in Indian removal.

Crosscurrents of Exilic Longing

Like the central figures in *The Forest Sanctuary* and "Pocahontas," Sigourney's and Hemans's poetry crisscrossed the Atlantic. Hemans's work was as popular in the United States as it was in England. The *North American Review* praised her poems for moral lessons well suited to American civil society, noting "throughout a great part of this country there is not a family of the middling class, in which some of them have not been read."[16] Her poem "The Landing of the Pilgrim Fathers in New England" (1825) became a standard for classroom recitations and public ceremonies. Critics found special significance for American readers in *The Forest Sanctuary;* when it was republished in Boston in 1827, one anachronistically argued that Hemans's hero "imbibed the spirit of our own fathers" in his sixteenth-century struggle for religious liberty.[17] Sigourney's poetry also traveled. In 1840, she hand-carried the manuscript for *Pocahontas, and Other Poems* to London, where it was published the following year. The American was already famous enough in Europe to be welcomed into the parlors of literati such as William Wordsworth, though she lamented that she was "too late" to meet Hemans, who had died five years earlier.[18] The poets' influences on one another flowed across the ocean as well. Hemans cited Sigourney's *Sketches of Connecticut* as inspiration for her poem "Edith, a Tale of the Woods."[19] Sigourney expressed her admiration for Hemans's poetry in an 1827 letter that singled out *The Forest Sanctuary* for special praise.[20] That poem left a lasting impression: her 1840 paean to "The Genius of Mrs. Hemans" recalls its "full, sustained, sublime inspiration."[21]

The influence of *The Forest Sanctuary* on "Pocahontas," in particular, becomes clear in the poems' formal and thematic parallels. Both are long, heavily footnoted poems that open and lend their titles to the collections in which they appear. More tellingly, both use the same modified Spenserian stanza form. Invented for *The Faerie Queene,* the Spenserian stanza proper, a narrative form of eight lines of iambic pentameter followed by an alexandrine, had been revived by high romantic English poets. In *The Forest Sanctuary* Hemans adopted an uncommon variant that alters the rhyme scheme.[22] In taking up this complex form, she positioned herself among the ranks of serious poets and showcased her aesthetic sophistication. Her use of the modified Spenserian stanza may have been what Sigourney had in mind when she pronounced the "poetical genius" of her predecessor "too peculiar to be mistaken."[23] At any rate Sigourney took note because she applied the unusual variation for perhaps the first and only time in "Pocahontas." This formal correspondence has been overlooked despite scholarly interest in the figure of the "transatlantic poetess" and the transatlantic "traffic in poems."[24]

Both *The Forest Sanctuary* and "Pocahontas" dramatize the exile's sense of loss, alienation, and longing for home resulting from political or cultural conflict. The poems share plots in which a scene of religious or tribal-national violence leads to the main figure's religious conversion, political imprisonment, and transatlantic displacement. Hemans's Spaniard converts to Protestantism after he witnesses the martyrdom of a friend in the Inquisition. He is imprisoned for his beliefs but escapes and flees from Europe with his wife, Leonor, and son. Leonor dies at sea; the Spaniard and his son ultimately find the sanctuary of the poem's title in "the wilds of the red hunter's land" in North America.[25] Sigourney's poem describes Pocahontas's rescue of Captain John Smith, the English colonist sentenced to death by her father, the Powhatan chief. Despite her kindness, the colonists later kidnap her in an effort to manipulate her father. "Forced amid the invaders' homes to dwell" and "held as a hostage in the stranger's cell," she eventually "bow[s] her heart to learn a Saviour's will."[26] Her conversion facilitates her marriage to Rolfe and their journey to England. The conversions and imprisonments in the poems both precede and emblematize the alienation of displacement: even before departure, the Spaniard and Pocahontas become strangers in their own lands.

Nevertheless, the imprisonment plots serve different purposes in the two poems. For Hemans, imprisonment became a metaphor for Catholic oppression, which "strives to bind / With his strong chains to earth, what is not earth's—the mind!"[27] Her critique conformed to British mainstream anti-Catholic sentiment, giving her tale a decidedly nationalist slant.[28] In contrast, Sigourney's imprisonment scene brings to the surface a hidden history in order to challenge idealized views of the colonial encounter. Pocahontas's abduction was described in antebellum colonial histories, but it was rarely included in the many popular literary versions of her story that emerged in the first half of the nineteenth century.[29] The kidnapping story is one, Sigourney's speaker tells us, that "the indignant lyre declines to tell."[30] In bringing this story to light, the poet challenged the emphasis on cross-cultural cooperation in popular Pocahontas mythology. She also prepared readers for a different understanding of Pocahontas's exile across the sea, an experience tinged by the record of European colonial aggression.

If imprisonment makes the Spaniard and Pocahontas strangers in their own lands, conversion seems to release them from all ties to national or natural homes. In Hemans's poem, conversion frees the Spaniard from a spiritually stultifying national identity. Bringing "a blighted name" to the New World in his escape from persecution, he asks, "What part hath mortal name, where God alone / Speaks to the mighty waste, and through its heart is known?" Ties to the home country loosen where the speaker "feel[s] His presence in the vast, and dim, / And whispery woods."[31] As Charlotte Sussman points out, the vagueness of the vast, dim New World contrasts with the poem's detailed descriptions of the country left behind.[32] The difference suggests that distinctions of place no longer matter to the displaced subject who has found spiritual redemption; home becomes irrelevant in light of his closeness to God. "Pocahontas" depicts a similar transcendence, as the heroine's Christian conversion transforms her relationship to the home place. Pocahontas once worshiped the natural beauty surrounding her, the "fragrant shrubs and flowers," the "birds, whose warm hearts with living praise o'erflow." Conversion brings her to seek a "higher bliss," a heavenly "home unchangeable . . . / Where is no fading flower."[33] The convert relinquishes the earthly joys of her forest home to embrace an afterworld as indeterminate as the New World forest that the Spaniard enters. At least momentarily, religious transformation conditions a separation from place, whether nationally or environmentally defined.

Both Hemans and Sigourney emphatically gendered this release from bonds to nation and environment, albeit in very different ways. *The Forest Sanctuary* draws a stark distinction between the Spaniard's experience of exile and that of his unconverted wife. Men, the poem suggests, are made for exile.

> Strange heart of man! That ev'n midst woe swells high,
> When thro' the foam he sees his proud bark sweep,
> Flinging out joyous gleams to wave and sky!
> Yes! it swells high, whate'er it leave behind.[34]

Leonor, in contrast, exhibits an intense and profoundly feminine connection to place:

> Not thus is woman. Closely *her* still heart
> Doth twine itself with ev'n each lifeless thing,
> Which, long remember'd, seem'd to bear its part
> In her calm joys. For ever would she cling,
> A brooding dove, to that sole spot of earth
> Where she hath loved, and given her children birth,
> And heard their first sweet voices. There may Spring
> Array no path, renew no flower, no leaf,
> But hath its breath of home, its claim to farewell grief.[35]

Unlike her husband, who is "wedded to the far futurity," Leonor clings to the past, and her memories cement her psychically to the place of origin.[36] Importantly, her attachment is generated by familial affection that materializes in her desire for "ev'n each lifeless thing" that defines her life in Spain. Love for her husband and child sends her into exile, but she cannot stop longing for the concrete objects—the paths, flowers, and leaves—of the home place. In anchoring Leonor to a "spot of earth," the poem departs from gender conventions that relegate women to an extranational affective sphere; the bond here is to family as situated in a specific geographical space, one defined by its natural and man-made features. This feminine attachment to home has dire consequences: unable to leave it all behind, Leonor suffers, her spirit, "worn / By its dull brooding weight, [giving] way at last."[37]

In "Pocahontas," on the other hand, woman's heart would seem, at first, to condition the same possibilities for transatlantic mobility that "the strange heart of man" grants to Hemans's Spaniard. Aboard the ship that speeds her away from her home, Pocahontas finds comfort in the presence of her husband and child:

> And this is woman's world. It matters not
> Though in the trackless wilderness she dwell,
> Or on the cliff where hangs the Switzer's cot,
> Or in the subterranean Greenland cell;
> Her world is in the heart. Rude storms may rise,
> And dark eclipse involve ambition's skies,
> But dear affection's flame burns pure and well,

And therefore 'tis, with such a placid eye,
She sooths her loved ones' pangs, or lays her down to die.[38]

"And this is woman's world" reverberates against Hemans's "Not thus is woman," suggesting a direct engagement with *The Forest Sanctuary* and an objection to its representation of women as fixed in place by their feminine attachments. The female heart that ties Leonor to Spain is precisely what makes Pocahontas's entire "world" portable, as woman's love transcends geographical boundaries and tribal-nationalist loyalties. The flame of her affection burns brightly no matter where she lands; her duty to loved ones *is* her home. If not "joyous" in her mobility as the Spaniard claims to be, Pocahontas can be "placid" in her displacement because of her love for her husband and child.

Yet any spiritual or gendered transcendence of place and tribe-nation turns out to be fleeting; for all three exiles, displacement produces a painful longing for home. Nostalgia emerges in the first line of *The Forest Sanctuary* as the exile in North America hears in imagination the "voices of [his] home," despite his efforts to "dash these fond regrets to earth."[39] Though the Spaniard does not suffer as acutely as his wife, he, too, aches for what has been lost: "Oh sweet and mournful melodies of Spain, / That lull'd my boyhood, how your memory thrills / The exile's heart with sudden wakening pain!"[40] Pocahontas feels the same nostalgic longing as she embarks on her journey: her "memory wandereth to her distant home, / To fragrant gales, the blossom'd boughs that stir, / To the sad sire who fondly dreams of her."[41] Retreating from the notion that Christian conversion or woman's love can free the exile from her attachment to home, Sigourney imagined Pocahontas feeling the pull of family history and the natural features of her home environment.

The Spaniard, Leonor, and Pocahontas all grieve the loss of home, but for the women the heartbreak is fatal. Just as Leonor does, Pocahontas suffers literal homesickness, a condition that recalls to us the earliest sense of nostalgia (from the Greek *nostos,* "homecoming," and *algos,* "pain") as a clinical malady produced by desire for the lost home.[42] Longing and illness intertwine in each woman's demise, and, as they approach death, each turns her sights not up toward heaven but back toward the earthly place left behind. Leonor's dying moments connect her to Spain; with her last breaths, she sings folksongs from the Spanish mountains and a Catholic hymn that seems to her husband to swell "From the far dust, wherein [his] sires were lying." She gathers strength to bless her son—"A long, long kiss she press'd" upon his cheek—and then dies.[43] Sigourney drew on the fictional Leonor's death scene to represent the historical Pocahontas's final hours in England. Imagined resonances tie her to her homeland:

Sweet sounds of falling waters cool and clear,
  The crystal streams, her playmates far away,
Oft, oft their dulcet music mock'd her ear,
  As, restless, on her fever'd couch she lay.[44]

Pocahontas, too, momentarily revives to deliver a blessing to her son, as (in a clear echo) she presses "One long, long kiss on his bright brow" before dying.[45]

The close correspondence between these death scenes confirms that Sigourney had *The Forest Sanctuary* close at hand while she was composing "Pocahontas," but what resonates in the latter is the poet's centralization of the catastrophic *female* experience of exile. Driven from his home by persecution, the Spaniard is nonetheless autonomous in his search for sanctuary; though burdened by the heavy weight of nostalgia, he commands his own passage between and across continents. He and his son continue their journey after Leonor's death, their New World liberty a partial compensation for loss of their loved one and their home. In contrast, Pocahontas and Leonor reflect a global mobility that is both involuntary and lethal. Carried away from home by marital and maternal obligations as well as by political circumstance, they do not control their own passage. The Spaniard survives his displacement to wander in the New World. For Pocahontas, as for Leonor, exile equals death.

Postcolonial and feminist theorists have imagined exile and diaspora as sites for the production of subjectivity and agency. According to Homi K. Bhabha, global migrations produce the interstitial third space from which the marginalized may speak, a space characterized by, among other things, an "exilic poetics" that is "the place from which *something begins its presencing.*"[46] Julia Kristeva finds conditions productive of resistance in both the literal exile of the person displaced from home by political or social conditions and the figurative exile of woman alienated from hegemonic language, both of which can be "a form of dissidence."[47] To different degrees, the poems disrupt romantic, masculinist representations of global mobility that is autonomous, liberatory, and redemptive, suggesting that the exile's experience depends on the way he or she is situated within social structures of power. Sigourney expanded on Hemans's gendered representation of exile, underlined in the contrast between the Spaniard's experience and that of his wife, to centralize the suffering of the disempowered figured removed from her homeland. In so doing she laid the groundwork for a protest against the mass dislocations of indigenous people in the United States.

The Romance of Exile and the Reality of Indian Removal

Leonor succumbs to a lethal homesickness midway through *The Forest Sanctuary;* the rest of the poem follows her husband's exilic wanderings. So while Hemans acknowledged the effects of exile on the disempowered woman, she did so in a limited way, returning to a romantic representation of masculine mobility. She also papered over the violent repercussions of European transatlantic crossing. The New World forests the Spaniard encounters are conspicuously unoccupied, and native inhabitants are present only in the abstract: once in memory, as the speaker recalls his martyred friend rescuing him from hostile natives during the conquest of Peru; once in fantasy, when the speaker imagines an indigenous hunter blissfully ignorant of the oppressive Catholic regime across the sea. The absence of actual native people reproduces a fantasy of the New World as available for European possession, thereby masking the violence of conquest. Though he retreats to what he calls "the red hunter's land," the Spaniard readily claims this space as his own "bower of refuge."[48]

In contrast, by focusing entirely on the experience of an indigenous woman, a figure marginalized by race as well as gender, Sigourney refused the romantic fantasy of uncontested European conquest that Hemans presented. The conflicts between natives and colonists that Pocahontas attempts to mediate underline the violence of colonization. Despite the "loftier destiny" they bring to the New World, the poem represents the colonists as anything but heroic:

> [They are] dejected men, with disappointed frown,
> Spoil'd youths, the parents' darling and their dread,
> From castles in the air hurl'd ruthless down,
> The sea-bronzed mariner, the warrior brave,
> The keen gold-gatherer, grasping as the grave.[49]

For Sigourney, colonization was not a romantic adventure but a project fueled at least in part by corruption and greed. More strikingly, when she reconfigured Hemans's drama to tell an American story, she emphasized the unequal conditions and costs of global dislocation—for her heroine and for Native Americans in the poet's own day. The last six stanzas of "Pocahontas" propel the reader back in space and forward in time: back to Pocahontas's North American home, where her heartbroken father is to die without seeing his daughter again, and forward to the forced displacement of eastern tribes by the U.S. government under the auspices of the Indian Removal Act of 1830.

These additions depart from the baldly nationalistic versions of the Pocahontas story circulating in the antebellum period, but they are in keeping with the poet's political activism. Sigourney was a founder of an unprecedented campaign by hundreds of middle-class white women to halt removal. She distributed (and possibly helped to draft) Catharine Beecher's "Circular Addressed to the Benevolent Ladies of the U. States," a call for women to intervene on behalf of Native people.[50] She protested through poetry, as well. In "Remonstrance of the Creek Indians against Being Removed from Their Own Territory" (1827), the speaker describes the Creeks' deep love for their homeland and pleads, "Drive them not hence!"[51] In "The Cherokee Mother" (1831), a speaker rails against the whites who are forcing her and her family into exile.[52] "Indian Names" (1834) is the best known of Sigourney's political poems; its final stanzas, excised in a second version published four years later, decry the policy that created the Trail of Tears, that "caravan of woe."[53] The end of "Pocahontas" reiterates a sentiment Sigourney had been expressing for years: addressing Native Americans, the speaker declares, "I would ye were not, from your father's soil, / Track'd like the dun wolf."[54]

In fact, the poem's last stanzas directly connect Pocahontas's colonial displacement and death to the suffering of Native Americans victimized by removal in the nineteenth century. Here, private exile begins to take on public significance. Pocahontas's father's lonely death occasions the speaker's reflection on the suffering in generations that followed.

> A little time thou found'st, O pagan king,
>   A little space, to murmur and repine:
> Oh, bear a few brief months affliction's sting,
>   And gaze despondent o'er the billowy brine,

And then to the Great Spirit, dimly traced
Through cloud and tempest, and with fear embraced,
In doubt and mystery, thy breath resign;
And to thy scorn'd and perish'd people go,
From whose long-trampled dust our flowers and herbage grow.

Like the fallen leaves, those forest tribes have fled:
Deep 'neath the turf their rusted weapon lies;
No more their harvest lifts its golden head,
Nor from their shaft the stricken red-deer flies:
But from the far, far west, where holds, so hoarse,
The lonely Oregon, its rock-strewn course,
While old Pacific's sullen surge replies,
Are heard their exil'd murmurings deep and low,
Like one whose smitten soul departeth full of wo.[55]

In these stanzas, a Christian note of regret that Pocahontas's father dies "in doubt and mystery" gives way to a more resounding political message about the "scorn'd and perish'd" Native American people. The sorrows brought about by Pocahontas's displacement, her longing for home and her father's lonely death, serve as preview to the suffering of Native American exiles in Sigourney's own time. This temporal and geographical shift politicizes Sigourney's Pocahontas story. In exile, Hemans's Spaniard hears the voices of home, and Pocahontas hears the music of the waterfalls in her native land. As a witness to nineteenth-century removal, Sigourney's speaker hears the "exil'd murmurings" of an entire people. Where *The Forest Sanctuary* idealizes exile, "Pocahontas" makes it devastatingly concrete.

Exile, Diaspora, and National Memory

The shading of individual exile into diaspora and genocide anticipates postcolonial efforts to de-romanticize exile by connecting it to mass displacements. Nico Israel distinguishes between a modernist understanding of exile as a private experience entailing "a coherent subject or author and a more circumscribed, limited conception of place and home" and a postmodernist, postcolonial conception of diaspora as a public process of group dispersal that "troubles such notions of cultural dominance, location, and identity."[56] Edward Said argues that aestheticized representations of solitary exile distract us from political oppressions. In "Reflections on Exile," he asks, "Is it not true that the views of exile in literature . . . obscure what is truly horrendous: that exile is irremediably secular and unbearably historical; that it is produced by human beings for other human beings; and that, like death but without death's ultimate mercy, it has torn millions of people from the nourishment of tradition, family, and geography?"[57] Whereas many twentieth-century representations glorify the individual experience of the exiled artist, Said insists on contextualizing such experiences within the mass migrations that result from war, imperialism, and totalitarianism. "You must first set aside Joyce and Nabokov," he argues, "and think instead of the uncountable masses for whom UN agencies have been created. . . . To reflect on exiled Muslims from India, or Haitians in America, or Bikinians in Oceania, or Palestinians throughout the Arab world means that you must leave the modest refuge provided by subjectivity and resort instead to the abstractions of mass politics."[58] Setting celebrations of writers in exile against a catalogue of displaced peoples, Said argues for acknowledging, as he expresses it elsewhere, the "worldliness" of exile, its circumstantiality and historical contingency.[59]

The difficulty for Said is that stories of mass displacement are "almost by design irrecoverable."[60] Untold and untellable histories of diaspora get buried beneath aesthetically pleasing representations of solitary exile. Indeed, Said himself seems to lose sight of the displaced masses he describes; as Caren Kaplan argues in her critique of "Reflections on Exile," he tends to fall back into the modernist language of exile and authorship. "The relationship between the exile . . . and the ever-expanding numbers of displaced persons remains uneasy and unresolved" in the essay, Kaplan notes, as Said appears to be "torn between the multiply located identities that a term such as 'diaspora' makes possible and the meaningful structure of sentiments that attach themselves to his preferred term, 'exile.'"[61]

I draw attention to Said's difficulties reconciling concepts of exile and diaspora to illuminate a similar problem in the final stanzas of "Pocahontas." Having connected the heroine's transatlantic journey and death to the removal of thousands of Native Americans from their homelands, Sigourney used the end of the poem to consider the place of these two stories in American memory. These stanzas contrast the commemoration of Pocahontas underway in the antebellum period with the already irrecoverable history Native American diaspora.

> Forgotten race, farewell! Your haunts we tread,
> Our mighty rivers speak your words of yore,
> Our mountains wear them on their misty head,
> Our sounding cataracts hurl them to the shore;
> But on the lake your flashing oar is still,
> Hush'd is the hunter's cry on dale and hill,
> Your arrow stays the eagle's flight no more;
> And ye, like troubled shadows, sink to rest
> In unremember'd tombs, unpitied and unbless'd.
>
> The council-fires are quench'd, that erst so red
> Their midnight volume 'mid the groves entwined;
> King, stately chief, and warrior-host are dead,
> Nor remnant nor memorial left behind:
> But thou, O forest-princess, true of heart,
> When o'er our fathers waved destruction's dart
> Shalt in their children's loving hearts be shrined;
> Pure, lonely star, o'er dark oblivion's wave,
> It is not meet thy name should moulder in the grave.[62]

Like the dislocated masses Said describes, the vanished natives remain "unremember'd . . . unpitied and unblessed," their stories silenced and evidence of their existence erased. Only the memory of the mythic Pocahontas survives "dark oblivion's wave" to be enshrined in the hearts of the colonizers' descendants.

The contrast between the memorialization of Pocahontas and the disremembering of the displaced Native Americans who came after her suggests that Sigourney must have recognized the limitations of her poem's political project. Though she recast Hemans's narrative of exile in a way that politicized the processes of colonial dislocation, her effort to draw attention to the tragedy of removal through the well-rehearsed story of Pocahontas contended with romanticized representations already deeply engrained in American culture. The final stanzas of her poem implicitly articulate the poet's dilemma: the story of Pocahontas's tragic journey serves as a platform to protest the forced exodus of thousands of Native Americans from their homes, but the memorialization of this mythic figure threatens to eclipse their suffering.

Still, the revision of Hemans's romanticized exile reflects Sigourney's significant aesthetic and political ambitions. Reading "Pocahontas" against *The Forest Sanctuary* helps us to reconsider Sigourney in two crucial ways. First, it shows us that the American poet was more of an activist than has been generally acknowledged. She presented the story of Pocahontas not to contribute to an idealized history of colonization but to contest that history and decry ongoing injustice. Second, it calls attention to Sigourney's self-conscious engagement with the literary protocols she took up. The transatlantic traffic in poems, it turns out, was not as smooth and fluid as we might have imagined. Sigourney drew on Hemans's form, theme, and approach but challenged the British poet's romantic representation of colonial exile. The two poets gendered experiences of transnational crossing in surprising ways, positing a female attachment to place that calls into question universalizing narratives of heroic global mobility. Yet Sigourney's departures from Hemans's model—notably by recasting the exile as an indigenous woman whose experience prefaces Indian removal—allowed her to deconstruct established myths of displacement. As the American poet moved from Pocahontas's voluntary transatlantic journey to the Trail of Tears, exile lost its romantic burnish to reveal the human cost of conquest. With "Pocahontas," that is, Sigourney began to formulate a literary and political theory of exile. The poem makes possible an interrogation of exile as both trope and historical reality—and even, more broadly, a meditation on the politics of poetics.

As Sean Epstein-Corbin argues in chapter 5, Sigourney's "sentimental cosmopolitanism" and capacity for cross-cultural exchange were foundations for national self-knowledge, universal sympathy, and justice. Hers was a cosmopolitanism deeply rooted in the cause of reform. Indeed, though I have described the ways in which "Pocahontas" Americanizes Hemans's theme of exile, the poem is anything but parochial. Rather, it draws on Sigourney's sisterhood with the English poet to develop literary strategies that contest settler colonialism, sexism, and racism. In connecting the Spaniard, Leonora, and Pocahontas as suffering exiles, Sigourney worked to strengthen the bonds of common humanity across lines of gender, nationality, and race. At the same time, by reimagining the colonial encounter from the point of view of the colonized, she problematized established fantasies of European and Euro-American ascendancy. As she linked Pocahontas's displacement to that of Native Americans affected by removal, she called attention to a monumental injustice being erased from national memory. Finally, by adapting European literary conventions, she developed a sentimental poetry that attends to the staggering consequences of western patriarchy. Much more than a mere imitator, that is, Sigourney used her status as "the American Hemans" to stage interventions both literary and political.

NOTES

1. Samuel Kettell's *Specimens of American Poetry* (2 [1829]: 207) includes an early reference to Sigourney as "the American Hemans" (Gary Kelly, ed., *Lydia Sigourney: Selected Poetry and Prose* [Peterborough, Ont.: Broadview, 2008], 24).
2. Wendy Dasler Johnson, "Reviving Lydia Sigourney," *Romanticism on the Net* 29–30 (February–May 2003), http://www.erudit.org.
3. "Critical Notices: Mrs. Sigourney—Miss Gould—Mrs. Ellet," *Southern Literary Messenger* 2 (January 1836): 112. The review is unsigned, but Gordon S. Haight attributes it to Poe (*Mrs. Sigourney: The Sweet Singer of Hartford* [New Haven: Yale University Press, 1930], 79).
4. Lydia Sigourney, letter to Edgar Allan Poe, April 23, 1836, in Haight, *Mrs. Sigourney,* 83–84.
5. Haight, *Mrs. Sigourney,* 88.
6. Dasler Johnson, "Reviving Lydia Sigourney."
7. Eliza Richards, *Gender and the Poetics of Reception in Poe's Circle* (Cambridge: Cambridge University Press, 2004), 67.
8. Paula Bernat Bennett, *Poets in the Public Sphere: The Emancipatory Project of American Women's Poetry, 1800–1900* (Princeton: Princeton University Press, 2003), 59–60.
9. Bryan Sinche, "Lydia Sigourney's Sailors and the Limits of Sentiment," *Legacy* 29, no. 1 (2012): 64.
10. Tricia Lootens, "Hemans and Her American Heirs: Nineteenth-Century Women's Poetry and National Identity," in *Women's Poetry, Late Romantic to Late Victorian,* ed. Isobel Armstrong and Virginia Blain (New York: St. Martin's, 1999), 245. Lootens usefully shows how Sigourney modified Hemans's positions but does not argue that this amounts to deliberate revision, as I do here.
11. Cindy Weinstein, *Family, Kinship, and Sympathy in Nineteenth-Century America* (Cambridge: Cambridge University Press, 2004), 7.
12. Haight, *Mrs. Sigourney,* 119.
13. [Edgar Allan Poe], review, *Graham's Lady's and Gentleman's Magazine* 20 (January 1842): 72.
14. Lydia Sigourney, *Letters of Life* (New York: Appleton, 1866), 327.
15. Charlotte Sussman argues that *The Forest Sanctuary* challenges idealistic representations of migration circulating in Hemans's moment ("Epic, Exile, and the Global: Felicia Hemans's *The Forest Sanctuary,*" *Nineteenth-Century Literature* 65, no. 4 [2011]: 481–512). I suggest "Pocahontas" goes further, presenting exile as a personal and collective death.
16. "Mrs. Hemans's Poems," *North American Review* 24 (April 1827): 463.
17. Ibid., 457.

18. Sigourney, *Letters of Life,* 320.
19. Felicia Hemans, "Edith, a Tale of the Woods," in *Records of a Woman, with Other Poems* (Edinburgh: Blackwood, 1828), 69.
20. Lydia Sigourney, letter to Jane C. Sigourney, March 10, 1827, in Kelly, *Lydia Sigourney,* 308–10.
21. Mrs. [Lydia] Sigourney, "Essay on the Genius of Mrs. Hemans," in [Harriet Hughes], *Memoir of the Life and Writing of Felicia Hemans: By Her Sister* (New York: Francis, 1845), xviii.
22. Hemans likely drew the variant from Lord Byron's 1812 poem "And Thou Art Dead, as Young and Fair," though it appeared earlier elsewhere. On Byron's influence, see Susan Wolfson, "Hemans and the Romance of Byron," in *Felicia Hemans: Reimagining Poetry in the Nineteenth Century,* ed. Nanora Sweet and Julie Melnyk (New York: Palgrave, 2001), 155–80.
23. Sigourney, "Essay on the Genius of Mrs. Hemans," vi.
24. Laura Mandell, ed., *The Transatlantic Poetess,* special issue of *Romanticism on the Net* 29–30, (February–May 2003), http://www.erudit.org; Meredith McGill, ed., *The Traffic in Poems: Nineteenth-Century Poetry and Transatlantic Exchange* (New Brunswick, N.J.: Rutgers University Press, 2008).
25. Felicia Hemans, *The Forest Sanctuary, and Other Poems* (Boston: Hilliard, Gray, Little, and Wilkins, 1827), 87.
26. Mrs. L[ydia]. H[untley]. Sigourney, *Pocahontas, and Other Poems* (New York: Harper, 1841), 23.
27. Hemans, *The Forest Sanctuary,* 53.
28. Susan Wolfson, *Felicia Hemans: Selected Poems, Letters, Reception Materials* (Princeton: Princeton University Press, 2000), 268.
29. For historical descriptions of the kidnapping, see John Frost, *History of the United States; For the Use of Common Schools* (Philadelphia: Cowperthwait, 1839), 47; and George S. Hillard, *Life of and Adventures of Captain John Smith* (New York: Harper, 1839), 189. Hillard's text was one of Sigourney's sources (*Pocahontas,* 33). I am aware of one other antebellum literary work that represents the kidnapping: Robert Dale Owens, *Pocahontas: A Historical Drama in Five Acts* (New York: George Dearborn, 1837). On nineteenth-century representations of Pocahontas, see Robert S. Tilton, *Pocahontas: The Evolution of an American Narrative* (New York: Cambridge University Press, 1994); Frances Mossiker, *Pocahontas: The Life and Legend* (New York: Da Capo, 1996); and Ann Uhry Abrams, *The Pilgrims and Pocahontas: Rival Myths of American Origins* (Boulder, Co.: Westview, 1999).
30. Sigourney, *Pocahontas,* 23.
31. Hemans, *The Forest Sanctuary,* 6.
32. Sussman, "Epic, Exile, and the Global," 500.
33. Sigourney, *Pocahontas,* 24.
34. Hemans, *The Forest Sanctuary,* 67.
35. Ibid.
36. Ibid.
37. Ibid., 69.
38. Sigourney, *Pocahontas,* 26.
39. Hemans, *The Forest Sanctuary,* 3, 5.
40. Ibid., 9.
41. Sigourney, *Pocahontas,* 26.
42. Marcos Piason Natali, "History and the Politics of Nostalgia," *Iowa Journal of Cultural Studies* 5 (Fall 2004): 10.
43. Hemans, *The Forest Sanctuary,* 74, 79.
44. Sigourney, *Pocahontas,* 28.

45. Ibid., 30.
46. Homi K. Bhabha, *The Location of Culture* (New York: Routledge, 1994), 5.
47. Julia Kristeva, "A New Type of Intellectual: The Dissident," in *The Kristeva Reader,* ed. Toril Moi (New York: Columbia University Press, 1986), 298.
48. Hemans, *The Forest Sanctuary,* 87.
49. Sigourney, *Pocahontas,* 17.
50. On the women's antiremoval campaign, see Alisse Portnoy, *Their Right to Speak: Women's Activism in the Indian and Slave Debates* (Cambridge: Harvard University Press, 2005); and Susan Zaeske, *Signatures of Citizenship: Petitioning, Antislavery, and Women's Political Identity* (Chapel Hill: University of North Carolina Press, 2003). Cherokee women's antiremoval activism preceded white women's involvement; see Tiya Miles, "'Circular Reasoning': Recentering Cherokee Women in the Antiremoval Campaigns," *American Quarterly* 61 (June 2009): 221–43. Catharine Beecher describes Sigourney's participation in the early stages of the movement (*Educational Reminiscences and Suggestions* [New York: Ford, 1874], 62–63). On the authorship of the unsigned "Circular," see Mary Hershberger, "Mobilizing Women, Anticipating Abolition: The Struggle against Indian Removal in the 1830s," *Journal of American History* 86 (June 1999): 27.
51. [Lydia Sigourney], "Remonstrance of the Creek Indians Against Being Removed from Their Own Territory," in *Poems: By the Author of "Moral Pieces in Prose and Verse"* (Boston: Goodrich, 1827), 76.
52. Mrs. L[ydia]. H[untley]. Sigourney, "The Cherokee Mother," *Cherokee Phoenix, and Indians' Advocate,* March 12, 1831.
53. Lydia Sigourney, "Indian Names," in *Heath Anthology of American Literature,* ed. Paul Lauter, John Alberti, Mary Pat Brady, Jackson R. Bryer, King-Kok Cheung, Kirk Curnutt, Anne Goodwyn Jones, Richard Yarborough, James Kyung-Jin Lee, Wendy Martin, Quentin Miller, Bethany Schneider, Ivy T. Schweitzer, and Sandra A. Zagarell (Boston: Wadsworth, 2009), B:1696–98.
54. Sigourney, *Pocahontas,* 31.
55. Ibid.
56. Nico Israel, *Outlandish: Writing Between Exile and Diaspora* (Stanford: Stanford University Press, 2000), 3.
57. Edward Said, *Reflections on Exile and Other Essays* (Cambridge: Harvard University Press, 2000), 174.
58. Ibid., 175–76.
59. Edward Said, *The World, the Text, and the Critic* (Cambridge: Harvard University Press, 1984), 34.
60. Said, *Reflections on Exile and Other Essays,* 176.
61. Caren Kaplan, *Questions of Travel: Postmodern Discourses of Displacement* (Durham: Duke University Press, 1996), 120, 121.
62. Sigourney, *Pocahontas,* 32.

10

"SEVERAL SIGOURNEYS"

CIRCULATION, REPRINT CULTURE, AND SIGOURNEY'S EDUCATIONAL PROSE

Amy J. Lueck

In her now-famous essay "Reinventing Lydia Sigourney," Nina Baym argued that Sigourney's literary range "inevitably allows for the construction of several Sigourneys who are unknown to modern criticism."[1] Since 1990, when Baym revealed Sigourney as a student of history and a writer of historical prose, scholars have filled the gap she identified with a variety of Sigourneys, identifying her "generic plurality" as a means to "achieve multi-positionality as a woman poet," as Paula Bernat Bennett writes, and noting that Sigourney's wide-ranging oeuvre does not readily lend itself to a reading of the author as a sentimental poetess.[2] Subsequently, scholars like Bennett, Wendy Dasler Johnson, and Elizabeth Petrino have taken up the call to reinvent, reconsider, or, as Dasler Johnson strives to do, revive Sigourney as a complex poet worthy of scholarly consideration. But while such scholars acknowledge Sigourney's range of genres, few have focused on her prose. Even as they acknowledge it, they leave it, as Allison Giffen says, "all but overlooked."[3]

In this chapter, I fill this gap by focusing on the reinvention of Sigourney as an educator who used her prose to advance her educational causes. Many scholars have remarked on her educational program, and she herself was "admittedly always the teacher," identifying herself as "a schoolmistress and a literary woman."[4] For example, in chapter 12, Ricardo Miguel-Alfonso pays similar attention to Sigourney's didactic use of history and biography, which connects hers to the educational projects of Ralph Waldo Emerson and the other transcendentalists. In *From School to Salon,* Mary Loeffelholz offers perhaps the most extended attention to the centrality of schooling to Sigourney's writing and life. Loeffelholz suggests that we "consider the school as the common social location . . . of Sigourney's poetic and prose genres, inseparable from their matrix of republican ideas."[5] That is, she frames schooling and Sigourney's identity as a teacher—rather than the home and motherhood—as central to the writer's work "as a whole."[6] In her attention to the school, Loeffelholz raises a question that is central to my own essay: "Is the authority of the teacher modeled on that of the mother, or that of the mother on the teacher?" She answers, "For Lydia Sigourney, the role of the teacher came first, not just biographically but historically, ideologically, and almost, it seems ontologically."[7] I would add that, while Sigourney positioned herself in relation to domestic culture in her early work, she developed an increasingly professional authorial persona in relation to education that drew on the authority of mothers but was increasingly distanced from the home. In other words, she spoke to maternal teachers in her earlier essays; but by the late 1830s and 1840s, as the schoolroom became an accepted site of practice for women students and teachers, she increasingly intervened in conversations about formal, extra-domestic schooling. Further, in Sigourney's broad circulation of her educational essays, we can clearly trace the evolution of her ideas about education and gender and about herself as a woman educator, which changed as the cultural terrain around women's education shifted, particularly in regard to what Loeffelholz calls the emergence of the "domestic-tutelary regime," in ways she did not always control.[8]

Although critics have focused on Sigourney's role as a writer of educational narratives, they have yet to explore how the culture of reprinting has affected her development as a writer and a thinker.[9] Since her own time, she has been well known for actively republishing her work. Often sending the same work to multiple magazines, she then periodically gathered them together to be issued as a book.[10] An essay might appear in some half-dozen forms over the course of a decade, traversing from magazine print to book and back again. Many scholars have discussed Sigourney's recirculation of her work, sometimes disparagingly, as in the early assessments of scholars such as Gordon S. Haight (1930) and Ann Douglas Wood (1972).[11] But Sigourney was not unique in this way. Instead, as Meredith McGill argues in *American Literature and the Culture of Reprinting,* recirculation was a significant practice in nineteenth-century literary culture, which was characterized by "its exuberant understanding of culture as iteration and not origination."[12] In this context, editors constructed distinct Sigourneys for their own and their publications' purposes, and Sigourney revised her own self-presentation, adapting and responding to various reader demands. As Jennifer Putzi demonstrates in chapter 2, "the composition, circulation, and publication processes involved in the production of a . . . poem [may be] . . . collaborative." This collaborative process was central to Sigourney's production, shaping what Putzi calls her "stages and styles of authorship" over the course of her career. As a perhaps less intentional extension of this process, the reprinting of Sigourney's essays reflected both authorial decisions and a culture of circulation that outstripped authorial and editorial control.[13]

The changes that Sigourney and her editors made to her essays as they were reprinted over time gesture to and participate in the revision of cultural beliefs about who had the authority to speak on educational matters and on what grounds. Sigourney and other nineteenth-century women authors understood those limits well.[14] Appeals to home education and to the mother's domestic role were strategies to enlist women readers' interest in education, the plight of teachers, and the need for advanced education for women—and to build community among those readers. That is, when we study Sigourney's periodical prose, we can observe that maternal teaching and domesticity are invoked in the service of increased educational and teaching opportunities for women and may not have been wedded to the literally maternal and domestic.

The evolution of Sigourney's engagement with education aligned with both the nation's growing trend toward public schools and her professionalization as an author. Through an examination of Sigourney's personal and business letters, Melissa Ladd Teed traces the emergence of a professional teaching persona that was evident in the circulation of her prose. In the 1830s-era transition from the model of the "genteel amateur" to a "commercialized literary marketplace," Sigourney was an "overlooked but important architect."[15] To follow this evolution, I have analyzed Sigourney's educational essays, which originally appeared in journals such as the *Juvenile Miscellany* (1830), the *Ladies' Magazine and Literary Gazette* (1833), and *Godey's Lady's Book* (1840) and were reprinted in a wide range of journals, including the *Southern Literary Messenger* (1838) and the *Maine Farmer* (1836). Like Giffen, I have concluded that, though "much of her work is the product of a conservative sensibility," her investment in traditional domestic values and codes "is more complex than scholars have given her credit for."[16] By attending to the changes in her educational ideas across their various iterations, we can recognize the progressive nature of Sigourney's educational writing and the ways she used—and was used by—reprint culture.

Though I will move through these essays in rough chronology, I begin here in the middle, with Sigourney's 1837 introduction to the third edition of *Letters to Young Ladies,* which lays out some key terms that link her earlier and later engagements with education, just as the volume itself spanned that period across reprintings. In this introduction, she established the link between mothers and teachers as audiences for her educational prose. She acknowledged that "only a small portion are engaged in the departments of publick and systematick instruction" but argued that "the hearing of recitations, and the routine of scholastick discipline, are but parts of education. It is in the domestick sphere . . . that woman is inevitably a teacher."[17] By extending the definition of teaching, Sigourney extended the definition of teachers; and by including all mothers under the mantle of teachers, she was able to argue for women's advanced education: "Of what unspeakable importance, then, is *her* education, who gives lessons before any other instructor."[18] This appeal, of course, was not hers alone but a popular argument mobilized by Mary Wollstonecraft, Emma Willard, and other advocates of women's education.[19] Yet the logical arrangement of this early essay suggests that Sigourney was also using maternal teaching to foster among the larger population of mothers a sense of value for and solidarity with teachers, which she accomplished in part by her alignment of "parents, preceptors, or legislators" as the guardians of education.[20]

When she added this essay to the third edition of her book, Sigourney most likely understood that it would not be read exclusively by young women but also by their "preceptors, parents, and legislators." Thus, the essay takes the opportunity to enforce the importance of female education, demonstrating Sigourney's responsiveness to her own circulation patterns and her ability to use revisions to attend to multiple audiences with different readerly investments. Even as she constructed herself as a staid supporter of a separate sphere for women, her prose demonstrates that she participated in redefining that sphere across reprintings. In particular, she used the trope of motherhood (biological and figurative) to advocate for increased educational opportunities for girls in both learning and teaching by blurring the distinctions between mothers and teachers. Writing about this same passage, Loeffelholz notes, "The category 'mothers,' for Sigourney, is a subset of the category 'teachers,' the second, broader category identical with womanhood itself."[21] The extension of the logic of republican motherhood beyond the family was not a new phenomenon, but writers like Sigourney played a role in transforming this rhetorical move into a social shift.[22]

Sigourney's essay "Biography of an Infant" exemplifies the complicated effects of recirculation on her educational project and the extension of domestic teaching into extra-domestic spaces.[23] In that piece, written for and published in the March 1830 issue of the *Juvenile Miscellany*, she described a boy of two and a half years who evidenced "a degree of learning and intelligence, to which infancy has usually no pretensions."[24] He showed remarkable development in literacy, natural history, and geometry in his early years, but his premature death cut short his progress. At the end of the biographical account, Sigourney articulated what was often an unstated motivation for her prose sketches—to entertain children while teaching their parents: "This sketch which was commenced for the entertainment of youthful readers, seems to bear a moral for parents."[25] The moral, of course, is the importance of parents' early instruction of young children. As with many of her periodical and book publications, she designed this piece for multiple audiences (children and their parents) and multiple purposes (entertainment and modeling), yet all of these audiences and purposes were firmly located in the home.

A month later, Sigourney's article was reprinted, with significant changes, in the *Western Recorder* of Utica, New York, under the title "Infant School System." The editor noted that "it is not indeed said that the subject of this article was a *member* of the infant school. He probably was not. Yet the method which was pursued in unfolding his mind was precisely that which distinguishes the infant school system of instruction."[26] This version excised Sigourney's account of the young boy's death as well as her moral at the end, instead embedding the piece into an adjacent discussion about so-called infant schools for young children, which were usually organized outside the family home and which Sigourney had not mentioned in her original piece. Though publications such as the *Western Luminary* (of Lexington, Kentucky), the *Philadelphia Recorder*, and the *New York Observer* reprinted Sigourney's original essay, the changes in the *Western Recorder* were an early extension of Sigourney's theory for teaching reading outside the home, though Sigourney herself had not yet written about that extension. The situation exemplifies how reprint culture could outwit the vigilant literary management of authors like Sigourney, who was known for her cautious negotiation of the literary marketplace.[27]

Although the reprinting in the *Western Recorder* seems to have been beyond Sigourney's designs, even the original version of "Biography of an Infant," as published in the *Juvenile Miscellany,* was part of the conversation about extra-domestic schooling. At that time the magazine was edited by Lydia Maria Child, who had a distinct interest in promoting female educational opportunities and extending women's domestic instruction beyond the home. Sigourney's essay appeared in the company of articles such as "School Hours; Chapter Two. The Solar Microscope," in which female students discover the structures of a housefly's wing by examining it under a microscope in a classroom, and "Letter to a Sister," in which a schoolteacher encourages his sister to study chemistry and offers many facts about that science for the benefit of eavesdropping readers.[28] Thus, Sigourney's piece became part of a larger conversation about expanded educational opportunities and education reform, and the editor who decided on its placement suggested a connection between her domestic essay and formal schooling that later exchange editors picked up on and extended.

By examining these articles in their original context, we can see how Sigourney's project linked to the rhetorical and political work of the magazines in which she appeared. As Lorinda B. Cohoon has argued, children's periodicals like the *Juvenile Miscellany* allowed authors to draw on "the domestic sphere to meditate on public issues," for they "depicted women commenting on childhood citizenship and intervening in the educations of boys and sometimes girls."[29] Borrowing from the work of Gilles Deleuze and Félix Guattari, Cohoon frames children's literature as a "smooth nomad space" in which women authors could negotiate the "striated sedentary space" of political discourse and advocate for change.[30] Within the "smooth" space of children's publications such as the *Juvenile Miscellany,* authors like Sigourney directed the educational pursuits of both mothers and children. I identify a similar "smooth nomad space" in the reprinting and recirculation of Sigourney's work, whereby editors, often male, reframed and extended her ideas into more political and progressive contexts. Paul B. Ringel also discusses these subtle processes of cultural transformation, arguing that the key to success in the children's magazine industry was its ability to construct an editorial formula that could "monitor and adapt its appeals" in a "gradual and intermittent" process of shaping values in the face of "constantly changing relationships with the expanding market economy."[31] In other words, while many of Sigourney's essays use the domestic scene and women's responsibilities as their backdrop, essays like "Biography of an Infant," nominally directed at mothers in their domestic practice, moved readily into other educational debates because Sigourney's rhetorical project was ultimately reform-minded. She was looking forward toward advances in education rather than backward toward conserving the home, and the editorial formula of the magazines in which she was featured supported and extended this agenda.[32]

This point is exemplified by Sigourney's essay "On Domestic Industry: Adressed [*sic*] to Young Ladies," published in the *Ladies' Magazine and Literary Gazette* in 1833, in which she explicitly connected her domestic focus with her educational project. Turning from a catalogue of domestic activities that "combine amusement with utility," she "entreat[ed]" her young readers "to show that love of books is not inconsistent with what republican simplicity expects from his daughters, and that knowledge need be no hindrance to duty."[33] While the article's early paragraphs about sewing, knitting, spinning, and cooking assume a tone of casual advice and reflection, the final paragraphs transform suddenly into polemic, beginning with "It need not follow that a thorough knowledge of housekeeping is incompatible with intellectual tastes and attainments."[34] The structure of the piece reveals Sigourney's awareness of and anxiety about the claims of opponents who pitted the cultural value of the home against the extension of female education. Her autobiography expresses this same anxiety about her own professional activities: "It was my desire to bear a part in [the household] operations, and to prove that the years devoted to different pursuits had created neither indifference nor disqualification for domestic duty."[35] This fear was shared by women writers and women learners, who were both "unwelcome" in the dominant culture and therefore, as Dasler Johnson writes, "Always conscious of the eye of the beholder."[36] Sigourney's concern that young women might affirm the fears voiced by critics of women's education and writing by squandering their educations or dedicating themselves too thoroughly to their intellects at expense of the home appears too often in her work to overlook. It suggests (as Teed does) that Sigourney attended to the domestic scene strategically, at least partly anticipating a critical audience that would be averse to her educational project.

Sigourney's "Duty of Mothers," reprinted in the *Southern Literary Messenger* in 1838, shares this anxiety about hostile criticism and supports female education through appeals to the notion of republican motherhood that her southern audience may have found particularly persuasive, "repeatedly urging" young educated women to demonstrate "that by a participation in the blessings of education, you are made better in every domestic department, in every relative duty."[37] This message was reinforced by the magazine's publisher and editor, Thomas Willis White, who departed from the publication's rule of "leav[ing] our readers to form their own judgments upon the labors of our contributors, without comment or commendation from ourselves" with the hopes that "by so doing, it shall arrest the attention of our readers generally."[38] His editorial intervention relocated Sigourney's essay, pushing it toward formal school settings, perhaps in recognition of the larger educative project of her work. Indeed, the essay's placement in this particular journal already implies that it had a general audience beyond mothers, but White also explicitly recommended that female schools use Sigourney's essays as "chaste models of composition, or repositories of all that is pure in sentiment and sublime morals."[39] Importantly, however, this extension into the schoolroom was accomplished not by the writer but her editor.

The ease with which Sigourney's essays circulated across audiences and contexts suggests that her contemporaries, unlike modern readers, might not have seen her work as clearly gendered. This difference may have allowed the writer and her editors to reposition her arguments for various audiences. But some editorial interventions push her work more forcefully into alternative conversations. One such case involved her essay "Domestic Employments." As far as I can tell, it first appeared in the 1834 edition of *Letters to Young Ladies,* though it may have circulated in another form first. In 1836, however, it was repositioned by the following commentary in the *National Intelligencer* (commentary that was reprinted in the *Maine Farmer* and elsewhere):

> [Sigourney's essay] is addressed to her own sex. . . . The general conclusions apply, if possible, with more force to the opposite sex, upon whom the sterner duties of life depend. In softening and sweetening the duties of private life, are the obligations less binding on men than on women? The fact is, that it demands exactly the same amiable qualities in every member of a family, to make the domestic hearth the heaven of happiness.[40]

The essay is about preparing young middle-class women to earn a wage in the event of a reversal of fortune. Yet the editor's framing commentary alters the rhetorical context of the piece, undercutting its political tenor by changing the inflection of gender from feminine to masculine and thus redirecting it to men. By claiming that the essay's conclusions "apply, if possible, with more force to the opposite sex" (that is, to young men), the editor effectively reclaimed wage earning as a male domain.[41] Simultaneously, he extended the concluding lesson that "there is no need that domestic duties should preclude mental improvement or extinguish [the] mental enjoyment" of both young women and young men.

While Sigourney often wrote about domestic employments, contextualizing those writings in a network of circulation helps us to understand how her essays would have been received and repositioned to favor either her own or her editor's opinions about women's education. A pointed example is her essay "Maternal Effort," published in *Ladies' Garland and Family Wreath* in 1839. The piece, which tells the story of a family that learns to work after a reversal of fortune, opens with "It is the duty of mothers to instruct their daughters how to sustain reverses of fortune." Sigourney's preface and title provide a strong frame for interpreting the narrative, and they are followed by several paragraphs that pursue the importance of "active industry" in females.[42] In other versions, however, the essay does very different work. For instance, the version in the *Common School Journal*, published nine years later in 1848, excises the final paragraphs of the original essay, which pin the issue most clearly to women. Moreover, while the piece still begins with an emphasis on mothers' duty, either Sigourney or the editors retitled it as "The Father—An Instructive Sketch."[43] Another version, in the *Christian Observer* (1850), excises all framing commentary, leaving a narrative that emphasizes the actions of the family unit and the dangers of wealth. It, too, has a new title—"Don't Become Rich Again," a line drawn from the story.[44]

Though it is not clear if Sigourney oversaw those particular changes, similar shifts in other essays during the late 1830s and 1840s suggest that she may have been adapting her work to the changing culture and her own changing circumstances. For instance, as more young women began attending school during this period, the agenda of her essays shifted from advocating for advanced learning to supporting teachers and schools more specifically. Even if, as seems likely, she did not oversee the changes in the examples I cited earlier, those revisions would have shown her that the reading public was receptive to her as not only a maternal figure but also a professional teacher and author. As Loeffelholz argues, Sigourney "monitored her own reception and shifted her own self-construction as an author, including the field of her own interdependent literary genres, in response to a changing field of literary possibilities."[45] Teed reports that Sigourney's representative George Griffin even advised her in 1835 "to speed up her work on female education so that she would not be preempted," advice that hints at Sigourney's strong affiliation with this issue in the literary marketplace as well as the shifting terrain in which she engaged with it.[46]

Sigourney remained on the forefront of educational writing through the updating of her essays, whether or not those updates were to her credit (or even to her liking). Russ Castronovo notes that "form is a dynamic process, an ongoing adjustment to and engagement with social and historical content."[47] Put into conversation with reprint culture, the shifting form of each of Sigourney's essays demonstrates this insight. They adjust to and engage with social and historical content and context across each reprinting. In this way, acknowledgment of reprint culture confounds any straightforward reading of authorial control, distributing the author function across various unknown agents. Sigourney was swept along with the tides of circulation as much as she was directing them. Over time, though, she did adjust her rhetorical strategies to suit the changing rhetorical context.

Rather than arguing that mothers need education to teach their families, Sigourney's essays by the late 1830s were increasingly directed at teaching as a wage-earning activity, and her most common refrain became an appeal to "reverses of fortune."[48] In essays such as "Charity of Wages" (1838) and "Superficial Attainments" (1840), she drew a strong connection between education and women's ability to sustain themselves in poverty, highlighting teaching and learning in relation to extra-domestic economies, though she did not leave the powerful warrant of the home far behind. For example, in "Charity of Wages," published in the *Ladies' Companion,* education is depicted as enriching domestic economies when the daughter of an unfortunate family brings home a book that her female teacher has loaned her, which the daughter will read to her mother while she works.[49] As the daughter reads to the mother, she is reversing the domestic scene of instruction: now the daughter is the instructor, with the aid of her teacher's insight. Both the domestic economy and extra-domestic work of the schoolteacher and the students are validated in this narrative moment, which has become the inverse of what Sarah Robbins calls a "domestic literacy narrative."[50]

It is no coincidence that "Charity of Wages," hinging as it does on the increasingly important notion of women's labor after the financial crash of 1837, was reprinted by at least six periodicals.[51] Other essays, such as "Superficial Attainments," which appeared in the July 1840 issue of *Godey's Lady's Book,* similarly directed Sigourney's readers toward more serious study in the face of uncertain futures, admonishing them to "be studious to prepare yourselves, for every duty that may devolve upon you."[52] The audience, however, was not only the family that might face a reversal of fortune but also the wealthy family that might support education by advocating for fair wages for teachers and the establishment of schools to train students in the useful arts. True benevolence, she suggested, is in such training for future work. Positioning the discussion of women's wages in terms of middle-class women's benevolent activities is a prime example of how Sigourney invoked larger political and social concerns in her writing while remaining within the accepted norms of discourse for female authorship.[53]

The growing connection between education and the possibility of earning a wage de-centered the domestic economies that were so clearly tied to mothers and home learning in Sigourney's earlier essays, but a focus on the morality and importance of mothers remained a powerful strategy as Sigourney began to address teachers. While she was no longer speaking to or about mothers when she discussed teachers in her article "Primary Schools," published in *Godey's Lady's Book* in 1840, she made a case for the increased "honour" owed to teachers and relied on the trope of motherhood for its effect: "Teachers of primary schools! have you ever thought that the words which you utter to the little ones at your feet, the counsels which now they seem so lightly to regard, may grave themselves as with the point of a diamond, and go with their souls to the judgment of the Great Day? Have you not, indeed, a dignified vocation, standing as you do, next to the mother, and she next to God?"[54] This call to the teacher highlighted the connection Sigourney had made between mothers and teachers throughout her essay career, in which the female teacher, as moral guide and model, stood in for (and next to) the mother in an educational role that was nothing short of divinely directed. But significantly, this particular appeal was made to and on behalf of teachers themselves. In this way, the equivalency of mothers and teachers persisted but in the form of its own mirror image: whereas once mothers needed education because they were teachers, now teachers needed support and respect because they were like mothers.

Sigourney's mobilization of the tropes of family and motherhood increasingly enabled movement of the female body beyond the family home. More precisely, as Jessica Enoch argues, it enabled the movement of the school into the feminine sphere.[55] While this development can be read as an extension of women's sphere beyond the home, Enoch explains that the movement to accept women in the classroom was accomplished by bringing the realm of teaching within the privatized realm of the mother, "renovating" the nineteenth-century school "both discursively and materially, from a public, exposed, masculine space to an enclosed, private, and feminine space."[56] Indeed, we can see in essays like "Primary Schools" the evidence of this rhetorical move to renovate schools discursively by placing women and their associated morality at the center of the educational project through their relation to mothers.

Sigourney also sought to intervene in the material renovation of schools. During 1840, as she was composing "Primary Schools" for *Godey's Lady's Book,* she published "The Perception of the Beautiful" in the same journal. Exemplifying Enoch's claim about "renovating," this essay argues that the design of schoolhouses should "aim at somewhat of the taste and elegance of the parlour."[57] While her arguments were couched in material concerns about unhealthy structures and ventilation, Sigourney was also focused, as the title suggests, on designing schoolhouses that would cultivate students' perception and appreciation of beauty as an area of study and development, not merely as spatial ornament. In later versions in the *Common School Assistant* (1840) and the *Connecticut Common School Journal* (1840), Sigourney reframed the essay, foregrounding the issue of schoolroom design as an increasingly hot reform issue. Fifteen years later, a significantly abbreviated version circulated again in the *Connecticut Common School Journal* (1855) retitled this time as "The Beautiful and Tasteful in Education."[58]

The frequent changes in Sigourney's reprinted essays gesture to her concerns about reform but also to her vulnerability to the literary marketplace and reprint culture. While her educational project remained consistent in its attempt to align mothers and teachers for the benefit of advanced education, the function of motherhood as a signifier for her readers shifted as women's education became increasingly common. As Loeffelholz affirms, Sigourney lived and wrote through transitions in the literary cultural field, particularly in relation to cultures of schooling, and "shaped her career to them as they, in turn, took some of their form from her widely popular example."[59] In short, we cannot understand her educational and rhetorical project without considering the multiple genres in which she wrote and the audiences for whom she wrote as well as the ways in which her writings and her name circulated and took on meaning in the economies of literary exchange. Even as her essays (and sometimes her imaginative work) build on the established ground of domestic teaching, they reveal the complex discursive field into which Sigourney wrote, highlighting how editorial commentary, decisions, and placement framed the works' reception and shaped their effect. Because each essay inflects and is inflected by the conversation that occurs across the pages of a publication, the reprinting and recirculation of essays can extend and sometimes produce important shifts in that conversation. Examining her essays as they circulated across periodical venues provides insight into how Sigourney responded to and was received by the larger culture of publication and democratic discourse on the subject of education, placing her in the network of literary and cultural forces to which she belonged and that she so ably navigated, even if she did not always control them.

NOTES

1. Nina Baym, "Reinventing Lydia Sigourney," *American Literature* 62 (1990): 390.
2. Paula Bernat Bennett, "Was Sigourney a Poetess? The Aesthetics of Victorian Plentitude in Lydia Sigourney's Poetry," *Comparative American Studies* 5, no. 3 (2007): 274.
3. Allison Giffen, "Dutiful Daughters and Needy Fathers: Lydia Sigourney and Nineteenth-Century Popular Literature," *Women's Studies* 32 (2003): 261. Not everyone other than Giffen overlooks Sigourney's prose, though by and large scholars do not focus on it specifically or exclusively. On Sigourney's didactic stories, see Ken Parille, "'What Our Boys Are Reading': Lydia Sigourney, Francis Forrester, and Boyhood Literacy in Nineteenth-Century America," *Children's Literature Association Quarterly* 33 (Spring 2008): 4–25; and Sarah Robbins, *Managing Literacy, Mothering America: Women's Narratives on Reading and Writing in the Nineteenth Century* (Pittsburgh: University of Pittsburgh Press, 2004). On her histories, see Sandra A. Zagarell, "Expanding 'America': Lydia Sigourney's *Sketch of Connecticut*, Catharine Sedgwick's *Hope Leslie*," *Tulsa Studies in Women's Literature* 6, no. 2 (1987): 225–45; and Baym, "Reinventing Lydia Sigourney."
4. Barbara Downs Wojtusik, "Lydia Huntley Sigourney" in *Dictionary of Literary Biography: The American Renaissance in New England*, ed. Wesley T. Mott (Detroit: Gale, 2001), 243–92; Lydia Sigourney, *Letters of Life* (New York: Appleton, 1867), 268.

5. Mary Loeffelholz, *From School to Salon: Reading Nineteenth-Century American Women's Poetry* (Princeton: Princeton University Press, 2004), 36.
6. Ibid., 35.
7. Ibid., 36.
8. Ibid., 33.
9. Parille, "What Our Boys Are Reading"; Robbins, *Managing Literacy, Mothering America.*
10. Melissa Ladd Teed, "A Passion for Distinction: Lydia Huntley Sigourney and the Creation of Literary Reputation," *New England Quarterly* 71 (March 2004): 63.
11. Gordon S. Haight, *Mrs. Sigourney: The Sweet Singer of Hartford* (New Haven: Yale University Press, 1930); Ann Douglas Wood, "Mrs. Sigourney and the Sensibility of the Inner Space," *New England Quarterly* 45 (June 1972): 163–81. For an example of scholarship that does attend to different versions across reprintings, see Paula Bernat Bennett, "Emily Dickinson and Her Peers," in *A Companion to American Literature and Culture*, ed. Paul Lauter (Chichester, U.K.: Wiley-Blackwell, 2010), 307.
12. Meredith McGill, *American Literature and the Culture of Reprinting, 1834–1853* (Philadelphia: University of Pennsylvania Press, 2003), 4.
13. Sigourney was not alone in being subject to such shifting valuations. Tracing the literary reception and legacy of Frances Sargent Osgood, Mary G. DeJong demonstrates how an author's literary reputation intersects with those of other authors and with the shifting currency of terms like *woman poet* ("Her Fair Fame: The Reputation of Frances Sargent Osgood, Woman Poet," *Studies in the American Renaissance* [1987]: 266).
14. In discussing Sigourney's employment of "sentimental poetic conventions of her day," Elizabeth A. Petrino emphasizes her ability to "challenge political injustices" from "within the dominant rhetoric" ("Nineteenth-Century American Women's Poetry," in *The Cambridge Companion to Nineteenth-Century American Women's Writing*, ed. Dale M. Bauer and Philip Gould [Cambridge: Cambridge University Press, 2001], 128). The same insight can be gleaned from Sigourney's mobilization of tropes of femininity and domesticity, which served as a powerful rhetoric from within which to advocate change.
15. Teed, "A Passion for Distinction," 58.
16. Giffen, "Dutiful Daughters and Needy Fathers," 256.
17. Lydia Sigourney, *Letters to Young Ladies* (New York: Harper, 1837), 11. *Letters to Young Ladies* was originally published in 1833, without the introductory essay quoted here: "Address to the Guardians of Female Education." The essay was republished as "To the Guardians of Female Education," *Literary Emporium* 3/4 (September 1846): 265–68.
18. Sigourney, *Letters to Young Ladies,* 13.
19. Mary Wollstonecraft, *A Vindication of the Rights of Woman: With Strictures on Political and Moral Subjects* (Boston: Edes, 1792); Emma Willard, *An Address to the Public; particularly to the members of the Legislature of New-York, Proposing a Plan for Improving Female Education* (Middlebury, Vt.: Copeland, 1819).
20. Sigourney, *Letters to Young Ladies,* 15.
21. Loeffelholz, *From School to Salon,* 36.
22. On Sigourney's domestic literacy narratives and their appeals to republican motherhood, see Robbins, *Managing Literacy, Mothering America.*
23. Lydia Sigourney, "Biography of an Infant," *Juvenile Miscellany* 4 (March 1830): 40–50. It was quickly republished in the *Youth's Companion* 3 (March 1830): 166–67; and as "An Extraordinary Child" in both the *Western Luminary* 6 (April 1830): 164, and the *Philadelphia Recorder* 8 (April 1830): 4. All of my subsequent quotations refer to the *Juvenile Miscellany* version.
24. Sigourney, "Biography of an Infant," 48.
25. Ibid., 49.
26. Lydia Sigourney, "Infant School System," *Western Recorder* 7 (April 1830): 60.

27. Teed, "A Passion for Distinction," 61.
28. "School Hours; Chapter Two. The Solar Microscope," and "Letter to a Sister," *Juvenile Miscellany* 4 (March 1830): 13–25, 71–75.
29. Lorinda B. Cohoon, "'A Just, A Useful Part': Lydia Sigourney and Catharine Maria Sedgwick's Contributions to *The Juvenile Miscellany* and *The Youth's Companion*," in *Enterprising Youth: Social Values and Acculturation in Nineteenth-Century American Children,* ed. Monika Elbert (New York: Routledge, 2008), 3.
30. Ibid. Also see Gilles Deleuze and Félix Guattari, *A Thousand Plateaus* (New York: Semiotext(e), 1987).
31. Paul B. Ringel, *Commercializing Childhood: Children's Magazines, Urban Gentility, and the Ideal of the Consumer in the United States, 1823–1918* (Amherst: University of Massachusetts Press, 2015), 5.
32. The very choice of the prose form suggests a progressive agenda if we follow Russ Castronovo's argument that prose itself is "progressive." Recognizing "formal choices as emblematic of a deeper political concern for disseminating information and propagating opinions," he uses a charming analogy to explain the significance of the form: "If verse and prose were electoral candidates, verse would be the incumbent and prose would be the voice of change and new ideas." In this way, we are encouraged to read Sigourney's prose productions as forward-looking even in their mobilization of incumbent images of the home ("Poetry, Prose, and the Politics of Literary Form," in *A Companion to American Literary Studies,* ed. Caroline F. Alexander and Robert S. Levine [Chichester, U.K.: Blackwell, 2011], 20).
33. Lydia Sigourney, "On Domestic Industry: Adressed to Young Ladies," *Ladies' Magazine and Literary Gazette* 6 (July 1833): 292.
34. Ibid.
35. Sigourney, *Letters of Life,* 267–68.
36. Wendy Dasler Johnson, "Reviving Lydia Huntley Sigourney," *Transatlantic Poetess* 29–30 (February–March 2003): n.p. Also see Teed, "A Passion for Distinction."
37. Lydia Sigourney, "Duty of Mothers," *Southern Literary Messenger* 4 (December 1838): 787.
38. Ibid. On the journal-related relationship among Sigourney, White, and Edgar Allan Poe, see Robert D. Jacobs, "Campaign for a Southern Literature: The Southern Literary Messenger," *Southern Literary Journal* 2 (Fall 1969): 66–98.
39. Sigourney, "Duty of Mothers," 787.
40. Lydia Sigourney, "On Domestic Employments," *Maine Farmer* 4 (December 1836): 360.
41. Ibid.
42. Lydia Sigourney, "Maternal Effort," *Ladies' Garland and Family Wreath* 2 (January 1839): 153–54.
43. Lydia Sigourney, "The Father—An Instructive Sketch," *Common School Journal* 10 (September 1848): 268.
44. Lydia Sigourney, "Don't Become Rich Again," *Christian Observer* 29 (May 1850): 72.
45. Loeffelholz, *From School to Salon,* 36.
46. Teed, "A Passion for Distinction," 59.
47. Castronovo, "Poetry, Prose, and the Politics of Literary Form," 19.
48. Sigourney, "The Father—An Instructive Sketch," 268.
49. Lydia Sigourney, "The Charity of Wages," *Ladies' Companion* 12 (December 1838): 81.
50. Robbins, *Managing Literacy, Mothering America,* 2.
51. "Charity of Wages" was reprinted in the [New York] *Family Magazine* 6 (May 1839): 358; [Philadelphia] *Ladies' Garland and the Family Wreath* 2 (February 1839): 191; *Christian Register and Boston Observer* 18 (March 1839): 1; [Cincinnati] *Western Christian Advocate* 6 (June 1839): 28; [Lowell] *Ladies' Pearl* 2 (March 1842): 212; and [Philadelphia] *Friends' Weekly Intelligencer* 6 (March 1849): 5.
52. Lydia Sigourney, "Superficial Attainments," *Godey's Lady's Book* 21 (July 1840): 29.

53. Teed, "A Passion for Distinction." Also see Paula Bernat Bennett, who traces the role of sentimentalism in social reform efforts, particularly among "high sentimental difference feminists" such as Sigourney (*Poets in the Public Sphere: The Emancipatory Project of American Women's Poetry, 1800–1900* [Princeton: Princeton University Press, 2003], 51).
54. Lydia Sigourney, "Primary Schools," *Godey's Lady's Book* 5 (May 1840): 219.
55. Jessica Enoch, "A Woman's Place Is in the School: Rhetorics of Gendered Space in Nineteenth-Century America," *College English* 70, no. 3 (2008): 275–95.
56. Ibid., 276.
57. Lydia Sigourney, "The Perception of the Beautiful," *Godey's Lady's Book* 20 (January 1840): 9.
58. Lydia Sigourney, "On the Perception of the Beautiful," *Common School Assistant* 5 (March 1840): 35; Lydia Sigourney, "On the Perception of the Beautiful," *Connecticut Common School Journal* 2 (February 1840): 117; Lydia Sigourney, "The Beautiful and Tasteful in Education," *Connecticut Common School Journal* 2 (April 1855): 240.
59. Loeffelholz, *From School to Salon,* 33.

11

SIGOURNEY'S POETRY OF DEATH

Paul Lauter

Whereto answering, the sea,
Delaying not, hurrying not,
Whisper'd me through the night, and very plainly before daybreak,
Lisp'd to me the low and delicious word death,
And again death, death, death, death,
Hissing melodious, neither like the bird nor like my arous'd child's heart,
But edging near as privately for me rustling at my feet,
Creeping thence steadily up to my ears and laving me softly all over,
Death, death, death, death, death.

—Walt Whitman, "Out of the Cradle Endlessly Rocking"

It is hard to avoid death in the poetry of Lydia Sigourney. Then again, one might make the same statement about the poems of Edgar Allan Poe. In fact, probably a higher proportion of Poe's poems concern death, generally of a loved woman—for instance, "The Raven," "Annabel Lee," "Ulalume," "The City in the Sea." And then there is Whitman's death-obsessed boy in "Out of the Cradle Endlessly Rocking."[1] So what has made Sigourney's death works—and, until recently, her entire corpus—so obnoxious to contemporary taste? What do her death poems tell us about her work as a writer and the culture that her poetry both responded to and helped to shape? Most of all, how do Sigourney's death poems provide a lens through which to view not only the changes in how Americans experience death but also the changes in how we understand the parallel shift from an earlier world of imaginary rural virtue to our own metropolitan culture?

Let's begin with some particulars. A number of tropes and details characterize Sigourney's death poems. Death is often presented as a respite, a release from struggle, indeed a relief from the cares of a threatening, often dangerous world:

> Yet wrong we not that messenger
> Who gather'd back the breath,
> Calling him ruthless spoiler, stern,
> And fell destroyer, death?
> His touch was like the angel's
> Who comes at close of day
> To lull the willing flowers asleep
> Until the morning ray.[2]

Here and elsewhere in Sigourney's writings, death's touch is gentle and compassionate. Death is a long sleep that leads not to dissolution but to the triumph of immortality, in which "the pure of heart wake to eternal life." Sigourney was by no means alone in posing death in these terms. Alice Cary, for example, spoke this way of death in her conclusion to volume 2 of *Clovernook* (1853):

> All things are beautiful in their time. Even Death, whom the poets have for ages made hideous, painting him as a skeleton reaper, cutting down tender flowers and ripe grain, and binding them into bundles for his dark garner, heedless of tears and prayers, is sometimes clothed with the wings and the mercy of an angel . . . and how many, who have trembled with terror at his approach, have found the dearest rest in his embraces, as a frightened child has forgotten fear in wildest joy on discovering that some frightful being was only its mother, masqued for playing.[3]

But at the same time, and somewhat in contradiction to such comforting notions, Sigourney also presents death as a "woe," a "shuddering pathway," a "Dread hour." Speaking to a now-dead friend whose last word was "mother," she asks for an explanation:

> Fain would we hear thee tell,
> But ah!–the closing eye,
> The fluttering, moaning sigh,
> Speak forth the disembodied friend's farewell,

We toil to break the seal, with fruitless pain,
Time's fellowship is riven:—earth's question is in vain.[4]

Death often appears as a person in Sigourney poems, as, for example, in what is probably her most famous work on the subject, "Death of an Infant":

Death found strange beauty on that cherub brow,
And dash'd it out. There was a tint of rose
On cheek and lip;—he touch'd the veins with ice,
And the rose faded.—Forth from those blue eyes
There spoke a wishful tenderness,—a doubt
Whether to grieve or sleep, which Innocence
Alone can wear. With ruthless haste he bound
The silken fringes of their curtaining lids
For ever. There had been a murmuring sound
With which the babe would claim its mother's ear,
Charming her even to tears. The spoiler set
His seal of silence. But there beam'd a smile
So fix'd and holy from that marble brow,—
Death gazed and left it there;—he dared not steal
The signet-ring of heaven.[5]

According to the search engine of LION, the phrase "death of an infant" appears in twenty-seven poems, almost all from the late eighteenth and early nineteenth centuries, and almost all proposing that the infant is fortunate in having arisen to heaven before corruption and pain can set in. Most of these poems are dreadful, but that is not the case, I think, with Sigourney's poem, despite the conventional "tears," the "tint of rose," the "beamed," and the concluding "Heaven." Her success depends partly on her systematic and clever use of enjambment and related expressive tactics. For example, in line 2 finality is conveyed by the very abruptness of the phrase "And dash'd it out," particularly after the lyricism of line 1, "Death found strange beauty on that cherub brow." Similarly, the cadence of line 4, "And the rose faded," suggests irrevocability, especially after the continued smooth, even charming movement from lines 2 and 3, "There was a tint of rose / On cheek and lip." Lines 9, "For ever," and 12, "His seal of silence," show a similar tactical use of enjambment and abruptness of tempo. An enjambment (line 7: "which Innocence / Alone can wear.") also calls attention to the ambiguous quality of "Innocence": *only* innocence "can wear" or innocence *lonely* "can wear" such a look. Finally, the self-contained last line—"The signet-ring of heaven"—works by breaking away from the iambic pentameter in which the poem is primarily written into a rhythm that is not abrupt, as earlier, but settled, complete.

Sigourney portrays death here and elsewhere in her work as definitively male, threatening and intrusive. He "arose between" the lover and his bride ("Burial of the Young"); a "Spoiler Spirit," he trespasses "Within that blissful bower" to steal away the lady therein ("Sudden Death of a Lady"). In particular, death intrudes upon mother and child, the primary relationship at the emotional center of most Sigourney death poems (and many others). Usually, in her world, the child leaves the despairing mother behind, though sometimes the deserted consciousness is that of the child, abandoned by the demise of the parent. In either case, the poem offers a conventional religious consolation: mourn not, because, to use the phrasing of 1 Corinthians (54–56), "When the perishable has been clothed with the imperishable, and the mortal with immortality, then the saying that is written will come true: 'Death has been swallowed up in victory. Where, O death, is your victory? Where, O death, is your sting?" It is to this eschatological vision that the death poems point, and that, more than their Christian morality, distances them from most serious twenty-first-century critics of poetry. After all, we who read poetry for the pleasures of its language, form, and structure, and not particularly for its consolatory or moral functions, are among those least likely to take seriously the resonances of "Where, O death, is thy sting?" We are more inclined to share in the fun of the line from the musical *Oh! What a Lovely War* (1967): "Oh! Death, where is thy sting-a-ling-a-ling?" I write this not to criticize my colleagues or my own secular self but to begin pointing toward how Sigourney's relationship to her own audience both distances her from us yet intrigues us.

What are we to make of the effort to mitigate the sting of death, on the one hand, and the almost obsessive attraction to it, on the other? The contradiction between death seen as terror and death as release? The need to mourn and to be joyful? Before I try to answer those questions, I want to underline what distinguishes Sigourney's approach to death. Nineteenth-century poets dealt with the subject in markedly different ways from the way contemporary writer's approach it. In "Death Scene" (1854), Phoebe Cary, for example, focused on dying, as distinct from death:

Dying, still slowly dying,
  As the hours of night wore by,
She had lain since the light of sunset
  Was red on the evening sky,—

Till after the middle watches,
  As we softly near her trod,
When her soul from its prison fetters
  Was loosed by the hand of God.

. . . .

When we thought how with feet unshrinking
  She came to the Jordan's tide,
And, taking the hand of the Saviour,
  Went up on the heavenly side.[6]

While the religious sentiment is reasonably conventional, Cary evokes the experience of the watcher of the dead, whose faith is tested by the death of her friend and then strengthened. The weight of the poem lies with the experience of the observer, as in poems like "Entering Heaven," which ends "And at daybreak she had entered / On a better life than ours." Even a poem like her "The Life of Trial," which talks about the pain of a woman whose pathway is "choked up" with "sharp thorns," begins "I am glad her life is over."[7] In Phoebe Cary, as in the stories of her sister Alice, the observer is never absent. Our experience of the dying person is mediated by the observer's feelings and comments.

Emily Dickinson, by contrast, was more interested in the perception of the dying person, as in poems like "I felt a Funeral, in my Brain," "Because I could not stop for Death," and "I heard a Fly buzz—when I died—":

I heard a Fly buzz—when I died—
The Stillness in the Room
Was like the Stillness in the Air—
Between the Heaves of Storm—

The Eyes around—had wrung them dry—
And Breaths were gathering firm

For that last Onset—when the King
Be witnessed—in the Room—

I willed my Keepsakes—Signed away
What portion of me be
Assignable—and then it was
There interposed a Fly—

With Blue—uncertain stumbling Buzz—
Between the light—and me—
And then the Windows failed—and then
I could not see to see—[8]

Dickinson's gift lies in imagining what cannot be communicated: dying itself. In describing the fly, she captures the revolting physicality of dying and the distinctiveness of its every instance.

To understand the specific contradictions I noted as characterizing Sigourney's death poems, one needs to consider both biography and the differing experiences of death in the nineteenth century. Her success as a poet—and she certainly was successful in aesthetic terms as well as in social position and money—had in significant measure to do with her ability to write occasional verse responding to the emotional needs of her readers. Large families were more the norm, along with plagues such as cholera. Families had little understanding of disease and suffered more deaths, particularly of young children. Even in clean, comfortable homes infant mortality in the antebellum period was something like eighty to one hundred people per thousand. In poorer urban districts it would have been as high as three hundred people per thousand. As late as 1870 in Chicago, a "child had a 50% chance of reaching the age 5. . . . Today the odds are better than 98%."[9] According to another authority:

> In 1850, each male had a 2 percent chance of dying in the next year. By 2000, each male had a 1 percent chance of dying in the next year. Over this 150-year time span, the death rate was cut in half. . . . Medical technology has had its greatest impact to date in preventing infant mortality, especially between the ages of 1 to 4. In the year 1850, a young child in this age cohort had a 2.4 percent probability of dying in the next year. Today, the probability of dying in the next year for these children has been reduced from 2.4 percent to 0.04 percent. That's a phenomenal 60-fold reduction.[10]

So death was much more a presence then than now.

Moreover, death in the nineteenth century was a more immediate, indeed intimate, experience. Dying people were watched over by friends and relatives, and corpses were often laid out at home by those same relatives and friends. In rural areas home burial was hardly unusual, perhaps the rule, and graves were dug by those same closely connected folks. Death was not mediated by hospital, hospice, funeral home (as it's strangely called), undertaker (another wonderful euphemism) as it is for us. And while shootings, stabbings, outbreaks of cholera, and war were hardly absent from the lives of antebellum Americans, they were not part of an overwhelming visual culture of daily horror projected into our lives by internet media, television, and movies. For us, individual death has been placed at a distance. For nineteenth-century Americans who did not know the mass deaths of terrorism, the gun in the street, missiles in the air, bombs in the train, death remained personal, immediate—an unaccountable stranger, a stalker who could not be kept away when he chose to arrive. Perhaps that is why the distant yet too close Civil War struck many Americans' consciousness so profoundly. We do not, on the whole, experience death in ways that might be constructed metaphorically as the actions of some kind of person. The difference is marked by the rarity in twentieth-century verse of a phrase such as e. e. cummings's "how do you like your blue-eyed boy / Mister Death," in which part of the comedy of the line has to do with the impossible presumption of addressing such a special "person."[11] Poets may decline to be resigned, refuse to mourn, or "rage against the dying of the light," but Mister Death makes few personal appearances.[12] The material conditions of modern death are today experienced in the hospital, on the battlefield, on the beleaguered street corner; these do not lend themselves to personification.

In Sigourney, the hostile actions of death may, of course, through faith, be eased:

Love yields the grave its idol-trust,
   While the rent heart-strings bleed,
But Faith, whose pinion scorns the dust,
   Blames not the Spoiler's deed;
A new and tuneful lyre she hears,
   Where joys forever bloom,
And bids us through our blinding tears
   Write *blessed* on the tomb.[13]

The sentiment here is not markedly different from that in John Donne's "Death be not proud": "why swell'st thou then; / One short sleepe past, wee wake eternally, / And death shall be no more; death, thou shalt die." What separates Sigourney's poem from Donne's is style—and certain limits of propriety. Donne's speaker boldly challenges death—"Death be not proud"—a character consistently addressed and belittled within the poem: "poor death," "Thou art slave to Fate, Chance, kings, and desperate men, / And dost with poyson, warre, and sicknesse dwell."[14] Sigourney's poem "The Sudden Death of a Lady" consistently uses the image of death as one who rifles a "bower," but she cannot elaborate upon this suggestion of death as a malign masculine intruder. Instead, she chooses undeveloped and more conventional images of bleeding heartstrings and "blinding tears," a heaven of tuneful music and blooming joys. Style here, it seems to me, reflects not her own limits as an inventor but the consolatory functions of her verse for an orthodox audience: more than a hint of death as ravisher would disrupt such a purpose. Sigourney's professional aspirations to speak consolation to a wide audience—on which her standing and income depended—work against her bringing to visibility in her verse her doubts about and rather hostile reactions to the masculine—for instance, her husband and her publishers, about whom her letters are, to say the least, ironic. In March 1834, she wrote to George Griffin, a New York lawyer who had been of assistance to her in negotiating contracts: "As a body of men, I have feared the Publishers, ever since I have had anything to do with them. They seem to me wily & not liberal, neither disposed to be the natural allies of the authors, but rather to forage upon them."[15] If death is for her male—and he is—she will maintain an ambivalent attraction and repulsion toward him. Male publishers and even a husband are the inescapable, indeed obligatory accoutrements of a successful female poet; one accepts but doesn't necessarily *like* them, any more than one likes the specter of death. But to pursue the trope of death as masculine ravisher would be to place the poet and her speaker at grave odds with most of her audience, not to speak of her own sense of propriety.

These psychological issues are deeply connected with Sigourney's experience of American society as moving away from the possibility of a community of Christian rectitude, materialized in the world of the village. From her perspective, the village world remains the domain of life, whereas the city augurs the decline of values and ultimately, in a certain metaphorical sense, death. Sigourney is well aware that behind—or perhaps beneath—the village lie the Native Americans, victims of Christian hypocrisy and settler violence. The question is the direction in which the new nation might move. A basic test of America for her remains the treatment of Indians: as a poet and organizer, she worked to prevent Cherokee removal. With Catharine Beecher, she helped organize the 1829 "Ladies' Circular," a petition signed by thousands of women across the country, into a crucial tool for shaping antiremoval sentiment, especially in the religious community.[16]

Stephen Brandon and John Andrews argue that evangelical Christians like Sigourney and Jeremiah Evarts—who headed missionary activity directed toward Indians—saw removal as an evil in itself. But also they perceived it as symbolizing "forces such as the emerging marketplace economy, party politics, and individualism which, if left unchecked, would ultimately undermine" the specifically Christian community they believed to be central to maintaining civic morality in the American democracy.[17] Those promoting removal, from this perspective, not only violated the treaty and human rights of Indians but threatened American democracy itself. The failure of the antiremoval campaign, as well her audience's hostile sentiments toward Indians, clearly shows in Sigourney's Indian poems.[18] I believe that they also generate at least some of her apparent obsession with the omnipresence of death in her world. Particularly in the 1830s that world is sliding downward, if not literally toward death—though there is plenty of that associated with the Trail of Tears—certainly toward the loss of earlier values, toward what is imaged for Sigourney by the city. The language and imagery in her "Morning, in Rural and City Life" from her 1854 volume *The Western Home* express the discomforting, if not altogether fearsome, idea of the city that exists as the antithesis of her center and source of values, the village. Yet in "A Cottage Scene," the village one sees immediately "a cradle at a cottage door," an image of future life.[19] While in "The New-England Village" are preserved metaphors of

> good old times,
> When hospitality, with grasp sincere,
> Led to her board the unexpected guest,
> And, careless of the pomp of proud array
> Or servitude of menials, warm'd the heart
> To social joy.[20]

Now the village sustains only "hoarded memories, / Pleasant, yet mournful." Mournful because the "frank fellowship / Of simpler days" is disappearing before the "blight of ill," of change, of a new world wherein "a sigh of pain shall steal / O'er the pure mingling of congenial souls."[21] Sigourney's own language from "The New-England Village" expresses well the negative side of Jeffersonian ideas about the value—and values—of an agrarian republic, a set of ideas nicely deconstructed by a long line of American studies scholars but still very much alive in the rhetoric of today's politicians.

Against this nostalgic but powerful image of village purity and piety—that is, social and cultural homogeneity—lies the city. The details Sigourney in "Morning, in Rural and City Life," it seems to me, metaphorically represent not so much the city as the fears of those who see a whole way of life under assault:

> —Morn cometh to the cottage. Through its door
> Peep ruddy faces. Infant mirth awakes.
>
> . . . .
>
> Joy breathes around, while Health, with glowing lips
> And cheek embrowned, and industry with song
> Of jocund chorus, hail the King of Day.
>
> —Morn is upon the city. See, how slow
> Its ponderous limbs unfold. On arid sands
> Thus the gorged boa, from some dire repast,
> Uncoils his length.
>
> . . . .
>
> Flame hath fallen
> Wherewith to kindle incense; still man locks
> His bosom's altar. And doth sell for sleep,
> What Esau sold for pottage.
>
> . . . .
>
> —Hark! Life doth stir itself. The dray-horse strikes
> His clattering hoof, eyeing with quivering limb
> The tyrant-lash.
>
> . . . .
>
> Half-famished Penury from its vigil creeps,
> The money-seeker to his labour goes,
> Gaunt Avarice prowls—but where are Wealth and Power—
> The much-indebted, and the high-endowed?

> Count they heaven's gifts so carelessly, that Morn
> With glowing blush, may claim no gratitude?
> Lo! From their plentitude Disease hath sprung—
> The dire disease that ossifies the heart,
> And Luxury enchains them, when the soul
> With her fresh, waking pulse should worship God.[22]

It is not the rush and crowding of the city that Sigourney points to as she does in *Lucy Howard's Journal* (1858). Here, she emphasizes overindulgence, the accoutrements of slavery—lash and chains—sleep, silences, and disease—death, metaphorically. To be sure, that is partly a function of the moment she is dramatizing: dawn. But more, she is setting these qualities against those of the Christian agrarian community she could see, or wished to see, still a shadow presence in Hartford and in the other towns of her native Connecticut.

Hartford, we need to remember, was—and really still is—decidedly not a city on the model of New York, not even the 1850s New York of some 120,000 people. Nor was it really a Boston or Philadelphia. While it was no longer a village, neither was it during Sigourney's life yet a city in the pejorative sense she presents in "Morning." Prior to 1860 it had no police force, only a constable and citizen patrols. The Phoenix Insurance Company, a backbone of Hartford's main industry, had been founded in 1851 as the American Temperance Life Insurance Company to serve the needs of teetotalers. It was a place of social and cultural obligations: Daniel Wadsworth, Sigourney's patron, had founded his Athenaeum—museum, library, historical society—in 1842 to offer aesthetic pleasure and instruction to the citizenry. This citizenry, it should be said, had been pushing steadily at the ethnic, cultural, and religious boundaries that had largely defined Hartford since the seventeenth century. Manufacturing had begun to be a presence, along with trade. Eli Whitney had his plant there; in his factory the first large order for Colt revolvers was produced. Soon, of course, Sam Colt established his own striking factory building, with its blue and starry dome. And the city moved ever further from that world of "peaceful dwellings," "hallow'd temples" and "snowy spires" that Sigourney celebrated and tried to sustain in the nostalgia of her verse.[23]

An older way was dying, even as the new was becoming powerful enough to be born—to revise Matthew Arnold's formulation.[24] This may help us understand why so much of Sigourney's poetry is about death, especially the death of a child—that is, of the future, as in the cottage cradle. The parabola of Sigourney's life is in some powerful sense implicated in a dying world. If the death of innocence is a phenomenon of the village community, now passing, death as a metaphorical function of indulgence, of consumption, of bourgeois life itself is, of course, a metropolitan phenomenon.

And here I want to return to one of my initial questions about how Sigourney's poems lead us to think about why the city is so heavily on our cultural agenda today. One could cite Hamlin Garland's "Up the Coulée," or Willa Cather's "A Wagner Matinee" or Theodore Dreiser's *Sister Carrie,* among many other texts, to argue that it has always appeared and reappeared in the American schema. But I want to suggest that the tension between a self-defined, red-state countryside and an ambivalently fabricated blue-state metropolis is—as the reconstruction and whitening of post–Katrina New Orleans suggests—powerfully with us again. American politics is a politics of nostalgia and threat, again and again played out along the village-city axis we are trying to understand in one of its formative symbolic moments. In this respect, Sigourney leads us interestingly not only to the nineteenth but to the twenty-first century.

From this perspective, her death poems fit Freud's definition of *mourning:* a reaction "to the loss of some abstraction which has taken the place of one, such as one's country, liberty, an ideal, and so forth."[25] I introduce Freud here because his distinction between *mourning* and *melancholia* illuminates the very different psychological dynamics of Sigourney's death poems and those of Poe. David Kazanjian and David L. Eng write:

> In Freud's initial conception of melancholia, the past is neither fixed nor complete. Unlike mourning, in which the past is declared resolved, finished, and dead, in melancholia the past remains steadfastly alive in the present. By engaging in "countless separate struggles" with loss, melancholia may be said to constitute, as [Walter] Benjamin would describe it, an ongoing and open relationship with the past—bringing its ghosts and specters, its flaring and fleeting images, into the present.[26]

Thus, Poe's women, specters all, continue to live, like the raven itself, in the speaker's room, or he in theirs, as in "Annabel Lee."

For Sigourney, death exacts closure, as in "The Knell":

> Thou silent, changeless one,
> The seal is on thy virtues now no more,

Like ours to tremble in temptation's hour,
Perchance, to fall.[27]

Her problem, the problem of consolation, is to detach desire, libido, from the lost object, the "silent, changeless one." That can be accomplished within her specifically Christian framework only by an eschatological leap into the last of days. In contrast, for Poe's speakers, forever melancholic, the beloved object remains a daily torment—and a nightly pleasure, the continuing core of existence:

And so, all the night-tide, I lie down by the side
  Of my darling, my darling, my life and my bride,
  In the sepulcher there by the sea,
  In her tomb by the sounding sea.[28]

His poems testify to their continued, if imaginary, living, whereas Sigourney's poems aid in getting her real-life readers through the extinction of real loved ones.

One final comparison: The link between sex and death that one finds in the work of many male writers—among them, Poe—resembles the common adolescent male experience of the discovery of one's own death as coincident with, and in some degree a function of, the onset of sexuality. Poe dramatizes that again and again, perhaps most transparently in his story "Eleanora," in which the central female figure starts dying the moment passion enters into her previously Platonic relationship. The wages of sin, it is said, are death, and the image of sin—as Milton, for example, stages it in *Paradise Lost*—is sex. Many of Sigourney's death poems seem to me to shadow out a fear of male intrusion, at bottom a (sexual?) act that cuts off childhood and betrays female innocence. Is this a significant developmental fantasy of female adolescence in a patriarchal society, parallel to the adolescent masculine imaginary we encounter in Poe? However that might be, these are scary and deeply submerged fantasies, perhaps too scary for a public poet already troubled by a furious and failing husband and anxious about a demanding audience with deep suspicions about scribbling women.

Far better, then, to help initiate her audience's mourning rather than exciting its melancholia. The village memories are "Pleasant, yet mournful."[29] Writing both to and for those patrons, Sigourney is not free to indulge her fantasies, even if she were inclined to do so. But for us, mourning is the work of the hospice; fantasy is the work of the filmmaker, the painter, the poet. Alas, poor Lydia, she is not a fellow of infinite melancholic fantasy, like brother Edgar, but a woman of practical bent, earning her bread by focusing us *past* the grave, the skull, or the tomb by the sounding sea and, as she writes, toward "the feet of God," where the "strife of battle [is] o'er" and "where Death is a king no more."[30]

NOTES

1. Part of my concern in this essay is to understand Sigourney in relationship to her now better-known, and certainly better-appreciated, male contemporaries. That is particularly important because writers like Poe and Whitman have been central to our construction of ideas of nineteenth-century poetic value. A similar rationale, I think, helps inform Ricardo Miguel-Alfonso's essay in chapter 12. Ideas of value are, of course, also inflected by ideas of gender.
2. Lydia Sigourney, "Death of a Father," in *Pocahontas, and Other Poems* (New York: Harper, 1841), 126.
3. Alice Cary, "Conclusion," in *Clovernook, or Recollections of Our Neighborhood in the West,* 2nd series (New York: Redfield, 1853), 361.
4. Lydia Sigourney, "The Last Word of the Dying," in *Poems* (Philadelphia: Key and Biddle, 1834), 102.
5. Lydia Sigourney, "Death of an Infant," in *Landmark Anthologies: Specimens of American Poetry,* ed. Samuel Kettell (Boston: Goodrich, 1829), 2:209.
6. Alice Cary and Phoebe Cary, *The Poems of Alice and Phoebe Cary,* ed. Katharine Lee Bates (New York: Crowell, 1903), 387.
7. Phoebe Cary, *Poems and Parodies* (Boston: Ticknor, Reed, and Fields, 1854), 4, 10.
8. Emily Dickinson, "I heard a Fly buzz—when I died—," in *The Poems of Emily Dickinson,* ed. R. W. Franklin (Cambridge: Belknap Press of Harvard University Press, 1999), 265–66.
9. Ellen O'Brien and Lyle Benedict, *19th and 20th Century: Infant and Childhood Mortality* (Chicago: Chicago Department of Health, 1911–18), 270.
10. Robert A. Freitas, Jr., "Death Is an Outrage," lecture delivered at the fifth Alcor Conference on Extreme Life Extension, November 16, 2002, Newport Beach, Calif.
11. e. e. cummings, *Tulips and Chimneys* (New York: Liveright, 1923), 84.
12. Dylan Thomas, "Do Not Go Gentle into That Good Night," in *The Collected Poems of Dylan Thomas* (New York: New Directions, 1952), 122.
13. Lydia Sigourney, "The Sudden Death of a Lady," in *Poems,* 131.
14. John Donne, Holy Sonnet X, in *Donne's Poetry, Authoritative Texts, and Criticism,* ed. A. L. Clements (New York: Norton, 1966).
15. Lydia Sigourney, letter to George Griffin, March 11, 1834, in Melissa Ladd Teed, "A Passion for Distinction: Lydia Huntley Sigourney and the Creation of a Literary Reputation," *New England Quarterly* 77 (March 2004): 61.
16. Mary Hershberger, "Mobilizing Women, Anticipating Abolition: The Struggle Against Indian Removal," *Journal of American History* 86 (1999): 15–40.
17. Stephen Brandon, "Sacred Fires and Sovereign Rhetorics: Cherokee Literacy, Nationalism, and the Emergence of Professional Authorship in America" (Ph.D. diss., University of North Carolina, Greensboro, 2003), 200.

18. Paul Lauter, "Teaching Lydia Sigourney," in *Teaching Nineteenth-Century American Poetry,* ed. Paula Bernat Bennett, Karen Kilcup, and Philipp Schweighauser (New York: Modern Language Association, 2007), 109–24.
19. Lydia Sigourney, "A Cottage Scene," in *Poems,* 51.
20. Lydia Sigourney, "The New-England Village," in *Pocahontas,* 200.
21. Ibid., 201.
22. Lydia Sigourney, "Morning, in Rural and City Life," in *The Western Home, and Other Poems* (Philadelphia: Parry and McMillan, 1854), 136–38.
23. Sigourney, "The New-England Village," 201.
24. Matthew Arnold, "Stanzas from the Grande Chartreuse," in *The Poems of Matthew Arnold,* ed. Miriam Allott, 2nd ed. (London: Longman, 1979).
25. Sigmund Freud, "Mourning and Melancholia," in *The Standard Edition of the Complete Psychoanalytic Works of Sigmund Freud,* trans. and ed. James Strachey (London: Hogarth, 1957), 14:243.
26. David Kazanjian and David L. Eng, *Loss: The Politics of Mourning* (Berkeley: University of California Press, 2003), 3–4.
27. Lydia Sigourney, "The Knell," in *Poems,* 146.
28. Edgar Allan Poe, "Annabel Lee," in *The Complete Poems of Edgar Allan Poe,* ed. Thomas Ollive Mabbott (Urbana: University of Illinois Press, 2000), 468 ff.
29. Sigourney, "The New-England Village," 201,
30. Lydia Sigourney, "On the Death of a Mother, Soon after Her Infant Son," in *Poems,* 122.

12

TEACHING THROUGH OTHERS

SIGOURNEY, EMERSON, AND THE DIDACTIC CULTURE OF TRANSCENDENTALISM

Ricardo Miguel-Alfonso

> They are the living, they alone
> Whom we thus call *the dead.*
>
> —Lydia Sigourney, "The Holy Dead" (1849)

The transcendentalist movement never had a coherent educational theory—that is, an agreed-upon set of principles and rules that served as a foundation for its practical reforms. Even though the transformation of public education and the access of women to culture were among the transcendentalists' most urgent actions, their attempts often materialized as private rather than collective efforts. There were theorists of education, like Ralph Waldo Emerson, and practical educators, like Margaret Fuller and Lydia Sigourney, but the connection between them was sometimes unclear, given the gap between the ideals of the former and the social and educational conditions that the latter had to face. The most abstract, idealistic visions of education could not always be transformed into practical principles, so each educational reformer created his or her own way of teaching, which ran the gamut from the Socratic dialogues of Fuller and Bronson Alcott to Sigourney's more religiously inspired, imitative method. In addition, the educational level of nineteenth-century American audiences did not make it easy to apply—even to understand—such theoretical concepts. In a late essay on the subject, Emerson declared, "Whilst thus the world exists for the mind; whilst thus the man is ever invited inward into shining realms of knowledge and power by the shows of the world, which interpret to him the infinitude of his own consciousness, it becomes the office of a just education to awaken him to a knowledge of this fact."[1] To teach the infinitude of human consciousness and its symbolic presence in the occurrences of nature was, for him, a noble and necessary pursuit—perhaps the noblest—but for a public that often lacked both a proper philosophical formation and the time for reflection, it was barely comprehensible. The transcendentalist model of education, at least in this neo-Platonic form, required a training that only a continued practice of reading and interpretation could afford.

This does not mean that a real, useful education was unattainable or that it held a secondary role in the reforms of the American romantics. Education was a tool, and most of them acknowledged its transformational power. Thus, it comes as no surprise that many of these romantics, mostly women, devoted an important part of their lives to its practice. The democratic ideals of the Constitution could be fulfilled only through an egalitarian education that cultivated the image of men and women as equal members of society. As Wesley Mott has argued, the didactic impulse was pervasive in the writings of most transcendentalists and was conceived of as a necessary precondition not only for the intellectual formation of new generations but also, and more importantly, for the construction of a personal and public self-culture that would allow for the independence of thought and action that the new nation demanded.[2]

Writers such as Sigourney devoted their life to providing children (and, indirectly, adults) with such a pedagogical practice. From her early work as a teacher in Norwich and Hartford between 1811 and 1814, to her later books on the theory of education, some of them in the form of retrospectives and personal recollections, she strove to articulate an educational background that merged the theory provided by the lives of eminent men and women with the practice of self-culture that nineteenth-century thinkers from William Ellery Channing and Theodore Parker to Emerson and Fuller encouraged in their philosophical-educational works. In that sense, her connection to the transcendentalist movement is clear. Her method was relatively simple and consisted of readings of history and philosophy, on the one hand, and commentaries on passages of the Bible, on the other. These readings were neither random nor disconnected. Their aim was to reinforce a preexisting, even metaphysical, notion of goodness: religion provided the theory of moral knowledge; history and philosophy confirmed that theory. Chronologically, Sigourney's oeuvre constitutes an early version of transcendentalist culture's reformist aspirations. Although she continued to publish until the early 1860s, her first educational works appeared between 1815 in *Moral Pieces, in Prose and Verse* and 1838 in *Letters to Mothers,* and in these books she laid out the foundation of the vision and method that would complement the works of other transcendentalists. In them she anticipated a notion of teaching and learning that would resurface in the creators of the movement, notably Emerson, but also, and more importantly, in the efforts of educational activists such as Fuller and Elizabeth Peabody. In other words, the work of Lydia Sigourney helps us understand the formation and growth of transcendentalism, its didactic spirit, and its meaning for education.

In this chapter, I examine how this educational model parallels that of Emerson and other transcendentalists in its use of history and biography as didactic tools and, consequently, to what extent Sigourney was a precursor of certain romantic reformist practices. Her work as a whole differed from the works of some of these reformers in its strongly Christian inspiration, yet its relentless (quasi-Aristotelian) confidence in the powers of emulation as an educational instrument allows her to stand as an important antecedent of the didactic ambition of American transcendentalism. In short, it is essential to recover Sigourney's work and reinscribe it within the history of nineteenth-century American culture to understand better the development of education, women's rights, literary culture, and transcendentalism.

In her famous Boston conversations, a series of educational meetings held in the late 1830s, Fuller is reported (by Peabody) to have declared that poetry is "the ground of . . . the true art of life; it being not merely truth, not merely good, but the beauty which integrates both."[3] This is a typically romantic idea, to be sure, similar to Henry David Thoreau's claim in *Walden* that "to affect the quality of the day . . . is the highest of arts."[4] To "affect the quality of the day," in the sense of transforming private and public life, was one of the underlying tenets of romantic philosophy and politics; and it seemed particularly pertinent in the antebellum years, when social and political conflicts—including the state of education—were abundant and pressing in both Europe and the United States. The possibility of regarding one's personal life as a beautiful object that could be shaped, refined, and continually renovated remained one of the aesthetic and ethical principles of romanticism. In this view, art—and poetry, in particular—could serve as a mediator between the private and public spheres, mainly by imaginatively re-creating situations that demanded a degree of responsiveness from the audience. In other words, by contemplating the lives and contexts of others, whether real or imagined, readers could reshape their beliefs and transform their response to actual situations. Art, in this view, was an instrument of self-transformation that, if universally understood, had the potential of changing a society's collective beliefs.

The best example of this vision can be found in the work of the German philosopher and poet Friedrich Schiller. His *Letters on the Aesthetic Education of Man* argues that only through self-culture and education can human beings attempt to achieve freedom and, as a consequence, social justice. Freedom and reason, Schiller claimed, are the foundation of a balanced and egalitarian individual and social life. In particular, reason has the power of "transforming the work of blind compulsion into a work of free choice, and of elevating physical necessity into moral necessity."[5] In more abstract terms, once this work has been accomplished, an ideal self should be revealed that exists in every human being and is the basis of a harmonious existence. A person's task is therefore to remain, "through all his changing manifestations, in harmony with the unchanging unity of this ideal."[6] This ideal self can come into view in different ways, but, Schiller argued, we can best contemplate and scrutinize it through art because artists can more easily get rid of the material necessities of existence and work on abstract models of personhood. Artworks, like science, "rejoice in absolute immunity from human arbitrariness" and thereby must aspire to "produce the Ideal out of the union of what is possible with what is necessary."[7] Or, as he wrote in his poem "The Artists," humanity progresses "through Beauty, to the land where Knowledge lies."[8] This ideal of wisdom through art is a moral model that transcends time and place because it unites what is necessary to do with what we can actually do, thereby confronting what is vital to achieve with what we can actually attain. In other words, it is a way of knowing and articulating the range of human possibilities starting from its necessities. The ideal shows the path of change and reform by presenting images of what human beings can become.

Fuller is probably the best representative of the American reception of Schiller. She not only read and translated the works of Johann Wolfgang von Goethe, Schiller's close friend and intellectual companion, but also assumed some of the most important philosophical principles of his poetics and his politics. In particular, she relied on the idea of aesthetic education that Schiller developed in his famous series of letters. In *Women in the Nineteenth Century* and other works, Fuller attempted to offer a vision of education as suitable and necessary for both sexes and, more generally, a conception of art as a practical refutation of the socially accepted discontinuity between them. Reading and the criticism of literary works provide insights into not only the beliefs and values established (and sometimes perpetuated) in the act of writing but also certain strategies and mechanisms of understanding that transcend gender and class. In other words, aesthetic education offers a set of symbolic, ideal selves that embody the best in each of the sexes and symbolizes the hope for a different future.

Fuller was not the only one to be influenced by German aesthetic thinking. In a tone reminiscent of Schiller's, Peabody claimed in the introduction to her *Aesthetic Papers* that "the 'aesthetic element' . . . [is] a component and indivisible part in all human creations which are not mere works of necessity; in other words, which are based on idea, as distinguished from appetite."[9] Using a literary metaphor to comment on the different natures of man and woman, Madame de Staël argued that "women endeavour to set themselves out like a romance; men like a history."[10] Peabody voiced a distinction that Fuller had already elaborated on: as Peabody reported, the latter had urged her readers to "cling to the truth that poesy was the natural life of the soul; and never yield inwardly to the common notion that poesy was a luxury, . . . but maintain in word and life that prose carried the soul out of its track."[11] Similarly, Julia Ward Howe repeated decades later that, "as education is enlarged, as freedom becomes more general and entire, the agreement of mankind becomes greater in the objects to be attained for the promotion of their best interests."[12]

Two main ideals underlie this attempt at self-cultivation through art. First, as I have pointed out, the cultivation of a beautiful self is both a private effort at perfectionism and a means of achieving the same effect at a public level. Second, that beauty necessarily leads to freedom and moral virtue. This redemptive purpose was shared by most romantics, including Sigourney, though it had its contradictions and limitations. The contrast between the ideal and the real was often seen as an obstacle rather than as a stimulus for improvement—an obstacle that women themselves sometimes accepted as a natural cause for their public invisibility. For women in nineteenth-century American culture, the constraints of reality were the result of a set of beliefs that often included a male-dominated ideology, a religious inflexibility thinly disguised as holiness, and sometimes women's own complicity with their accepted role as a central pillar of the domestic world.[13] One way to escape that contradiction, and a way that Sigourney assumed as her personal and public project, was to instruct women and make them aware of their potential as members of the community beyond the walls of their daily lives. Sigourney attempted to expand women's education so that it would embrace intellectual disciplines such as art, history, mythology, or philosophy. If, for Fuller, art provided women with a glimpse into their practical potential as social beings, for Sigourney this role was played by history and biography. Yet the ultimate objective of education was both personal and social, or, in Tiffany Wayne's words, "to free the very idea of 'Woman' from public discourse and popular culture by encouraging women to pursue diverse individualized *selves,* including pursuit of what each determined as her true vocation in life."[14] This new self derived mostly from the contemplation and emulation of historical characters. Emerson had already provided the basis of this imitative education in his 1835 lectures on biography. Sigourney, unlike Emerson, did not alter her conviction that emulation of great characters was the most efficient educational instrument for children. In her view, the piety of these characters made them solid, worthy, existential models not only in childhood but throughout one's life.

"Every line in his biography might be read to the human race with wholesome effect," Emerson said of Michelangelo in one of his early lectures on biography.[15] Such a statement will not surprise anyone because the idea of individual genius and its representative value figured prominently in his philosophy from its earliest stages and is a central principle of transcendentalist philosophy in general. Emerson placed great confidence in the subject as the source and objective of both knowledge and action. The most perceptive and active subject (who, in his work, appears in different disguises, such as the scholar, the visionary, and the genius) was for him the center of social life, the realization of the highest potential that is latent in every human being. The creative and regenerative power of certain individuals makes them stand as symbols of our common humanity. The great geniuses of history—literary, political, religious—change the course of progress by multiplying the potential of the whole social body and shifting our angle of perception and our understanding of their disciplines or arts. "An institution," Emerson famously reminded us in his essay "Self-Reliance," "is the lengthened shadow of one man."[16]

However, Emerson's individualism was not confined to a personal and subjective vision of reality to be imposed on others or to become dogmatic; rather, it was mainly intended to create social bonds and provide some common benefit. Even though he frequently spoke of the relation between genius and society in vague and abstract terms, he believed that the influence of eminent personalities starts at the personal level and is communicated individually. The relation of the genius to his society is something like an act of contagion, one that spreads until it becomes institutionalized and is ultimately sanctified in the eyes of his or her public. Abraham Lincoln for the Americans, William Shakespeare for the British, Miguel de Cervantes for the Spanish: all are symbols of the values, virtues, ideologies, or artistic expressions of an age but also of humanity, to such an extent that they have become national and universal icons. These "lenses through which we read our minds" are "constructive, fertile, magnetic, inundating armies with [their] purpose, which is thus executed."[17] The public plays the role of vehicle to disseminate moral behavior and our common heritage, a dissemination that constitutes the aim of biography. As a civil body, humanity is the medium of the work of genius. As an ethical ideal, it is its ultimate end. Understood in this way, the relation between the genius and the public is two-way. We tend to personalize certain virtues in what Emerson called *representative men* by seeing in them their practical incarnation; yet these men make those virtues available to everybody through their beautiful example—that is, they socialize them. Each one of them incarnates a universal virtue that is independent from time and place. Emerson's view of history and progress was, in this sense, hagiographical.

This is why it is crucial that the lives of great men (the lives of the *dead* as Sigourney insists) should always have some "wholesome effect" on readers. Geniuses have to be influential and contribute to the moral progress of society. This was an aim of Emerson's general philosophy and of his views about art and biography. Especially in his younger years, his thinking relied heavily on the idea that the individual was able to transform the world and the lives of others, turning them into beautiful objects for contemplation. We can call this concept of individualism *aesthetic* in the sense that it creates a version of the subject as a transparent medium that contemplates the world in a mystical way, constructing the everyday experience as a process of achieving harmony with nature and therefore making personal expression inseparable from the perception of reality. The world is, in this sense, a product of the individual's mind. The Emersonian genius may not be a literary writer or an artist, but his or her vision of the world is aesthetic. This applies to both the poet-genius and the reader. Regarding objects as beautiful or as creating beauty, even if only in texts, was the basis of Emerson's ideas about thinking and reading. His philosophy was, in this sense, panpoetic.

A quick look at Emerson's work reveals how much he relied on the influence of other minds for his own philosophy, including Plato's, Shakespeare's, Goethe's, and the mystics'. In many ways, he considered himself to be the continuation and perfection of the tradition before him, but in an American style. In this sense, biography emerged as the most didactic kind of writing, often more than philosophy itself, insofar as it provided the example for others to follow, the vision of a beautiful life and a beautiful work. As I have discussed, he also saw biography as the most suitable way to create spiritual cohesion in society because the example set in biographical texts is universal. No distinction of time, place, gender, or social class is a barrier for the work of genius, whose chief value, not to be surpassed by any other social agent or institution, lies in contributing to the advance of what Emerson called "the constant mind of man."[18]

Emerson's early lectures followed the traditional, descriptive model of biography. They usually began as narrative accounts of eminent subjects and the incidents of their lives but soon expanded to reach a general, universal meaning for the reader. Emerson tried to keep a delicate balance between the materials of these lives and their significance, but the latter seemed to have been the most important in the end. The lectures opened as historical accounts (especially in the cases of Michelangelo and Martin Luther) and then were transfigured into moral tales. In most cases, they progressed from purely anecdotic facts to the figure's momentous contribution to human life, understood as a process of unfolding certain virtues and making them available to the community.

The moral element in these early biographies lies not only in the portrayal of exemplary lives. That is the purely representational side of the genre. What most interested Emerson is the extent to which a genius can overcome the human limitations that nature imposes on humanity—or, at least, those limitations that the human being thinks are imposed by nature. These limitations vary from one generation to the next, and paradoxically they are created by each genius. For instance, the world was disordered until Plato provided it with a new organization, but this organization would (in time) limit human beings until another mind, such as Michelangelo's, Shakespeare's, John Milton's, Emanuel Swedenborg's, or Immanuel Kant's, could provide a different, renewed order. Instead of continuous progress, history advances by means of dramatic changes. Shakespeare, for instance, was capable of subordinating nature to expression, while Edmund Burke provided new associations and harmonies to the disordered facts of nature.[19] Thus, geniuses provide the highest example of a beautiful existence while also surpassing the work of even the greatest poets. The poet may be able to name the order of nature, but the geniuses in Emerson's early biographies created that order. In other words, the poet, as visionary and receiver, expresses what the genius builds.[20] In Emerson's early theory there is never a sense of spiritual discontinuity or inconsistency among the historical ages, of which biographies serve as a record.

In this sense, biography works as an aesthetic and a moral text, idealizing the subject and turning that life into a model of common humanity and universal interest. Biography is the witness of progress and shows the way toward more improvement. To be aesthetically and ethically useful, the subject's life has to be perceived as beautiful, honorable, and therefore worthy of imitation. Using Michelangelo as an example, Emerson's lectures remind us that the aim of genius is "Beauty in the largest sense, Beauty inward and outward, comprehending grandeur as a part, and reaching to Goodness as its soul."[21] Of Milton they say that "the old eternal goodness finds a home in his breast, and for once shows itself beautiful."[22] Understood in this way, biography affords the reader a vision of perfectionism—that is, the gradual approach to the ideal (aesthetically educated) self postulated in theory by Emerson and especially Fuller.

In Emerson's view, so overwhelming is the moral influence of the genius's exemplary life that, in the end, no account of that existence seems to be wholly satisfactory. A mysterious aura of intractability surrounds the figure. For example, "Shakespeare we cannot account for, no history, no 'life & times' solves the insoluble problem. . . . And so is Genius ever total & not mechanically composable."[23] Even biography is a poor instrument when confronted with human life. Facts, dates, events—including their interpretation—cannot ultimately convey genius. It is an experience that cannot be explained. So in the end, biography is a mimetic kind of writing whose enlightening character remains in doubt. In spite of his complete reliance on the figures of the past, Emerson retained a certain tendency to mistrust the genius. The same early lectures that celebrated the power of example in life also reiterated that "there are few lives of eminent men that are harmonious."[24] For Emerson, the idolatry of eminent people seemed to be ultimately undeserved. They did not satisfy him as being wholly representative. "There are," he said, "few [lives] that furnish in all the facts an image corresponding with their fame."[25] This is why he urged his readers not to become Shakespeares or Platos but to translate their visions and adapt them to the reality of a new country.[26]

Few critics have established a connection between Sigourney and the culture of transcendentalism, not even in the field of educational reform.[27] Looking at the vast critical literature on the transcendentalist circle, we might note that its main figures (and most of its followers) were not even aware of her existence. Perhaps because a number of her important works were published before several of the masterpieces of transcendentalism appeared (notably, Emerson's 1836 *Nature*), she has not been associated with its central figures, even though her published work sometimes appeared alongside that of transcendentalist writers such as Emerson and Thoreau.[28] Nevertheless, I argue that she anticipated some of the theoretical principles of education that they and other romantic reformers would employ later, despite the differences between them. (Sigourney, for instance, remained an idealist, far from the more pragmatic character of Emerson in the early 1840s and onward.)

In one of the most important re-introductions to Sigourney's work from the 1990s, Nina Baym argues that, along with the poet, there is "Sigourney the preceptress, . . . [in whose] conversational works she assumes the persona of trusted sisterly or motherly guide . . . in a home space at once within and apart from the larger social body."[29] In the introduction to her *Evening Readings in History*, for example, Sigourney claimed that "History is useful to the young mind, by enriching it with knowledge, and furnishing it with subjects of thought. By judicious instruction it may convey those lessons to the heart, which confirm goodness, and stamp vice with abhorrence."[30] History *confirms* what seems to be a natural habit in people toward goodness and away from corruption. This supposedly natural tendency is to be guided by the educator, whose most efficient instrument is the use of examples. Therefore, the study of historical figures is an informative and moral endeavor at the same time, intended to guard "against the blindness of affection, the lassitude of indolence, and the enervating example of modern indulgence."[31] Sigourney compared the salutary effect of reading history and biography with the reading of novels, which she saw as "extremely injurious in a variety of ways" because fiction "has the worst possible effects upon the mind, by unfitting it for every other kind of intellectual enjoyment."[32]

Her method was not a passive one, and her use of examples was not intended to foster sheer contemplation and emulation. She desired a certain sympathy to emerge that would move the reader to *want* to follow the example. In her view, the experience of reading is not purely informative but formative inasmuch as it *moves* to action. It is ethical rather than technical, productive rather than reproductive. In a rather different context, this notion would emerge again in Thoreau's idea that "we do not learn by inference and deduction, and the application of mathematics to philosophy, but by direct intercourse and sympathy."[33]

Whereas Emerson emphasized the value of biography for education and civic life, Sigourney stressed the religious value and moral commitment of the characters she chose for her several biographical and historical books. Her interest was not so much the great deeds or intellectual achievements of these characters but their endurance in times of despair, for she believed that only in dire circumstances are the faith and fortitude of a person put to the test. As a token of what greatness is, Sigourney emphasized the effort and determination of maintaining faith in the face of adversity. Rather than extolling the creation of a new cosmogony or the refinement of literary style, as Emerson had done in his lectures and essays on Plato and Milton, she chose to focus on the religious convictions of her exemplary characters. In this sense, she practiced a religious-idealist education that, rather than being at odds with Emerson's and Thoreau's visions of didacticism, complements them by adding a Christian dimension. In this respect, there was no contradiction between the ideas of Sigourney and those of many of her fellow transcendentalists. All desired to fulfill the transcendental element in their philosophy, which could be attained only by giving it an ultimately religious meaning.

Sigourney, though, differed from the Emersonian model of emulation in another respect. Rather than providing models for the expansion of personality and the creation of a new national character, her historical figures taught lessons in self-control and restraint, especially about resisting the temptation of ceasing to believe and thus falling into the hands of radical skepticism. She also worked to reinforce the faith of her readers as they turned their lives into paths toward virtue:

> To those who may contemplate these examples, the question is submitted, whether that religion is not worthy of persevering search, of ardent prayer,—which can render the illusions of prosperity harmless, and the pains of sorrow salutary,—make life's pilgrimage a scene of virtue, and beautify death as an angel of repose,—exchange the coveted and perishing goods of time for an eternal heritage in the heavens. And to the young,—to whose perusal these pages are particularly and affectionately dedicated,—do they not offer additional inducement to "remember their Creator," ere the period of that promise shall expire, "those that seek me *early* shall find me?"[34]

Again, in contrast to Emerson, *reinforcing* was the key word in Sigourney's process. Just as readings of history tend to confirm a person's beliefs, so her teachings were meant to remind her students of these same beliefs rather than creating faith anew. This is why it was essential to stress the radically human nature of these historical figures, to move away from idealization and show their strengths as well as their weaknesses (as Emerson did more dramatically in *Representative Men*). Looking back on her years as a teacher, Sigourney recalled the astonishment of her pupils at the manifold nature of personality, especially that of admired historical figures: "Even now I seem to hear, like the varying tones of music, their sweetly modulated voices, praising deeds of generosity or pity, or expressing surprise that the great were not always good, or amazement that artifice, revenge, or cruelty should sometimes have stained those names whom the world had pronounced illustrious."[35] To make these lessons more easily identifiable and understandable for students, Sigourney moved away from the Emersonian imperative of adaptation. The examples she provided were to be followed rather than adapted. Her aim was the transmission of proper behavior through the use of particular cases, sometimes just anecdotes, whose moral nature was immediately evident. This is why her sketches were often simple and vague and tried to excite the imagination, because "the reflecting mind may also perceive the Hand of God."[36] In the end, the goal was "to transplant the same virtues into the lives of students."[37]

What was most appealing for readers in Sigourney's educational project was the degree to which she became involved in the exemplary lives that she used as role models. Many times the characters she chose for her lessons mirrored her own aspirations as a teacher and a poet. Sometimes the vagueness of her sketches may have encouraged different visions, but she always resorted to the most traditional interpretation of their lives and their faith to provide what she called "not only a cheering sympathy but a controlling pattern."[38] This was not a fixed position, as Amy J. Lueck has argued in chapter 10, but one that fluctuated as Sigourney grew professionally, so that in her educational writings we can trace the development of a didactic culture for women that gradually "distanced from the home."

As Baym suggests, the ultimate objective of this historical education was to form citizens, especially women, who were both integrated into and alienated from the social body. Sigourney's teachings fostered "self-control," "disinterested benevolence," "silent excellence," and "humble piety." In other words, they "educate[d] inhabitants for the kingdom of Heaven."[39] These inhabitants were for the most part women—whom she described as "angels," using the era's popular metaphor—who needed to learn that their place in society consisted of expanding their education while also confining it within the limits of the domestic world. Sigourney therefore attempted to create educators in her own image. By limiting the example of her chosen historical figures to their religious struggles and their victories over "the atheist lore," she was attempting to replicate herself in others. Her use of history and biography, in this sense, seemed to be reproductive rather than inspirational. Her didacticism was passive, dictating the difference between wrong and right without allowing for other possible interpretations. However, we cannot forget Sigourney's audience. Her students were mostly children, unaccustomed to philosophical speculation. Her use of history and biography was a practical strategy to achieve what she called a "judicious instruction" but also a way of avoiding Emerson's later skepticism toward the examples of others.[40]

The educative project of transcendentalism can be viewed as a way to enlarge reason, the faculty that we employ to find the meanings of and connections among real objects; and Sigourney used reading exactly in that sense: as a way of enriching the young mind "with knowledge, and furnishing it with subjects of thought."[41] In the words of another transcendentalist reformer, Lydia Maria Child, she aspired to reveal to her students the harmony between love and wisdom that makes for a beautiful and moral life.[42] The difference is that Sigourney found a more powerful hand than that of nature, which in the end is more a metaphysical than a methodological distinction. In that sense, she was not only looking for a way of educating that would take the young mind beyond the real phenomena and into the wonders of God's creation but also trying to broaden the horizon of many of her contemporaries by providing yet another horizon for our understanding (another "circle," as Emerson explained in his essay of the same title). But despite the similarities she shared with many transcendentalists, not many of her contemporaries were able to recognize her contribution.

NOTES

1. Ralph Waldo Emerson, "Education," in *Lectures and Biographical Sketches* (Boston: Houghton Mifflin, 1891), 108.
2. Wesley T. Mott, "Education," in *The Oxford Handbook of Transcendentalism,* ed. Joel Myerson, Sandra H. Petrulionis, and Laura Dassow Walls (Oxford: Oxford University Press, 2010), 153–71. On the efforts of transcendentalist women in the field of educational reform, see Derek Pacheco, *Moral Enterprise: Literature and Education in Antebellum America* (Columbus: Ohio State University Press, 2013).
3. Ralph Waldo Emerson, James Freeman Clarke, and William Henry Channing, eds., *Memoirs of Margaret Fuller Ossoli* (Boston: Phillips, Samson, 1852), 1:342.
4. Henry David Thoreau, *Walden,* ed. J. Lyndon Shanley (Princeton: Princeton University Press, 1971), 90.
5. Friedrich Schiller, *On the Aesthetic Education of Man in a Series of Letters,* trans. Elizabeth M. Wilkinson and L. A. Willoughby (Oxford: Clarendon, 1967), 10.
6. Ibid., 17.
7. Ibid., 55, 57.
8. Friedrich Schiller, "The Artists," in *The Poems and Ballads of Schiller,* trans. Edward Bulwer Lytton (Edinburgh: Blackwood, 1852), 286.
9. Elizabeth Palmer Peabody, ed., *Aesthetic Papers* (New York, 1849), 1. The table of contents of the book is a telling example of how the idea of the aesthetic was amplified during the romantic period. While contributors such as S. G. Ward and Sampson Reed write on matters related to art (criticism and genius, respectively), the book also includes Emerson's "On War," Thoreau's famous "Resistance to Civil Government," and Nathaniel Hawthorne's sketch "Main Street."
10. Madame de Staël, *Germany* (London: Murray, 1813), 3:235.
11. Emerson et al., *Memoirs of Margaret Fuller Ossoli,* 1:342.
12. Julia Ward Howe, *Modern Society* (Boston: Roberts Brothers, 1881), 10.
13. See Glenna Matthews, *"Just a Housewife": The Rise and Fall of Domesticity in America* (New York: Oxford University Press, 1987).
14. Tiffany K. Wayne, *Woman Thinking: Feminism and Transcendentalism in Nineteenth-Century America* (Lanham, Md.: Lexington, 2005), 81.
15. Ralph Waldo Emerson, *The Early Lectures of Ralph Waldo Emerson,* ed. Stephen Whicher and Robert E. Spiller (Cambridge: Harvard University Press, 1966–72), 1:99.

16. Ralph Waldo Emerson, *The Collected Works of Ralph Waldo Emerson,* ed. Alfred R. Ferguson, Joseph Slater, Douglas E. Wilson, and Ronald A. Bosco (Cambridge: Harvard University Press, 1971–2013), 2:35.
17. Ibid., 4:5.
18. Emerson, *Collected Works,* 1:186.
19. Ibid., 1:292, 190.
20. In this sense, Emerson speaks of the genius as one who "repairs the decay of things" and of the poet as "the Namer" who gives things their "own name and not another's" (*Collected Works* 3:13). My inference is that the poet names objects after the genius has restored them to their original meaning.
21. Ibid., 1:100.
22. Ibid., 1:154.
23. Ralph Waldo Emerson, *The Journals and Miscellaneous Notebooks of Ralph Waldo Emerson,* ed. William H. Gilman et al. (Cambridge: Harvard University Press, 1960–82), 7:17–18.
24. Emerson, *Early Lectures,* 1:99.
25. Ibid.
26. Although this is not the place to discuss it at length, we must remember that Emerson changed his views on biography and imitation substantially in his later work *Representative Men* (1850). After the crisis provoked by the death of his son and his philosophical reorientation toward naturalism, his suspicion about the "wholesome" effect of emulating others increased, and he became highly skeptical of the actual symbolic value of great men. See David M. Robinson, *Emerson and the Conduct of Life: Pragmatism and Ethical Purpose in the Late Work* (Cambridge: Cambridge University Press, 1993), 89–111.
27. Myerson et al.'s *Oxford Handbook of Transcendentalism* mentions Sigourney only once—in the chapter about the *Dial,* as an example of the poetry that Emerson and Fuller did not welcome in their journal (379).
28. In the *Dial* 3 (July 1842), a poem "From Uhland. The Castle by the Sea" appears alongside Emerson's "Lecture on the Times" and Thoreau's "Natural History of Massachusetts." The signature "H." accompanying the poem makes it plausible to believe that it is Sigourney's, although there are other contenders for authorship. I am grateful to Elizabeth Petrino for this reference.
29. Nina Baym, "Reinventing Lydia Sigourney," *American Literary History* 62 (1990): 390–91. Baym is among the first to deal with Sigourney as a relevant figure in the culture of transcendentalism. Her work has inspired other scholars, including Allison Giffen, Dorothy Baker, Wendy Dasler Johnson, Gary Kelly, and the contributors to this volume.
30. Lydia Sigourney, *Evening Readings in History* (London: Ward, 1834), vii. Later in her life, looking back on her work as a whole, Sigourney declared that the study of history is the most appropriate for "domestic instruction" because it is "adapted to the mind in its earliest stages of development" (*Letters of Life* [New York: Appleton, 1866], 331).
31. Sigourney, *Evening Readings in History,* ix.
32. Lydia Sigourney, *Moral Pieces, in Prose and Verse* (Hartford, Conn.: Sheldon and Goodwin, 1815), 56.
33. Thoreau, "Natural History of Massachusetts," 40.
34. Lydia Sigourney, *Biography of Pious Persons; Abridged for Youth* (Springfield, Mass.: Merriam, Little, 1832), iv.
35. Sigourney, *Letters of Life,* 204.
36. Sigourney, *Biography of Pious Persons,* 36.
37. Sigourney, *Letters of Life,* 331.

38. Ibid., 362. In this sense, Ann Wood's characterization of Sigourney's poetry as a process of "strenuous sublimation" can also be applied to her didactic works ("Mrs. Sigourney and the Sensibility of the Inner Space," *New England Quarterly* 45, no. 2 [1972]: 167).
39. Sigourney, *Evening Readings in History,* ix–x.
40. Ibid., vii.
41. Ibid.
42. "The two creative principles of the universe are Love and Wisdom. Their union, and perfect proportion, constitutes Beauty" (Lydia Maria Child, "What Is Beauty?" *Dial* 3 [July 1843]: 490).

13

LYDIA'S LEGACY

MY JOURNEY AS A POSTMODERN POETESS

Annie Finch

"Now, listen, Annie. Speaking of women poets, have you ever heard of Lydia Sigourney?"

I didn't think we had been speaking of women poets. But either way, my father didn't wait for an answer.

"The Sweet Singer of Hartford. Lydia Sigourney! The Sweet Singer of Hartford! Now, there's a woman poet for you, Annie!"

My professor father made those comments on a Thanksgiving afternoon when I was fifteen, and for decades afterward the name and sobriquet stayed with me. In all of our long conversations about poets during my youth—Yeats, Valéry, Herbert, Vaughan, Shakespeare, Eliot—Sigourney was the only woman he mentioned aside from Dickinson (and the occasional recommendation that I should affect a large Marianne Moore–like hat if I really intended to succeed as a poet).[1] No reference to Millay, a favorite of my mother's and mine, ever passed his lips; in fact, Mummy always claimed that he had surreptitiously thrown out most of her Millay books soon after they married, to make more space for books of "real" poetry.

So it was uniquely significant for him to mention Lydia Sigourney, even if he didn't have a single one of her books to offer me out of the 40,000 volumes in his library. Today, of course, I would have googled her as soon as the dishes were cleared. But that wasn't possible in 1971. And even if I'd had the focus of mind to try to track down her books, they had long been out of print and wouldn't have been easy to find. My mother, who often shared with me poems by her own female (along with, of course, male) poet influences—Wylie, Thaxter, and Bogan as well as Millay—never mentioned Sigourney at all.[2]

So, although I had no idea as a young woman poet what Sigourney would eventually mean to me, thanks to my father's chance comment, I was curious enough about this "poetess" to keep an eye out in used bookstores for her gilt-bound volumes. For decades, in fact, I carried her name in me secretly as in a hidden vessel. The books of hers I began to discover gradually, on sagging shelves in the small back rooms of junk stores in half-empty New England towns, were private troves, volumes I opened occasionally to breathe in the acrid gift of their scent. Her flowery images and breathless lines were so alien to what I was learning about how poetry should be that they might have been composed on another planet. I think the strange voices of Sigourney's books and those of poetesses like her, some found on those dust-heavy junk store shelves and some inherited in faded volumes from my mother, may have impelled me almost obsessively to explore issues of poetic voice as I became educated in literary theory. In my undergraduate papers, whether on Spenser, Milton, Shelley, or Hardy, I came back again and again to questions of poetic subjectivity, parsing out the discredited ways in which poets had once established their authority to speak in the world.[3]

By 1986, when I was finishing up a graduate program in creative writing at the University of Houston, I had become certain that a postmodern poet sensitive to the imperialistic potential of language needed to forgo poetic subjectivity. I equated the hefty poetic egos of Keats, Shelley, and other romantic poets with a kind of spiritual and psychological militarism, and that period was, thankfully, over. But as an enlightened person, a feminist, I seemed to be stuck. I felt that my poems had a responsibility to inhabit self-consciously the fringes of *author*-ity and that I needed to complicate each word and line as I wrote until it crossed itself out in the process of inhabiting the page. But then how could I find a voice for myself and help heal the silence from which women poets had suffered? Though I did fashion a path to speaking up in verse drama—by inhabiting multiple perspectives at once—as a lyric poet committed to nurturing a post-patriarchal world, I had not found a comfortable way to express myself directly, as myself, to my readers. "Why can't you just marry the world like the other students in the program?" one of my poet-professors, Stanley Plumly, asked in desperation one day. I was a lost cause.

My poetic voice was at something of a stalemate when I arrived at Stanford to pursue a Ph.D. in English and American literature; I was writing only the nonrepresentational metrical work I now call "the lost poems," crossing myself out with each word I wrote.[4] But at Stanford, I had an idea that would end up carving a space for me to have a poetic voice of my own after all. I approached the teacher of my antebellum literature class, the brilliant Americanist Jay Fliegelman, about writing a term paper on Sigourney. I had already discovered that meter and form were important to my work. Now I was adding another piece to the puzzle of my emerging poetics. After many hours of research in Stanford's microfiche archives of nineteenth-century magazines and many hours absorbed in my own collection of gilt-edged volumes, I was startled to find the voice of this neglected poetess starting to speak to me—and later on, even starting to speak *in* me.

Far from understanding Sigourney as a poet of short-lived popular appeal, as she was usually categorized at that time, I came to see her as a far-reaching beacon when I read her through the lens of feminist and poststructuralist theory. She provided a genuine alternative to the limited choices that canonical Romantic poetics offered to women—an alternative so radical that it carved a doorway in the seamless wall that surrounded my poetic voice. Around this time, I convened a Modern Language Association conference panel titled "Nineteenth-Century Women Poets Other Than Dickinson" where I discussed my Sigourney work and Mary Loeffelholz and Cheryl Walker offered essays on what I was still referring to as "the sentimental tradition."[5] That conversation was a rare chance to discuss Sigourney with others who took the poetesses seriously; it helped me to understand Sigourney's significance as ambassador of a far broader aesthetic, some of whose roots I now believe may extend directly back to a matriarchal, oral-based social structure.

Much of Sigourney's importance to me as a poet lay in the fact that she was such an unabashedly female writer. The only women poets I had been taught in college to respect were Dickinson, H.D., Moore, and Bishop (Sexton and Plath were considered an embarrassment at Yale at that time, and women poets of color were invisible). These four poets all seemed to handle their femaleness with reserve. Their dry, careful intelligence navigated precisely through the overwhelmingly male literary world; the surfaces of their poems frequently struck me as cool, solitary, and disembodied. Sigourney was utterly different. Many of her poems spoke to me with woman-to-woman warmth as if she were a neighbor—direct, welcoming, and full of assurance that being female and a poet at the same time was really okay. She wrote of puddings and linen and flowers, of love for children, of the value of kindness and respect for relationships among women. Though Sigourney's concerns overlapped with Dickinson's, unlike Dickinson, she seemed to be a woman with little to fear or to hide.

Yet the most crucial lifeline Sigourney offered me was her approach to something even more foundational. The majority of her poems demonstrated a metaphysics of subjectivity that contrasted strikingly with that of the romantic poets of the early nineteenth century and their heirs—the only models of how to be a poet that I had been offered during my education to that point. Sigourney's despised poems on their crumbling, brittle pages promised a fresh solution to the concerns about subjectivity that had obsessed me since my undergraduate days at Yale.

Not having a clue yet how to bring these bizarrely domestic and transparent influences into my own postmodern poems, I focused first on writing a critical essay exploring Sigourney's aesthetic. Published in 1988 as "The Sentimental Poetess in the World: Metaphor and Subjectivity in Lydia Sigourney's Nature Poetry," it traced a model of poetic subjectivity based in a different idea of selfhood than the solitary ego searching for meaning that still monopolizes our ideas of the poetic self. Flipping through those gilt-edged volumes with their frontispieces, comparing the strategies of poems such as "The Coral Insect" and "Oak in Autumn" with those of canonical romantic nature lyrics such as Keats's "Ode to a Nightingale" and Bryant's "Thanatopsis," I had developed an understanding of an approach to poetic subjectivity that felt not only new but complete—a poetics with its own integrity and worldview, not dependent on a response to romanticism.[6] "Poetess poetics," as I called it, revealed itself as a way of engaging with nature that was polyvocal, interactive, and questioning rather than solipsistic and ego-centered.[7]

For example, most of us would consider "Ode to a Nightingale" or Bryant's "To a Waterfowl" as expressions of a typical poetic way to approach a natural scene. In both poems, a solitary speaker with much on his (I use the pronoun consciously) mind stands alone, using nature as a conveniently passive metaphor for his own thoughts about lofty and difficult subjects. Musing to himself so that we can overhear, he turns often to the subject of his own death. Finally, thanks to the lessons that the obliging surroundings seamlessly provide, he attains some peace of mind.

Compared to this model, long entrenched in our culture, Sigourney's way of approaching nature is so different that it is no wonder some seem to have had trouble even classifying poets like her as poets at all.[8] As my 1988 essay explores in detail, "Thanatopsis" could be called a "poet-centered" poem; everything revolves around one central speaker who appropriates nature at will—describing, for example, the ocean as "melancholy" and the brooks as "complaining" simply to reflect his own mood, with no acknowledgment that this kind of emotional imperialism could be problematic. Sigourney's poems, on the other hand, tend to be "poly-centered." There is often another subjectivity in the poem besides the poet-speaker's, sometimes more than one, and the poet often acknowledges the independence of the other subjectivity. Sigourney's literary devices, such as asking questions of natural objects, tend to endow them with the sense of having separate identities from the poet's.[9]

Yet for all its strikingly postmodern qualities of permeability and multivocality, the poetess's self was not invisible like the post-authorial self of twentieth-century experimental poetics with which I was struggling to come to terms as a young poet. Sigourney's poetess poetics offers a third way, an option that falls somewhere between the imaginary isolation of the domineering solitary ego and the full dissolution of individual consciousness evoked by postmodern poetics. Her poetics and those of other poetesses, including, I suspect, Longfellow (for, just as genetically female poets can write in the male-generated romantic idiom, so can poets of any gender write from the poetess model) is one of community—and further, perhaps, one of the spirit.[10] Near the end of my essay, I posit that Sigourney's idea of God allows her to open herself to nature without complete loss of self. Because her poetic identity operates in a spiritual framework, its boundaries can remain permeable yet coherent.[11]

I found Sigourney's subjectivity markedly different from that of the other pre-twentieth century woman poet whose work I knew best at that point: Dickinson. Comparing the two approaches, I found that, though Dickinson did absorb many influences from the poetesses of her era, she grafted them onto a romantic core. I felt her as a bridge, if anything, from the poetesses to a male-centered tradition. As I wrote in my essay "Mother Dickinson," she "became perhaps the most intimate male influence on my poetry. . . . She did me good by showing that a woman could dare to call herself a man as far as poetry was concerned, and that in the neutral world after death, perhaps a woman's poems could have as much dignity as a man's."[12]

But it was through Sigourney's aesthetic that I developed the chance to bask and flourish in the sense of being part of a centuries-old poetic approach, a position usually reserved for male poets, or male-identified poets, during the twentieth century. Her example helped me clarify where my own mother's poetry was coming from, and Millay's, and Teasdale's, and Bogan's, and even Kizer's, as well as the poems of Longfellow, Phillis Wheatley, Helen Hunt Jackson, Frances Osgood, Alice Cary, Alice Dunbar-Nelson, and others.[13] Without this understanding, I could have easily ended up poetically motherless, with large portions of my poetic root system missing.[14] Without this understanding, I'm not sure how I would have survived. Looking back, I recognize that my reading of Sigourney was far more than an act of literary criticism. It was an act of survival for me as a young woman poet—one that has continued to shape my poetry and my life.

During the twenty years after I first began exploring poetess poetics, I did come to find that essential aspects of my voice, tradition, and roots—my sense of poetic mother-lineage—had sprouted from the populist, innocent, and much-maligned literary soil of the poetesses, incongruous as such a heritage might seem for a highly-educated postmodern writer. Needless to say, I had claimed these poetess roots in spite of lack of support at Stanford. In 1989, when I proposed to expand my Sigourney article into a Ph.D. dissertation on poetesses' poetics with the inimitable feminist biographer Diane Middlebrook as my adviser, I was forced to drop the idea. I couldn't find a single other poetry professor in the English department who was willing to serve on such a dissertation committee. From the Americanist Albert Gelpi to the postmodern poetics scholar Marjorie Perloff, each refused on the simple grounds that Sigourney and the other poetesses were so bad that they could never repay serious study.

If there was little support for my scholarly interest in the poetesses, there was even less support for my aesthetic or literary connection with them. I learned not to examine my feelings about this situation too closely, because the sense of extreme isolation I suffered when I thought about it was painful. Instead, for many years, though I continued to explore poetess poetics in critical essays, I left my own poetic relationship with Lydia, as I increasingly thought of her, tucked away into a safe part of my creative self. I knew it was there, though, glowing quietly in my poetic heart like a shocking gift that I was afraid to open or to look at too closely.

And in spite of my hesitations, inexorably Sigourney's influence seeped into my poetic awareness and became a genuine influence on my work. She was always there for me, forgiving and supporting me for writing in all the ways I naturally felt like writing, and I became increasingly, and openly, grateful for her help. She opened a way for me to write poems to honor occasions that matter to me, to write in a positive way about my faith in the sacredness of nature and my belief in love and communities, to play with multiple perspectives and voices and the physical pleasure of form, and to address subjects such as friendship and childhood from a female perspective.

And she has proven to be an enduring model. As I have grown more deeply into womanhood, I have found more and more qualities in myself as a woman and a poet that tie me to her—to such an extent that, when reading Gordon S. Haight's 1930 biography recently, I was bemused to recognize myself in many of his condescending observations about Sigourney. Do I love to write poems for communities and groups of women? Check. Do I feel moved to share my sorrows with people around me? Check. Do I enjoy writing poems to commemorate shared occasions? Check. Do I sometimes find that such poems come to me easily on the spur of the moment? Check. Do I aspire to make a living writing poems for people who will enjoy them? Check. Furthermore, in reading Haight's book I was filled not with the expected contempt for these supposedly contemptible traits but with profound admiration for Sigourney's astounding industry, courage, ingenuity, kindness, and generosity.

I closed my 1988 essay with this sentence: "I hope that before too long it will be possible to see the sentimental tradition as a literary movement in its own right, as a movement having its own roots, its own aesthetics, its own world-view, and its own inheritors."[15] Surely a part of me then, at age thirty-two, was wondering if I would turn out to be one of those poetic inheritors. Ten years later, writing the closing sentence of another essay, I fully claimed the label of one of Sigourney's literary progeny: "I'm a poetess. It's a relief at last to admit it."[16] And twelve years beyond that, I called myself a poetess with a still deeper level of pride: "Now, after a further decade spent absorbing and meditating on the implications of the name [of poetess], I will say it again somewhat differently . . . : 'I am a poetess. It's an honor at last to admit it.'"[17]

In 2017, as I complete the essay in this book, I am experiencing yet another transformation in my life as a poetess. I am ready to complicate my claim and admit that it has been not only a relief and an honor to carry on Sigourney's lineage but also a problem, a real and distinct embarrassment. Interestingly, at this point the source of the mortification is not where I would have expected it to be: in the sentimental verse, the poems on flowers and dead infants for which Sigourney is so often mocked. Instead, I find I am now most humiliated by my encounters with the poet who feels to me like the less authentic Sigourney: the one trying desperately to be a "poet" with no "ess," to write with Miltonic or Shelleyan impact. Perhaps the best example of this type of poem is the highly embarrassing "Niagara," which, in spite of the regard in which it has long been held, is a far more mannered and derivative poem than any of Sigourney's supposedly more sentimental elegies. In short, I am now embarrassed by Sigourney to the extent that she was embarrassed by herself; I am made uncomfortable by her when she pretends to be what she is not, a poet-centered poet bent on making everything in the poem revolve around a strong single central ego.

Heide Göttner-Abendroth, the founder of the discipline known as matriarchal studies, posits in her book *Matriarchal Societies* that the four core aspects of such a society are consensus decision making, a gift economy, matrilineal social arrangements, and goddess worship (which also implies honoring the immanent spirituality of physical things and the sacredness of nature).[18] I believe that such a framework, along with Genevieve Vaughan's work on the gift economy as exemplifying the power and agency of the mother as a social construct, may illuminate Sigourney's matriarchal poetry (and perhaps her prose works for women as well).[19] In fact, I believe that matriarchal culture nourished her best poems. I now think of Sigourney, the first member of her family to be educated extensively, as the emissary of a venerable tradition of oral poetry, even though at times she tried to hide that legacy, to become a more "respectable" writer.

The differences between these two poles of Sigourney's poetics—the relaxed matriarchal poet who wrote for a community of women with playful imagination, deep emotion, rhythmic flexibility, and concrete domestic imagery, and the more patriarchal poet who wrote stiff and consciously impressive public poems, often in iambic pentameter and sometimes literally in a male voice—have yet to be teased out. (And of course there are other voices along the continuum, such as the ritualized Christian pious voice, a kind of hybrid perhaps resulting from the distortion the poet incurs by exploiting the matriarchal voice for the patriarchal voice's spiritual purposes).

Because the matriarchal Sigourney has not been edited or collected yet, I am in no position to dispute that the Sigourney we have now, a tangle of patriarchal and matriarchal voices, remains a deeply problematic model. But it is my belief that when the matriarchal Sigourney is peeled away from the patriarchal backdrop of her quasi-romantic blank verse, she will emerge as a more delightful and readable poet—in the same way that Paul Laurence Dunbar is far easier to appreciate when his more authentic poems are freed from the context of the "blackface" poems written to satisfy the biased expectations of the culture of his own time.[20] Perhaps, like Dunbar, Sigourney understood all too well the climate in which her work would need to be received in the century after her death: "Niagara" seems to have been the most consistently anthologized Sigourney poem during the long period of her effacement at the hands of patriarchal literary history, and, not surprisingly, even Wikipedia today calls it one of her (only two) "most successful" poems.

The more matriarchal Sigourney may well prove to be a far different poet from the Sigourney we currently know—not only in terms of voice, imagery, poetic self, and audience but also on the level of metrical strategy. Sigourney was an adept writer in two entirely different metrical idioms: the blank verse (unrhymed iambic pentameter) favored by educated male poets in the centuries after Milton and the noniambic and accentual metrical patterns of oral and popular verse, including ballad stanza, used largely by women poets who lacked formal higher education. Close analysis of her metrical strategies using a method of reading called metrical code analysis, which I develop in my book *The Ghost of Meter,* seems likely to uncover illuminating connections between these two opposed metrical idioms and

Sigourney's attitudes toward their corresponding cultural and spiritual attitudes.[21] Such connections may cast light on the intricate literary waters that Sigourney and other poets navigated as they worked to balance their poetic voice and authority on the divide between two traditions: the poet-centered/patriarchal tradition that I refer to in my 1988 essay as "romantic" and the poly-centered/matriarchal tradition that I would now call "sentimentist."[22]

Here's a brief example of how meter could play a part in such explorations. A metrical code reading of a passage from the (to my ear) insufferable "Niagara" reveals that Sigourney, as Dickinson would a few decades later, associates iambic pentameter with male-established conventions of literary power but triple rhythm (anapestic, dactylic, and other trisyllabic rhythmic patterns) with her own female agency.[23]

> Therefore I come, a listener to thy voice,
> And bow me at thy feet, and touch my lip
> To thy cool billow, if perchance my soul,
> That fleeting wanderer on these shores of time,
> May, by thy voice instructed, learn of God.[24]

In the phrases where the poetess refers to herself as an active subject, a "listener" and "a wanderer," she uses triple substitution (the only two anapestic substitutions in this passage). By contrast, when the speaker describes herself bowing and paying dutiful homage to the romantic icon of the waterfall, she does so in fully disciplined iambs. Such metrical subtexts align with metrical code patterns I discuss at length in *The Ghost of Meter*. This metrical balance is a physical embodiment of the literary maneuvering required of the poetess: a metrical code reading of the lines uncovers a hard bargain, showing how Sigourney purchased instruction in the dutiful, solitary rites of worship of the romantic sublime and the male God for the price of the transforming "improvement" of her own wandering, listening, triple meter soul.

Sigourney's charming poem "The True Friends," on the other hand, falls on the other end of the spectrum. It is written entirely in triple meter—a rhythm here powerful enough to alter a man's language, changing the word "wing" in the epigraph to "pinion" in the last line. In this poem, whose form reflects the oral-based traditions of poetesses' prosody, Sigourney uses a fluid combination of anapests and amphibrachs to embody the voices of the earth-goddesses Ceres and Pomona:

THE TRUE FRIENDS

"They leave no sting in the heart of memory, no stain on the wing of time."

—Hon. Marshall P. Wilder

Brown Ceres one day, with Pomona was meeting
Mid Autumn's inspiring smile,
So, giving each other a sisterly greeting,
They sat down to gossip awhile.

"I hope you are well, dear, this elegant weather—
How delightful the country,"—they said,
"And how do you prosper,"—both speaking together,—
"With regard to your business and trade?"

"Oh, where the rude thorn-bush and bramble were springing,
With fruitage the apple-tree bends,
The scythe of the mower at sunrise is swinging,
And the song of the reaper ascends.

"Let us walk hand in hand, for no obstacle caring,
Till the vine o'er the mountains shall grow,
Its suit of green velvet the brown heath be wearing,
And deserts with plenty o'erflow.

"The gold in its mine, with excitement and wonder
May gather an emigrant band,
And the chariot of Mars trample on its thunder,
But we're the true strength of the Land.

"For us, no lorn wife in her cottage is grieving,
Earth welcomes us both, in her prime;
No sting in the bosom of memory we're leaving,
No stain on the pinion of time."[25]

Here, two reclaimed classical goddesses survey the earth like matriarchs and tend to the land like mothers, fostering abundance through consensus and nurturing the gift economy without competition or fanfare.[26] Sigourney's mythical re-weaving sketches a clear, inspiring, and delightful scene of female agency and power leading to peace and harmony with the earth. Reading this poem, I feel it is no wonder that, as I have claimed my own path in earth-centered spirituality over the last several decades, I have come to think of Sigourney, piously Christian though she was, as a sister witch in disguise—that is, as a person claiming spiritual empowerment centered in nature and recognizing female aspects of spirituality.

Born in 1791, forty years before Dickinson's birth, Sigourney consistently honored the spirit in the natural world, the value in Native American traditions, and the power in women's communities. Her interest in Native American history and legend, her comparison of herself to a druid, her exuberant conversations extending subjectivity and voices to trees, coral, flowers, butterflies, and all manner of natural creatures are vibrant under the layers of Christian piety. And not only is this sense of sacred mission evident in Sigourney's themes; it informs her very conception of her art. The time-honored shamanic role of poets around the globe has been to honor and tend the culture's identities, traditions, and transitions in language heightened by repeating patterns. Although for most of the twentieth and twenty-first centuries, American poets have, by and large, abjured both the craft of poetic patterning and the responsibilities of what has come to be known disparagingly as "occasional poetry," during this period, as Sigourney's remarkable generosity with her poems bears witness, it has been the despised tradition of the poetess that has largely fulfilled the primal responsibility of the shaman-poet.

Sigourney's prolific stream of poems for occasions large and small, not to mention the staggering list of poems complete strangers requested her to write for them as reported in her autobiography *Letters of Life,* attest that this is the type of role she took on for her quickly modernizing society. Sigourney's occasional poems are part of the tradition of poetesses who wrote accessible, passionate poems that made full use of the ancient, magical tools of the art—rhythm and pattern—to mark and explore shared occasions and emotions. Longfellow's "Paul Revere's Ride" and "The Village Blacksmith," Lazarus's "The New Colossus," Hughes's "Harlem," Frost's "The Gift Outright," and Millay's "To Inez Milholland" are just a few further examples.

I am sometimes surprised now to realize how close I have now come to feel to Sigourney and the poetesses of the nineteenth century—and in ways I would never have predicted. The transformation was gradual. As a female-centered spiritual path, motherhood, and maturity brought me to appreciate the crucial importance of female community, I began, like the poetesses, to create more poems for use in daily life, hoping to weave poetry into the fabric of culture and to support everyday women in their paths. As my skill in meeting the challenges of poetic meter and form increased, I felt less need to weave linguistic and thematic challenges into my work and became more comfortable using clear language. And as unexpected career changes distanced me from university teaching, like the female poetesses who so often lacked educational opportunities, I opened further to the vulnerable possibility of addressing readers directly without academic mediation.

All these changes in focus combined to alter my self-identity as a poet. I feel myself now as a voice in community, stitching a carefully wrought spiritual connection between the worlds with a vocabulary and imagery that I hope anyone in my tribe (which now increasingly includes a nonliterary audience) may understand and enjoy. What a striking and delightful contrast this new image of the poet offers, as opposed to the solitary, angst-ridden version of the romantic poet-self I had tried unsuccessfully to make myself fit into for so many years!

Reading Ann Beebe's fascinating essay "Common Ground" (chapter 8) has helped me put these changes in my own life and art into a clearer context. I have come to understand how much my poetic self-identity connects—and perhaps has always connected—with Sigourney's model of the poet as a woman actively engaged on behalf of her community in the spheres of nature, public and political values, domestic life, and spirituality. Since publishing my initial essay on Sigourney in 1988, I have developed my understanding of the poetess beyond a mere alternative to the romantic poetic ego and into a far more active, socially engaged force that uses poetry specifically to call up and shape energies to heal and transform members of her tribe. The poetess, in other words, is a shamanic writer. And as a witch and a poet, I am increasingly proud to say that I aim to share in that work.

A few years ago, I was talking with a psychic medium about my efforts to create a poetic career outside of the university, among other issues. Out of the blue, she inquired if I knew anyone named Lydia. "The name "Lydia" keeps coming up. Is there a Lydia in your family?"

I said that there wasn't. In fact, I didn't know a single person named Lydia.

"Hmm, . . . well, this name is coming up very strongly. I think there is someone named Lydia in the spirit world who is looking out for you."

May Lydia Sigourney's communal, generous, nurturing spirit, rediscovered in the nick of time with the help of this current collection of essays, look out for all of us as we employ our goddess-given tools and gifts on behalf of a deeper connection with ourselves, with each other, and with nature.

NOTES

1. William Butler Yeats (1865–1939), Paul Valéry (1871–1945), George Herbert (1593–1633), Henry Vaughan (1621–95), William Shakespeare (1564–1616), T. S. Eliot (1888–1965).
2. Elinor Wylie (1885–1928), Celia Thaxter (1835–1894), Louise Bogan (1897–1970), Edna St. Vincent Millay (1892–1950).
3. Updated versions of several of my early essays will appear in Annie Finch, *How to Write Like a Witch,* Poets on Poetry series (Ann Arbor: University of Michigan Press, forthcoming).
4. A selection of the "lost poems" appears in Annie Finch, *Spells: New and Selected Poems* (Middletown, Conn.: Wesleyan University Press, 2013).
5. In 2001, my dear friend and mentor, the Pulitzer Prize–winning poet Carolyn Kizer, recoiled in horror at my use of the term *sentimental* to describe her work (Annie Finch, "Carolyn Kizer and the Chain of Women," in *The Body of Poetry: Essays on Women, Form, and the Poetic Self* ([Ann Arbor: University of Michigan Press, 2005], 77–85). In self-defense, she coined the more neutral replacement term *sentimentist,* which I find extremely useful and still use.
6. Lydia Sigourney, "The Coral Insect," in *Lydia Sigourney: Selected Poetry and Prose,* ed. Gary Kelly (Buffalo: Broadview, 2008), 99; Lydia Sigourney, "Oak in Autumn," in *Pocahantas, and Other Poems* (New York: Harper, 1841), 71.
7. In the last two decades wonderful new work has come out on the sentimentist tradition, including Paula Bernat Bennett's *Poets in the Public Sphere* (Princeton: Princeton University Press, 2003); Wendy Dasler Johnson's *Antebellum American Women's Poetry: A Rhetoric of Sentiment* (Carbondale: Southern Illinois University Press, 2016); and Elizabeth A. Petrino's *Emily Dickinson and Her Contemporaries* (Hanover, N.H.: University Press of New England, 1998). Now that talented scholars are recognizing Sigourney's value as well, so much so that a book such as this one as well as a respectable new edition of Sigourney's poems are finally available (Kelly, *Lydia Sigourney*), I am overwhelmed with gratitude that I don't need to feel alone anymore.
8. In the mid-1980s, when I was enrolled as graduate student in a program in creative writing, the poets who taught our workshops commonly drew a sharp distinction between poetry and verse, and learning to recognize and be properly horrified at verse seemed to be a foundational part of our initiation as poets. Thirty years later, John Barr makes the same distinction, defining verse as "not an instrument of exploration, but rather a tool of affirmation," while "serious" poetry, on the other hand, is written in pursuit of an open-ended goal" ("Is It Poetry or Is It Verse?," Poetry Foundation, September 18, 2006, https://www.poetryfoundation.org). A distinction along these lines

must be what Gordon S. Haight had in mind when he referred to Sigourney's poetry as "dilute, saccharine verse" (*Mrs. Sigourney: The Sweet Singer of Hartford* [New Haven: Yale University Press, 1930], 36).

9. Annie Finch "The Sentimental Poetess in the World: Metaphor and Subjectivity in Lydia Sigourney's Nature Poetry," *Legacy* 5, no. 2 (1988): 3–18.
10. For more on the poetess and the spirit, see Bennett, *Poets in the Public Sphere;* and Eliza Richards, *Gender and the Poetics of Reception in Poe's Circle* (Cambridge: Cambridge University Press, 2011).
11. In my essay "Coherent Decentering," I used readings of some of my own poems to illustrate the influence of this model of the poetic self on my practice. Annie Finch, "Coherent Decentering," in *The Body of Poetry,* 95–102.
12. Annie Finch, "Mother Dickinson," in ibid., 58–62.
13. See my essays "The Heart of Phillis Wheatley" and "Carolyn Kizer and the Chain of Women," in ibid., 64–68, 77–85.
14. For a powerful discussion of the importance of women's poetic traditions to women poets, see Jane Dowson, "Older Sisters Are Very Sobering Things: Contemporary Women Poets and the Female Affiliation Complex," *Feminist Review* 62 (Summer 1999): 6–20.
15. Finch, "The Sentimental Poetess in the World," 18.
16. Annie Finch, "Confessions of a Postmodern Poetess," in *The Body of Poetry,* 95–130.
17. Annie Finch, "What Is a Witch? What Is a Poet? What Is a Poetess," *American Witch* (July 2010), http://anniefinch.com.
18. Heide Göttner-Abendroth, *Matriarchal Societies: Studies on Indigenous Cultures across the Globe* (Bern, Switzerland: Lang, 2013).
19. Genevieve Vaughan, *For-Giving: A Feminist Criticism of Exchange* (Austin, Tex.: Plainview, 1999).
20. At least she will be more enjoyable—perhaps as good a benchmark as any for detecting poetic authenticity.
21. Annie Finch, *The Ghost of Meter: Culture and Prosody in American Free Verse* (Ann Arbor: University of Michigan Press, 1993).
22. Finch, "The Sentimental Poetess in the World," 3–18.
23. Finch, *The Ghost of Meter.*
24. Lydia Sigourney, "Niagara," in Kelly, *Lydia Sigourney,* 152.
25. Lydia Sigourney, "The True Friends," in *Gleanings* (New York: Appleton, 1860), 18
26. Sigourney's attention to Native American culture—for example, in her epic poem "Hobomok"—may also be fruitfully approached via this context.

AFTERWORD

Paula Bernat Bennett

In 1903, Grace Lathrop Collin published a retrospective essay on Lydia Huntley Sigourney in the *New England Magazine: An Illustrated Monthly.* An author herself as well as a scion of the Lathrop family that did so much to further Sigourney's early career, Collin accompanied the writer's biography with a critique of her literary efforts, most of which she found disappointing. Unlike other Sigourney detractors, however, she was not without sympathy for her subject. The poet, she observed, was "mistress of two literary styles": one that Sigourney "naïvely term[ed] 'the language of books'" which Collin condemns out of hand, and a second that she called "vernacular speech."[1] If Sigourney's exertions in the first linguistic mode were hopelessly marred by artifice and "flowery platitudes," Collin argued, in the second she admitted that Sigourney wrote surprisingly well: putting aside her poeticisms and allowing her "commendable common-sense," "like ledges of New England granite," to crop up here and there in her texts.[2] Pointing to exemplary passages in works such as "Gossip with a Spring Bouquet," "Myrtis and Other Etchings and Sketchings," "Past Meridian," and *Sketch of Connecticut, Forty Years Since,* Collin praised Sigourney's vernacular writing as equal to that of "any realist in rural New England dialect and temper."[3]

Collin is not alone in positing multiple Sigourneys in order to defend one or another aspect of the poet's output. Almost a hundred years later, Nina Baym refuted more than a century's worth of bad Sigourney press by employing the same tactic in "Reinventing Lydia Sigourney," an essay many scholars now consider foundational to modern Sigourney studies. Since Baym, this same strategy of reinvention, which effectively produces whatever Sigourney the scholar favors, has come to characterize Sigourney criticism generally, not just my own work but that of the majority of other contributors to this volume, including Jennifer Putzi, Joan R. Wry, Sean Epstein-Corbin, Gary Kelly, Angela Sorby, Janet Dean, and Annie Finch.

With this approach in hand, these scholars have found multiple ways to make sense of, and bring order to, the contradictions, excrescences, and moments of sheer genius in this writer's extraordinarily complex and multifarious oeuvre.

In choosing to present Sigourney in all her heterogeneity, however, Mary Louise Kete and Elizabeth Petrino have raised a number of metacritical issues that their contributors do not directly address. For example, does this diversity, so striking in their book, represent something basic to Sigourney's intentions as a writer, or is it the accidental outcome of an economic system that paid authors by the word or line? If the former, what, if any, are the consequences of emphasizing her variety as we have done? If the latter, how do we generalize, let alone theorize, about a writer who never settled on a particular aesthetic, a particular genre, or, as Collin pointed out, even a particular literary style or voice? What kind of writer was Sigourney in her own eyes, this "woman of all work in Parnassus's kitchen?"[4] Did she model herself on Felicia Hemans, as so many have believed? Or, as the nation's first major woman author of belles-lettres, did she see herself as a new kind of woman writer suited to a new world? If the latter, does this help account for the large role polyvocality plays in so much of her writing? Then again, can a writer like Sigourney—who never settled down to a single aesthetic or genre—find a place in the American literary canon? If she cannot, how do we justify teaching her? These questions are central not just to many of the essays in his volume but to our understanding of Sigourney's place in the nineteenth-century literary firmament generally, and as space allows, I will offer some thoughts on them here.

The idea that all books are divisible into one of three stable genres—poetry, fiction, or nonfiction—is a truism that, at least until the advent of poststructuralism, dictated how most twentieth-century authors saw themselves in relation to their audience, their craft, and their mission, with most writers opting to make one genre or another their own. This was far less true of nineteenth-century writers generally and not at all true of Sigourney, whose oeuvre embraces virtually every sort of literary genre extant in her period. In prose, she penned biographies of historical figures, sketches, satire, letters, advice literature, children's tales and essays, temperance literature, religious texts, memoirs and reminiscences, short fiction, local color narratives, and travel books. In poetry, the genre with which Sigourney is most often associated today, she not only composed a four-canto epic on the fate of America's aboriginal people, but satires, complaints, long narratives, jeremiads, biblical imitations, epitaphs and elegies, odes, hymns, parodies, nature poetry, historical poems, poems written in political protest, children's verse, poems about flowers, poems about the deaf, poems about sailors, works honoring other writers often by emulation (for example, Wordsworth and Hemans), and verses dealing with domestic life. Interestingly in light of Kelly's description of the factors leading to the break-up of Sigourney's marriage (chapter 6), the one genre she does not seem to have practiced was that staple of most nineteenth-century poetesses: love poetry.[5]

Along with writing in multiple genres, Sigourney also mixed poetry and prose in many of her books and varied her literary style, diction level, and meters in relation to the kind of poetry or prose she was writing. As a result, trying to classify the kind of writer she was, the school to which she belonged, or even how she conceptualized her own project may seem to be a hopeless endeavor. In a review of the last hundred years–plus of Sigourney criticism, what one finds instead is a pattern in which each scholar has his or her distinctive take on this elusive writer. Collin stresses her largely unrealized gift as a local colorist. Her biographer, Gordon S. Haight, dismisses her as a hack. Ann Douglas Wood damns her as an out-of-control dead-baby poet. Emphasizing Sigourney's writing on Native Americans, Baym calls her a historian. Sandra A. Zagarell puts her in the line of late eighteenth-century republicans. Petrino and Kete group her with sentimentalists. Mary Loeffleholz identifies her as a teacher. I think she was a political poet. Finch thinks she was a poetess. Karen Kilcup places her among early environmentalists, while Kelly classifies her as primarily a religio-domestic writer.

But what if, instead of seeking clues to Sigourney's authorial identity in her biography, her literary texts, or in what academics have said of her, we turn to what she herself relates about her evolution as a litterateur? Does this help explain the seemingly inexplicable dive she took into writings of every conceivable kind? In the posthumously published *Letters of Life* (1866), Sigourney provides a short but helpful description of her relationship to her period's literary market and to the impact this market had on her authorship. Her starting point, significantly enough, is not with her books but with her relationship to what was at least arguably the most important branch of this market: the efflorescence of periodical literature between 1820 and 1860.

Laying out the facts as she experienced them, Sigourney tells us about what she wrote, where she published, and who her readers were, identifying sample journals from the wide range of magazines and newspapers in which she published—some three hundred in all. Not only does she treat each sample as representative à la Whitman of the many different components within the American population, but she also highlights her own ability to appeal to each in turn:

> There was a long period, after I became a writer for the public, when periodical literature flourished abundantly. The monthly magazines in particular became almost a legion. Every position, occupation, and age of human life seemed to have its own exponent. . . .
>
> . . . On this sea of miscellany I was allured to embark, and, having set sail, there was no return. I think now with amazement, and almost incredulity, of the number of articles I was induced by the urgency of editors to furnish. Before I ceased to keep a regular catalogue, they had amounted to more than two thousand. Some of these were afterwards comprehended in selections [that is, collected for reprinting], though enough for several volumes must still be floating about, like sea-weed among the noteless billows. They were divided among nearly three hundred different publications, from the aristocratic "Keepsake" of the Countess of Blessington, and the classic "Athenaeum" and "Forget-Me-Not" of London, to the "Coachmakers' Magazine," the "Herald of the Upper Mississippi," the "Buckeye Blossom" of the West, and the "Rose-bud" of the factory girls at Lowell. . . .
>
> . . . With the establishment of a poetic name came a host of novel requisitions. Fame gathered from abroad cut out work at home. The number and nature of consequent applications were alike remarkable. Churches requested hymns, to be sung at consecrations, ordinations, and installations; charitable societies for anniversaries; academies and schools, for exhibitions. Odes were desired for the festivities of New Year and the Fourth of July, for silver and golden weddings, for the voyager wherewith to express his leave-taking, and the lover to propitiate his mistress. Epistles from strangers often solicited elegies and epitaphs; and though the voice of bereavement was to me a sacred thing, yet I felt the inefficacy of balm thus offered to a heart that bled.[6]

Whatever else these passages—so rich in lists of things achieved—do, they make clear that for Sigourney her commitment to diversity or what she called "miscellany" was the engine that drove her literary production. For her, if not for her husband Charles, who was appalled by her decision to write, as it were, or the masses, the real mise-en-scène for the nineteenth-century woman author was neither a lonely garret nor a room of her own nor even a kitchen on Parnassus or anywhere else.[7] Rather, her writing flourished in the editorial offices and amid the hurly burly of "hungering presses" that demanded, as she said, to "be fed."[8] Literally or figuratively rubbing elbows with men and women of every class and condition, she delivered her articles and poems and oversaw the manufacture of her books. Here, she found her voice—a voice, like Whitman's, designed to represent as well as to teach, cheer, console, castigate, and dozens of other things, consciously making herself thereby a "writer for the public."[9]

So what was this "sea of miscellany" like? For one thing, because of weak or nonexistent copyright protections, plagiarism was rampant, and the practice of author anonymity only added to the problem by making possible multiple contested claims of authorship. Because poems were both popular and convenient as fillers, newspaper poems, of which Sigourney wrote a great many, were regularly recirculated across the nation and even overseas without permission or remuneration. And then there was the cavalier behavior of editors, who had little investment in maintaining the integrity of texts. As Amy J. Lueck discusses in chapter 10, these individuals not only recirculated Sigourney's prose and poems but cut and spliced them in the process. Literary agents did not exist at this time, so authors had to negotiate salaries themselves. Unsurprisingly, most were paid very little, making Sigourney, whose audience base was enormous, one of an exclusive group of antebellum poets, male and female, with the bargaining power to make a living by writing alone. In such a market, every writer was on his or her own.[10] Authors wrote what and how they pleased, and publishers and readers either supported their efforts or they did not.

Yet for all this market's seeming drawbacks, it not only produced some of the nation's most revered writers but, just as important, it nurtured the talent of numerous others, in particular women, giving them a freedom to explore and still get published that comparatively few twentieth-century women authors would enjoy. In this experiment in democratic literary capitalism, anything was possible, even the rise of a so-called "gardener's daughter" to the nation's premier woman poet.[11] Authors of every sort—men and women, white and of color, educated and uneducated—took advantage of the opportunities such a market offered.[12] None understood this market better, however, or manipulated it more assiduously or to better effect than did Lydia Sigourney. In her biographical *Letters of Life* the poet claims that "two principles" guided her literary career—"not to interfere with the discharge of womanly duty, and to aim at being an instrument of good."[13] And these two principles characterized the greater part of her output. On them she built her reputation for religiosity and morality, carefully cultivating her following through an extensive personal correspondence that Putzi describes in this book. Those who wrote to her were her most loyal admirers, she did her best to meet their needs.

But just because she did benefit so greatly from her immersion in the popular literary market, the question that Paul Lauter once posed when challenging detractors of Frances Ellen Watkins Harper—namely, is she "good enough to teach?"—is all the more pressing.[14] Can a public writer—a writer who, as Kelly says, made her living by turning out "an extraordinary variety of religious and didactic prose, educational literature, and poetry and prose for everyday use"—also be a writer worthy of preservation?[15] Essays by Putzi, Wry, Zagarell, Epstein-Corbin, and Dean—not to mention Kete and Petrino's own comprehensive introduction—all complicate greatly and add nuance to the kind of writer Sigourney was, and their work makes any easy dismissal of her literary skills significantly more difficult.[16] Here I would like to conclude my brief contribution to this project of reconsideration by bringing forward two interrelated poems whose quality and complexity I believe argues strongly for Sigourney's place not just in the classroom but in the canon.

Both "The Alpine Flowers" and "The First Steamboat" conform to the kind of political writing that interests me most in Sigourney—poems and protest literature in which she challenges what she sees as moral threats to the nation. In "The Alpine Flowers," which I discuss first, Sigourney entwines an explicitly female-gendered sentimental vocabulary with the unambiguously masculinist vocabulary of British romanticism in order to critique male overreaching. Published in *Poems* (1827), "The Alpine Flowers" is among her most carefully crafted poems.

Meek dwellers mid yon terror-stricken cliffs!
With brows so pure, and incense-breathing lips,
Whence are ye?—Did some white wing'd messenger,
On Mercy's missions trust your timid germ
To the cold cradle of eternal snows?
Or breathing on the callous icicles,
Bid them with tear-drops nurse ye?—
—Tree nor shrub
Dare that drear atmosphere,—nor polar pine
Uprears a veteran front,—yet there *ye* stand,
Leaning your cheeks against the thick ribb'd ice,
And looking up with brilliant eyes to Him
Who bids you bloom unblanch'd, amid the waste
Of desolation. Man, who panting toils
O'er slippery steeps, or trembling treads the verge
Of yawning gulfs, o'er which the headlong plunge
Is to Eternity, looks shuddering up,
And marks ye in your placid loveliness
Fearless, yet frail, and clasping his chill hands
Blesses your pencil'd beauty. Mid the pomp
Of mountain summits rushing to the sky,
And chaining the rapt soul in breathless awe,
He bows to bind you drooping to his breast,
Inhales your spirit from the frost-wing'd gale,
And freer dreams of Heaven.[17]

Two of Sigourney's formal choices in this poem do a great deal to establish its seriousness. Most importantly, despite its flowery subject the poem is written in blank verse, a meter that Sigourney generally reserves for weighty topics such as historical events and the deaths of well-known persons. Along with this, in lieu of stanzas, she employs caesuras to give the poem shape, creating a four-part structure that subtly tracts the stages of her intellectual argument. Opening with an apostrophe to the poem's eponymous subject, she then loads her depiction of the rock-clinging edelweiss with an array of popular tropes for femininity—meek, pure, timid, placid, frail, and so forth—placing these banalities in direct opposition to the hyperactive language she associates with the poem's overachieving male actor, one "who panting toils / O'er slippery steeps, or trembling treads the verge / Of yawning gulfs, o'er which the headlong plunge / Is to Eternity." As in so much nineteenth-century sentimental poetry written in praise of women, whether authored by women or men, this female flower is not, however, what it seems. On the contrary, it is an agent of heaven, whose very qualities of meekness, purity, and frailty allow her to play a decisive role in generic man's salvation.

With this last thought, Sigourney concludes the poem, completing sentimentality's loop as a religious as well as a gendered discourse. Placid and frail the woman-flower may be, but she also possesses a spiritual strength without which man is lost. If in all these moves, "The Alpine Flowers" is well within the parameters that defined religio-domestic literary expression in Sigourney's day, its poetics give it a power significantly more sophisticated than that of most popular sentimental and religious poetry of the time, much of her own poetry included.

But while "The Alpine Flowers" appears to adhere to the sentimental gender conventions in some respects, in others, in particular the poem's deliberate setting in the preferred site for so much high romantic poetry, Sigourney goes well beyond the boundaries of what Kelly calls everyday religio-domestic verse. At stake here is not just women's spiritual power but precisely man's weakness and overreaching. Read with an eye to these issues, the poem represents a delegitimization of the cardinal tenets of Anglo-American romanticism. The search for inspiration in nature without reference to God, the identification with the heroic isolato, and, most importantly, the aspiration to transcend human limits in quest of the sublime ("awe")—were the triple pillars of Anglo-American romanticism's faith, and in "The Alpine Flowers" Sigourney engages all of them only to rebut each in turn. Long before Ahab met the white whale, Sigourney was asking a central question of Anglo-American culture: At what price aspiration?

It was a question she would pose again, albeit far more bitterly, in "The First Steamboat," among her most powerful and most difficult poems. Like the poem "Wealth" (1827), which Kelly discusses in chapter 6, "The First Steamboat" (1831) is about the value of money. But whereas Sigourney roots "Wealth" in the biblical story of Esau, "who sold / His birthright for the surfeit of an hour," in "The First Steamboat" there are no biblical injunctions to corroborate the author's point of view—nor does the narrator, who may or may not stand for the author, adopt an explicit point of view herself.[18] On the contrary, in this strange and troubling poem everything is ambiguous—from its 4/3 iambic beat, which is riddled with anapests, to the lengthy prolegomenon whose opening question is never answered. The result is a work that could mean one thing or its opposite, depending on how the reader feels about steamboats, money, the environment, and what we today call quality of life.[19]

For analytical purposes, I will divide the poem into two sections of eight and three stanzas respectively with a transition stanza serving as the link between them. The first eight stanzas describe Robert Fulton's steamboat as it makes its maiden voyage from New York City to Albany on August 17, 1807. In language dense with foreboding, the narrator's depiction emphasizes the terror that this bizarre machine inspired in those who witnessed its passage:

> Who thus o'er the foaming main doth glide?
> No sail propels her course,
> She heeds not the winds with their sway of pride,
> And asks no boon of the angry tide
> As she treads the breakers hoarse.
>
> No oar she plies with its measured sweep;
> But curling dark and high,
> Her volumed smoke to the clouds doth creep,
> While a snowy line marks the cleaving deep,
> A banner of flame on the sky.
>
> The sea, as in terror, uplifted her voice,
> From billow to billow it roll'd,
> The mermaidens lock'd up their bowers in a trice,
> And the monarch whale sought his palace of ice,
> While the tocsin of ocean toll'd.
>
> More close to its grotto the faint pearl grew,
> While the dolphins were waxing pale,
> Their warning shells the Tritons blew,
> And with urns overturned the river nymphs flew
> To tell father Neptune the tale.
>
> Old Hudson slept 'neath the curtain of night,
> But [she] furrow'd his heaving breast
> With a hissing sound like a serpent sprite,

And the Highlands kindled their beacon light
  At the torch of the wonderful guest.

A peaceful bark o'er the waters sped
  As this monster form drew near—
From his perilous post the helmsman fled,
And the hailing captain bade with dread
  From her demon-wake to steer.

Some heard piratical fetters clank
  As their vessels pass'd her side,
And they drifted apace towards the rocky bank,
As the poppy-fed Turks from Kanaris shrank,
  When his sparkling deck they spied.

From the fishermen's cabins the inmates burst,
  And were moved in their panic to say,
That the ghosts of the Dutchmen had risen from dust
To smoke their great pipes with a terrible gust
  And hasten from Gotham away.[20]

There are a number of oddities in these lines, but the most striking one is Sigourney's utilization of an assortment of pagan deities and spirits that, possibly for religious reasons, rarely, if ever, make an appearance in her verse. Why? Are these fictitious entities here simply for embellishment, or does she wish to suggest that the anxieties provoked by the steamboat are equally fictitious? If the latter, then the poem, which concludes with what sounds like a ringing endorsement of Fulton's invention, could be far more unified than it first appears. True, the steamboat terrifies man and beast now, but given world enough and time, people will overcome their imaginary terrors and they will value "Fulton's Folly" for the marvel it is.

But what if the reverse is true? What if the spirits and animals and the fishermen who depend on the Hudson for their daily bread are not empty tropes but beings vital to the river's ecology and hence to ourselves? Disconnected from both the world of the spirit and the world of nature, the steamboat, which is independent of both wind and tide, is utterly indifferent to the damage its "demon-wake" does to man and beast. It will destroy without even knowing that it is destroying. Viewed thus, Kilcup's assertion that "The First Steamboat" belongs to a group of poems in which Sigourney protests environmental destruction takes on considerable weight.[21] The steamboat is no marvel. It is the monster that the Hudson's real and imaginary denizens believe it to be—and it is also something more.

In the poem's pivotal ninth stanza, we are told that for the Native people the steamboat was "the prophet bird of death." Having set this prophecy before us, the speaker shifts to a prophecy of her own in some of the most powerful and terrifying, and at the same time, ambiguous lines that Sigourney ever wrote:

She seem'd like the prophet bird of death
    To the gazing Indian's thought:
The swift weird sisters, whose pestilent breath
And reeking caldron affrighted Macbeth,
    To this "water-witch" were nought.

Yet strangely her brood o'er the waters spread
    With a bold prolific birth!
From the frigid north to the tropics red,
Their furrowing feet of fire do tread
    The thousand floods of earth.

But where is the mighty hand that taught
    This wingless bird to fly?
Say, where is the breast whose inventive thought
This mine of wealth for the world hath wrought?
    Land of his birth, reply!

He hath fallen. The lofty tree is dead:
    But it hath a living stem;
O'er its roots young saplings their verdure spread,
And the golden fruits which on us it shed,
    We may render back to them.[22]

How do we interpret this steamboat and the future it embodies: as a curse that others have mistaken as a blessing (the first nine stanzas) or as a blessing that others misread as a curse (the last three stanzas)? And where does Sigourney stand: with the horrified speaker of stanzas 1 through 9 or with the putatively optimistic speaker of stanzas 10 through 12? Is her speaker reversing herself and praising a technology whose "golden fruits" will make us all wealthy, or is she reckoning up the cost that its spreading "brood" will have for life on this planet, "frigid north to . . . tropics red"? In a way that seems to deny everything we know of Sigourney's piety as a Christian, she has pushed God out as an actor in this poem, and we are left to decide where we stand on the value of money without aid of biblical wisdom and with only nature (and its spirits) to guide us.

At least that is what I thought when I first began working with this poem. But as I tried to make sense of those last three stanzas I found myself wondering if this poet, who was renowned for nothing if not for her transparency, was in fact double-voicing, hard to believe though that seemed. What led me to this possibility was the gothic string of images in the last three stanzas and the gothic literary associations that trailed in their wake: a machine that can reproduce itself, filling the world with its prolific "brood"; a wingless bird that flies; an ever-bearing "mine of wealth"; a "living" tree that even after death puts forth "golden fruits," which we render back again so that it can breed yet more gold. Whose was the "mighty hand" and "inventive thought" that brought this unnatural being, this parody creation, into existence? If not God, who? A man who apes God's creative power, unnaturally breeding monsters that unnaturally breed money? Frankenstein's unnatural son? Midas and his daughter? Jacob and his sheep? Jason and his golden fleece? The builders of the good ship *Enterprise*?

All these stories are squeezed into these few lines. In our passion for increasingly effective and powerful machines and ever-greater wealth, we, like Fulton with his steamboat, have rolled over the multiple networks of interdependence and reverence that once sustained animal and human life on this planet and, as we now know to our sorrow, sustained the planet as well. Sigourney published this poem twenty-three years before Henry David Thoreau published *Walden.* If we make her our starting point for environmental awareness, it has taken us 186 years to catch up to where she was then.

As Kete and Petrino note, scholars have labeled Lydia Sigourney many different things: "historian, essayist, infant elegist, social reformer, educator, literary entrepreneur, cosmopolite, and more."[23] But who or, more precisely, what was she? In this collection of essays, as over the course of the past two centuries, we have been given an assortment of terms by which to know her. Some, like *poet, educator,* and *social reformer,* broadly refer to her chosen vocations and avocations. Others, like *historian* and *elegist,* are offshoots of those vocations, and still others, such as *literary entrepreneur* and *cosmopolite,* are modern labels that nonetheless fit the way in which Hartford's "sweet singer" managed her life and career.[24] Such words help flesh out who and what Sigourney was, as do many of the other terms mentioned in this book or elsewhere: *wife, mother, daughter, devout Christian, philanthropist, letter writer, prose stylist, spokesperson for America's aboriginal population, temperance advocate, environmentalist,* and, I would add, *comedian.*[25] Truly she was a remarkable woman, to whom every professional woman and certainly every professional woman poet in the United States owes a sizable debt. She broke the ground we build on.

But was this extraordinarily versatile woman also a writer of worth, one in the American grain, whose work—like Whitman's and Thoreau's—we cherish because it helps us understand ourselves and thereby earns the right to be taught and preserved? Or, as some think, did her diversity sap her writing, and particularly her poetry, of significance? Did she, as we are so often told, "write too much" and say too little?[26] Perhaps.

However, I would like to suggest that Sigourney's commitment to diversity and to the market has a deeper cause than the fact that she wrote to make a living. For her, as for Whitman, multiplicity was the essence of her literary mission because it was and is the essence of America in all its contradictions, excrescences, and moments of genius. As "a writer for the public," she wrote, first and foremost, as the American she was.

NOTES

1. Grace Lathrop Collin, "Lydia Huntley Sigourney," *New England Magazine: An Illustrated Monthly* 27 (1903): 28.
2. Ibid., 27, 26.
3. Ibid., 28.
4. Lydia Sigourney, *Letters of Life* (1867; reprint, New York: Arno, 1980), 376.
5. For useful discussion of Sigourney's dubious placing with respect to other nineteenth-century poetesses, see Eliza Richards, *Gender and the Poetics of Reception in Poe's Circle* (Cambridge: Cambridge University Press, 2004), 60–106.
6. Sigourney, *Letters of Life,* 365–66, 367–68.
7. Kelly's chapter, which provides a blow-by-blow account of the disintegration of Sigourney's marriage, makes it clear that Charles Sigourney's revulsion at his wife's move to the public market—not just his anxiety that she might fail at her wifely responsibilities—played a significant role in their break-up. See Gary Kelly, chap. 6.
8. Sigourney, *Letters of Life,* 366.
9. Ibid., 365.
10. Exceptions to this rule do exist, in particular, the Concord-Boston clique that dissed Poe. But Sigourney never seems to have belonged to such a group, nor did the majority

of other writers. Only the Boston and New York coteries were powerful enough to seriously impact careers.

11. I have put "gardener's daughter" in quotation marks because it is clear in *Letters of Life* (11) that Sigourney's father performed the functions of a caretaker and man-of-all-work around the Lathrop estate. The myth that he was a simple gardener was fostered by scholars who, beginning with Griswold, sought to treat Sigourney as a woman who climbed above her station. See also Paula Bernat Bennett, "Was Sigourney a Poetess? The Aesthetics of Victorian Plenitude in Lydia Sigourney's Poetry," *Comparative American Studies* 5 (September 2007): 271–72.
12. See Paula Bernat Bennett, *Poets in the Public Sphere: The Emancipatory Project of American Women's Poetry, 1800–1900* (Princeton: Princeton University Press, 2000), 1–85, for an extended treatment of the democratization of the literary marketplace and its role in enabling women poets in particular. See also Isabelle Lehu, *Popular Print Media in Antebellum America* (Chapel Hill: University of North Carolina Press, 2000).
13. Sigourney, *Letters of Life*, 324.
14. Paul Lauter, "Is Ellen Frances Watkins Harper Good Enough to Teach?" *Legacy* 5 (Spring 1988): 27.
15. Kelly, chap. 6.
16. I would note that Sigourney's ubiquitous presence in anthologies of nineteenth-century American literature designed for the classroom is a clear sign that the process of canonization has already begun. Whatever individual scholars think of her poems, she has become a necessary figure.
17. [Lydia Sigourney], "The Alpine Flowers," *Poems* (Boston: Goodrich, 1827), 54.
18. H. [Lydia Sigourney], "Wealth," in *Episcopal Watchman,* October 15, 1827, 236, as quoted in Kelly, chap. 6. In the poem, Sigourney equates Esau's trading of his birthright for a mess of pottage to a person who abandons intellectual and spiritual development in favor of making money.
19. My discussion of "The First Steamboat" is a shortened and much revised version of an earlier treatment of this poem in Bennett, "Was Sigourney a Poetess," 279–83. For another reading, see Karen Kilcup, *Fallen Forests: Emotion, Embodiment, and Ethics in American Women's Environmental Writing 1781–1924* (Athens: University of Georgia Press, 2013), 97–99. Like Kilcup, I believe Sigourney was a major voice for environmental justice.
20. Lydia Sigourney, "The First Steamboat," *Bouquet: Flowers of Polite Literature* 1 no. 12 (November 19, 1831): 96.
21. Kilcup, *Fallen Forests,* 40, 43, 47.
22. Sigourney, "The First Steamboat," 96.
23. Mary Louise Kete and Elizabeth Petrino, chap. 1.
24. Gordon S. Haight, *Mrs. Sigourney: The Sweet Singer of Hartford* (New Haven: Yale University Press, 1930). Haight uses this popular nineteenth-century soubriquet for local women poets as the subtitle for his corrosive biography of the poet as a literary social climber of no perceptible worth.
25. I do not have the room to discuss Sigourney's comic writing here, but it is a significant aspect of her writing that, like her use of vernacular crops, is here and there in her oeuvre. It is wonderfully apparent in two works—*Sketch of Connecticut, Forty Years Since* and *Letters of Life.*
26. Collin, "Lydia Huntley Sigourney," 30. Collin's final judgment on Sigourney's writing is extremely harsh: "she was in the main a hack writer, and the greater number of her works are potboilers." Sigourney's considerable output unquestionably contributed to this view.

CONTRIBUTORS

Ann Beebe is associate professor of English at the University of Texas at Tyler, where she teaches nineteenth-century American literature. Her scholarly work includes articles on E.D.E.N. Southworth's influence in Great Britain, Elizabeth Stuart Phelps, and the Civil War diary of Lizzie Hardin.

Paula Bernat Bennett is professor emerita at University of Southern Illinois, Carbondale. She is the author of *Emily Dickinson: Woman Poet* (University of Iowa Press, 1990) and *Poets in the Public Sphere: The Emancipatory Project of American Women's Poetry, 1800–1900* (Princeton University Press, 2003). She has published widely on a number of nineteenth-century American women poets, and she is the editor of *Nineteenth-Century American Women Poets: An Anthology* (Blackwell, 1998).

Janet Dean is professor of English and Cultural Studies at Bryant University. She is the author of *Unconventional Politics: Nineteenth-Century Women Writers and U.S. Indian Policy* (University of Massachusetts Press, 2016) as well as numerous articles on Native American writers and topics including literacy narratives, narrative authority, and the dime novel and the marriage plot in Western literature.

Sean Epstein-Corbin is assistant professor of English at Merced College, where he teaches nineteenth-century American literature. He has published articles in *Crossroads* and *Transactions of the Charles S. Peirce Society* and is at work on book-length study entitled "Secularizing Sentiment, Democratizing Virtue: A Genealogy of the Liberal Subject over the Long Nineteenth Century."

Annie Finch is the author or editor of more than twenty books of poetry, plays, translations, literary essays, textbooks, and anthologies, including award-winning collections of poetry such as *Eve* (1997), *Calendars* (2003), and *Spells: New and Selected Poems* (2013), and the long poems *The Encyclopedia of Scotland* (1982) and *Among the Goddesses: An Epic Libretto in Seven Dreams* (2009). As a feminist critic and poet, Finch's 1988 essay "The Sentimental Poetess in the World: Metaphor and Subjectivity in Lydia Sigourney's Nature Poetry" was one of the key works introducing Sigourney to the scholarly world and positing the concept of the "poetess" as a necessary critical term for discussing nineteenth-century women poets.

Gary Kelly is Distinguished University Professor of English and Film Studies at the University of Alberta, where he teaches eighteenth- and nineteenth-century literature. He has published extensively on many topics related to British and American women writers, including a history of romanticism, essays on bluestocking work (class, gender, and intellectual and domestic work); the popular novel 1780–1820; the spectrum of romantic fiction (genre); Austen and modernity; Austen and home; romantic counterfactuals (readers' uses of history); women's long poems in pre–Civil War United States; the gendered Atlantic (women poets in romantic Britain, republican United States). He published *Lydia Sigourney: Selected Poetry and Prose* (Broadview Press, 2007) and is currently coediting *The Oxford History of Popular Print Culture.*

Mary Louise Kete is associate professor of English at the University of Vermont, where teaches nineteenth-century literature and gender studies. She is the author of *Sentimental Collaborations: Mourning and Middle-Class Identity in Nineteenth-Century America* (Duke University Press, 2000) and the coauthor of *Women's Worlds: The McGraw-Hill Anthology of Women's Writing* (McGraw-Hill, 2007). Having published on a wide range of nineteenth-century American authors, she is finishing a book on the cultural poetics of the mode of ekphrasis in nineteenth-century America entitled "American Ekphrasis and the Problem of the Representative Self," and collaborating with Petrino on a critical biography of Lydia Sigourney.

Paul Lauter is Allan K. and Gwendolyn Miles Smith Professor of Literature at Trinity College in Hartford, Connecticut. He has served as president of the American Studies Association, and he is general editor of the groundbreaking *Heath Anthology of American Literature,* now in its sixth edition. He was also one of the founders of The Feminist Press and its treasurer and an editor for fourteen years. He has published extensively on the literature of nineteenth-century women and working class authors.

AMY J. LUECK is assistant professor of English at Santa Clara University, where she teaches nineteenth-century American literature. Her primary research area is nineteenth-century rhetorical education and literacy in American high schools, which provides a useful frame for her secondary research interest in nineteenth-century women's literature. She has presented her research at national conferences, including Modern Language Association, Conference on College Composition and Communication, and Rhetoric Society of America, and has published in journals such as *Kairos*, *JAC*, and *Currents in Electronic Literacy*.

RICARDO MIGUEL-ALFONSO teaches nineteenth-century American literature at the University of Castilla-La Mancha (Spain). He is the author of *El Romanticismo americano y la idea de la literatura* (Verbum, 2013). He has published essays on Robert Coover, Ralph Waldo Emerson, Margaret Fuller, Nathaniel Hawthorne, and Adam Smith. He has also translated Emerson's *Essays* and George Santayana's *Reason in Art* into Spanish. He has coedited *A Power to Translate the World: New Essays on Emerson and International Culture* with David LaRocca (Dartmouth College Press, 2014). He is currently at work on a book on the transformation of Emerson's aesthetics and philosophy between the 1830s and the 1880s tentatively titled "Emerson, the Aesthetic Vision and the Disenchantment with Modernity."

ELIZABETH PETRINO is professor of English at Fairfield University, where she teaches nineteenth-century American literature and gender studies. She is the author of *Emily Dickinson and Her Contemporaries: American Women's Verse, 1820–1885* (University Press of New England, 1998) and the coeditor of *Jesuit and Feminist Education: Intersections in Teaching and Learning for the Twenty-first Century* (Fordham University Press, 2012). She is exploring Dickinson's transatlantic influences and theories of influence relating to how the publication context might have structured the ways she responded to British and Continental writers. She and Kete are collaborating on a critical biography of Lydia Sigourney.

Jennifer Putzi is associate professor and director of women and gender studies at the College of William and Mary. Putzi has authored of *Identifying Marks: Race, Gender, and the Marked Body in Nineteenth-Century America* (University of Georgia Press, 2006) as well as edited several editions of Elizabeth Stoddard's work. Most recently she has coedited *A History of Nineteenth-Century American Women's Poetry* (Cambridge University Press, 2016) with Alexandra Socarides. She is the coeditor of *Legacy: A Journal of American Women Writers.*

Angela Sorby is associate professor of English at Marquette University. She is the author of *Schoolroom Poets: Childhood, Performance, and the Place of American Poetry, 1865–1917* (University of New Hampshire Press, 2005). She has also published numerous articles on nineteenth-century American poets, including Elizabeth Akers Allen, Emily Dickinson, Ella Wheeler Wilcox, and James Whitcomb Riley, and she has written on a range of topics, including class, popular poetry, animal poems, and children's rights. A practicing poet, she is the author of several books of poems, and most recently, she has coedited an anthology, *Over the River and Through the Wood: An Anthology of Nineteenth-Century American Children's Poetry*, with Karen L. Kilcup (Johns Hopkins University Press, 2013).

Joan R. Wry is associate professor of English at Saint Michael's College, Vermont, where she teaches nineteenth-century American literature. She has published essays on Shakespeare, Shelley, Emerson, Thoreau, Whitman, Margaret Fuller, and Lydia Sigourney in journals such as *Renaissance Quarterly* and the *Walt Whitman Quarterly Review.* From 2005–2013, she served as the associate dean of Saint Michael's College.

Sandra A. Zagarell is Donald R. Longman Professor of English at Oberlin College, where she teaches nineteenth- and early twentieth-century American literature and culture, nineteenth-century British literature, nineteenth-century transatlantic literature, and the history of the book. Her editions of novels by Caroline Kirkland and Elizabeth Stoddard brought these important nineteenth-century authors to critical attention. A senior editor of *The Heath Anthology of American Literature,* she has published numerous essays on Elizabeth Stoddard, Sarah Orne Jewett, Mary Wilkins Freeman, and other American regionalist writers.

INDEX

Page numbers in italics refer to photographs or their captions.